£19.95.

AF745143

University of Bristol Library
Tyndall Avenue, Bristol BS8 1TJ

Date due for return
UNLESS RECALLED EARLIER

NOT FOR LOAN BEFORE
17 SEP 1997

Econon

UNIVERSITY OF BRISTOL
WITHDRAWN

For Charly

Economic Theory and Sovereign International Debt

Ernst Mohr

Institut für Weltwirtschaft
The Kiel Institute of World Economics
Kiel, Germany
and
Department of Economics and Statistics
University of Konstanz
Konstanz, Germany

ACADEMIC PRESS

Harcourt Brace Jovanovich, Publishers

London San Diego New York
Boston Sydney Tokyo Toronto

HJ 8011 MOH

This book is printed on acid-free paper

ACADEMIC PRESS LIMITED
24–28 Oval Road
LONDON NW1 7DX

United States Edition published by
ACADEMIC PRESS INC.
San Diego, CA92101

Copyright © 1991 by
ACADEMIC PRESS LIMITED

All Rights Reserved
No part of this book may be reproduced in any form by photostat, microfilm, or by any other means, without written permission from the publishers

A catalogue
record for this
book is available
from the British
Library

ISBN 0-12-504165-9

UNIVERSITY OF BRISTOL

Typeset by MCS Ltd, Salisbury, England
Printed and bound in Great Britain by The University Press, Cambridge

0 6 NOV 2019

WITHDRAWN

UNIVERSITY OF BRISTOL LIBRARY

Contents

Preface

A book on the international debt problem requires no justification. A book on the theory of debt and credit relations does. There exists an enormous body of literature pertaining to theoretical issues of borrowing and lending at all levels of aggregation in many fields in Economics. A further monograph on the subject therefore ought to be well justified.

The outbreak and persistent smouldering of what has been dubbed the international debt crisis in the 1980s has triggered a fresh look into debt and credit relations – a look which, under a research effort comparable in scope, perhaps, with the research on exhaustible resources in the wake of the oil crises in the 1970s, is quickly evolving into a new theory of debt. To contrast this new theory with the traditional theory of debt and credit relations the latter may be labelled the theory of non-sovereign debt whereas the new body of literature may be called the theory of sovereign debt. This book tries to account for and expand on the theory of sovereign international debt.

The purpose of this book is threefold. The youth of this theory manifests itself as an inevitable nuisance. It is almost without exception recorded in article form. So anyone who wants to read, say, ten papers on the subject will have to get familiar with perhaps as many conceptual frameworks. The first purpose of this book is to present an overview of the theory of sovereign international debt in a single, unified framework. It therefore addresses researchers who want to inform themselves on the current state of the theory in a time-saving manner.

The international debt issue is discussed in circles with very different backgrounds whereas the theory of sovereign debt is to a great extent written by mathematical economists and is often available only to them. The second purpose of this book is to make the reasoning of this theory accessible to a wider range of people. In keeping with this purpose, the book has been written with an emphasis on special cases and on economic interpretation, keeping the formal analysis to the indispensable minimum, and avoiding generality when I felt it would distract the reader from the point I intended to make. However, it remains a formal book: rigour is not avoided. Nothing more than elementary mathematics is assumed. It is hoped that the book can thus serve as a guide through the theory for first-year graduate students in economic theory, applied economists and formally trained practitioners alike.

The third purpose is to take the theory of sovereign international debt a few steps further. Work has been conspicuously concentrated around a single or at best very few markets, notably credit markets. The theory is so far in partial equilibrium terms. Many questions pertaining to repercussions from sovereign debt onto other markets in creditor and debtor economies still remain unanswered or have found only faint reflection in the literature. This book tries to address some of these questions in the context of a general equilibrium analysis of sovereign international debt.

Perhaps I have not succeeded in writing this monograph to serve all or even some of these purposes. However, it was worth a try. Certainly it was not without costs. Most prominent amongst them is the recourse to specific functional forms and simplified scenarios at the loss of generality. I express here the standard scientific hope that major conclusions drawn from those special cases will be robust with respect to generalizations and the exigencies of the real world.

During the course of writing I have accumulated a substantial amount of debt. As the reader will certainly discover soon, this debt may qualify as being sovereign. However, at great variance with what will be presumed in the main body of this book I gladiy abstain from repudiation: instead, I gratefully acknowledge the thanks I owe to so many.

My friend Peter König directed my attention to the topic. I greatly benefitted from discussions with Axel Behrens, Jesko Hentschel, Bert Hofman, Joachim Keck, Michael Rauscher, Jonathan Thomas and Timm Worrall throughout all stages of the work. I am grateful to members of the faculty of Economics and the Sonderforschungsbereich 178 'Internationalisierung der Wirtschaft' at the University of Konstanz for the provision of a stimulating atmosphere in which to undertake the research which led to this book. Participants at research seminars at the Universities of Munich and Mannheim and members of the 'Studiengruppe für theoretische Nationalökonomie der SGStV' and of the 'Außenwirtschaftlicher Ausschuß des Vereins für Socialpolitik' provided valuable ideas.

I am most grateful to Horst Siebert who encouraged me to continue the work when the ideas surrounding it were still obscure, who saw to it that time was not too tough a constraint for me and whose academic advice was very valuable. He was also helpful in obtaining financial support to write up the book during a sabbatical. I gratefully acknowledge financial support for this by the Deutsche Forschungsgemeinschaft.

Different parts of the manuscript have been typed at the Kiel Institute of World Economics by Ludwig von Auer, Matthias von Bodecker, Heidemarie Brocke, Kerstin Stark and Karin Wachsmuth. Ursula Fett carefully drew the diagrams. However, this book would not have been completed so soon without Inga Franke, who never became tired of typing version after version and who skilfully organized and oversaw it all. I am indebted to her for this.

Ernst Mohr

CHAPTER 1

Preview

I. The Problem

Non-sovereign debt is nested in an institutional framework which makes it subject to laws regarding contract enforcement and bankruptcy provisions. The legal framework and institutions of contract enforcement are geared towards decoupling the benefit to a creditor from the good or bad intentions of a debtor. If debtors do not want to abide by the stipulations of a credit contract concerning the timely payment of interest or repayment of principal, legal mechanisms ensure that the debtors behave as if they wanted to meet their obligations. The credit relationship is not constrained by a debtor's willingness to pay, but is constrained solely by the debtor's ability to pay. This is the central paradigm of the theory of non-sovereign debt.

All private debts within the legal reach of a nation qualify quite easily for this class. Enforcement costs and legal limitations of collateral do not really complicate matters within the theory of non-sovereign debt. In modern societies jurisdiction is smoothly and efficiently at work and costs of contract enforcement to creditors are minor or negligible, or so the theory presumes. Legal limitations of collateral are public knowledge and can be taken into account when making a loan.

International debt is governmental debt issued abroad. It also includes debt raised by individuals or institutions within a country and owed to someone in another country. Frequently such private international debt is supported by guarantees from the home government. To a foreign lender this makes the loan in fact one to a foreign government.

Compared to domestic debt, matters with international debt are different and substantially more complicated. International borrowing and lending takes place in an institutional framework from which collateral and the seizure of assets upon default are absent or substantially restricted. This is so because countries are, one is inclined to say by definition, sovereign and cannot be therefore subjected to foreign bankruptcy and default provisions.

Enforcement under the jurisdiction of a debtor country promises very often to be similarly disappointing. It is unavailable with respect to public or publicly guaranteed debt. Enforcement of loans to private foreigners under the foreign law, if available, is all too often associated with prohibitive costs in money, time, and risk. Appealing to international courts or other higher authorities tends to be even more unpromising, testifying to the fact that countries jealously guard and protect their status of sovereignty. For all these reasons it is safe to say that international debt is above the law. In the remainder of this book we shall call debt of this type sovereign debt.

Debtor sovereignty and the issuance of sovereign debt can substantially alter the relationship between creditors and debtors. The lack of enforcement mechanisms enlarges the set of feasible actions for a debtor after a loan is made and it diminishes the range of feasible actions for a lender. Set free from being forced to honour debt contracts to the limit of her ability or obligation, the overriding criterion for a debtor's action, as far as the lenders are concerned, becomes her willingness to pay. This is the central paradigm of the theory of sovereign debt.

This is not to say that a sovereign country's ability to pay, her solvency, is of no importance. As with non-sovereign debt, solvency is a necessary condition for repayment. However, sovereign and non-sovereign debt differ in that for the former, solvency is not a sufficient condition for repayment of principal and interest. The willingness to pay is the bottleneck restriction if it ends well before a debtor's ability to pay comes to an end. This must be expected to hold for the majority of situations.

An official statement from the foreign ministers and finance ministers meeting of eleven Latin American debtor countries at the Cartagena Conference, held on June 21–22, 1984, may serve as an anecdotal illustration of the foregoing arguments. The countries involved asserted their 'intention to comply with the commitments relating to their external indebtedness' (Cartagena Consensus, paragraph 8, cited after Navarrete, 1985, p. 13). Rather than deliberating what the intentions or sentiments behind and the importance of this statement *in particular* may have been, *such* statements help to bring to the fore the basic difference between sovereign and non-sovereign debt. Lenders can afford to exhibit a very substantial insensitivity towards a non-sovereign debtor's determination to pay. In contrast, with respect to sovereign debt the debtor's determination to pay turns into a key factor in the relationship between borrowers and lenders.

II. An Agenda for the Book

The foregoing paragraph has described, admittedly in a rather sketchy form, the essential difference between sovereign and non-sovereign debt. There are many economically important problems that arise when debt is sovereign.

As has already been asserted, sovereignty provides a debtor with a degree of discretion that is absent from non-sovereign debt relations. A creditor's *ex-post* utility from a debt contract hinges on the debtor's behaviour after a loan is made. A debtor may decide to avoid altogether the costs from borrowing by repudiating all old debt. Other forms of debtor actions that can adversely affect the creditors' *ex-post* utility from lending include unilaterally announced moratoria on the repayment of interest or principal, or the limitation of debt servicing to no more than some specified percentage of export earnings.

This creates a strategic interdependency between the parties to a debt contract. It is a major task of any analysis of sovereign debt to investigate the strategic interaction between debtors and creditors – before and after a loan is made, but also before and after a contract is violated in part or in whole.

A fundamental question which is closely related to this issue is what determines the behaviour of decision-makers in strategic situations. In the main body of the book we will pursue this question in the spirit of dynamic game theory. The idea entertained is that debtors and creditors egoistically evaluate all pros and cons of a given action in rational anticipation of similar behaviour of the other parties to a contract, and act in accordance with their greatest advantage. This issue will be taken up again at the end of this chapter.

For a debtor who is faced with the two alternatives of correctly abiding by all stipulations of a contract or repudiating debt altogether, this behavioural presumption requires her to repudiate all old debt if the costs of abiding by the terms of the contract exceed the costs of repudiation. The former quite apparently depend on the size of a loan, the interest rate and the fees to be paid by the debtor. The costs of repudiation or, more generally, of any breach of contract, can depend on a number of factors. Exercising sovereignty may seriously harm a debtor's reputation and severely restrict access to, or raise the costs of, future loans. Besides diminished access to credit markets a debtor may suffer from seizure of financial assets held abroad or some kind of gunboat-technology, be it in the form of withdrawal of foreign expertise or seizure of goods in transit. The sum of these potential costs determines a debtor's inclination to pay and hence her credit-worthiness.

Historically, sanctions in response to repudiation have varied substantially, both in severity and duration. An enquiry into the theory of sovereign debt will have to take this into consideration. Furthermore, care must be taken as it must be expected that not all sanctions can act as a deterrent from taking the sovereignty option. Care is on the agenda because a rational debtor will take into account only those sanctions that constitute a credible threat. And what constitutes credibility is in itself an intricate question.

One must expect that lenders, be they banks, bond-holders, a government, or supra-national institutions, are aware of debtor sovereignty when making a loan. That is, the influence of sovereignty supposed will not be restricted to the post-contractual relationship or, to put it differently, to the time after a loan is made. Potential lenders will have an incentive to design contracts in such a way as to ensure that a rational sovereign will come down against contract violations when it comes to servicing the loan. The judicious design of self-enforcing debt contracts will therefore replace reliance on enforcement mechanisms when debt is judged sovereign. In the aggregate, such *ex-ante* considerations of potential creditors will determine the shape of the credit supply a debtor has to face. Presumably, the supply of loans to a sovereign will differ from the supply to a non-sovereign debtor. A sovereign may have to be rationed to ensure repayment, or she may face an upward-sloping supply schedule to compensate lenders for a higher risk of repudiation when debt is higher. One must therefore suspect that debtor sovereignty is a source of credit-market imperfections.

Back on the debtor side of a debt relationship, sovereignty itself can give rise to a number of interesting problems. When some source of uncertainty is present so that contract violations cannot be excluded with certainty, a debtor will have to face the fact that with a certain probability costs of repudiation will have to be incurred. A debtor may therefore have an incentive to allocate resources to the containment of future sanctions.

Such an allocation of resources can in turn negatively feed back into the credit supply. For one thing, less effective sanctions directly diminish a debtor's credit-worthiness. Moreover, lenders may have to face an adverse selection problem. Because in as much as a higher interest rate on loans increases the probability of repudiation – and hence of having to pay the price for it – a higher interest rate will entice the debtor to allocate even more resources to the containment of potential sanctions.

However, against this incentive works another incentive which supposedly becomes more important the smaller the risk involved in the debt relationship. If commitment to a certain investment programme is possible, a debtor can commit herself to a programme which increases her costs from a breach of contract, thus improving her credit standing and extending the credit line. Debtor sovereignty, however, should be expected to severely restrict a debtor's ability to commit. Aspects of sovereignty that directly impinge on the supply and demand side of credit markets, some of which have been outlined above, are at the core of the theory of sovereign debt.

Important aspects of sovereign debt can be analysed in rather abstract settings. Others require further refinements. It is the foreign debt of nations that makes the sovereignty issue potentially important as an empirical problem. It should therefore be interesting to investigate aspects of debtor sovereignty that go beyond the credit markets alone, and possibly affect markets and economic units in debtor and creditor economies other than those directly involved. What is the impact of sovereign debt on aggregate consumption and saving? How are portfolio decisions affected? Is sovereign debt issued used for investment purposes or is it diverted away from investment into consumptive activities? Does debt sovereignty affect capital accumulation in the creditor countries? These are some of the questions that will be taken up later.

The international aspect of sovereign debt calls for further refinements. There are several possibilities of financing international debt. Loans may be part of foreign aid from governments or from supra-national institutions. An important part of foreign debt, however, is owed to the private sector in creditor countries. This debt is financed either through the issuance of bonds that are held by private households abroad or, more importantly, through loans from foreign banks.

It is well known that financing is irrelevant for real economic activity when capital markets are perfect. However, as has already been noted, debtor sovereignty may be causal to credit market imperfections. An inquiry into the various forms of financing can therefore provide valuable insights into the problem of sovereign debt.

Foreign debt is itself but one form of international capital relations. An important alternative to attracting foreign capital through the debt is direct investment. Direct investment, that is the acquisition of real capital in a country by foreigners, is subject to a phenomenon similar to the repudiation of foreign debt. Foreign ownership of real capital runs the risk of expropriation by the host country. A comparison of debt financing with direct investment can therefore provide further insights into international capital relations.

A banking system acts as a financial intermediary. Banks make loans which are refinanced through the attraction of deposits. Many internationally operating banks are incorporated in countries which are net lenders to debtor countries. Banks engaged in international lending are in an especially delicate position. On the active side of their balance sheet they hold unenforceable claims from international loans, and on the passive side of the balance sheet they hold liabilities against domestic depositors that are subject to enforcement. Banks engaged in international lending are thus put through the mill of being a creditor to a sovereign debtor and at the same time being a non-sovereign debtor themselves. Default of internationally operating banks due to debtor discretion may be a consequence. This culminates in the sometimes voiced concern that the stability of the international banking system is in jeopardy from sovereign debt. Banking therefore deserves close attention when analysing sovereign debt.

It is not difficult to testify further to the delicacy of international bank lending. One can validly argue that one-time relationships between banks and sovereign debtors are the rare exception. Banks, rather, are engaged in long-term relationships with sovereign debtors, and international debt contracts have in fact become revolving credit agreements. With old debt up for repayment, banks may be especially lenient in providing fresh money in order to support repayment of old debt. New loans may become part of an overall administration of old debt. An economic analysis of the incentives arising from the idiosyncratic nature of international debt relationships can provide valuable insights into the issue at hand.

So far we have outlined some of the ramifications of two alternatives open to sovereign debtors, outright repudiation and sticking to the letter of the contract. In fact, there may be many more options open to sovereign debtors, options which lie somewhat in between these extreme alternatives.

A sovereign may decide to honour some clauses of a debt contract and violate others. Obligations may be acknowledged in principle but payments delayed. Or she can violate one contract and honour others. This list could be enlarged at will. What is more interesting, however, is to ask what could entice a debtor to choose only a partial violation of a contract she decides not to honour in full.

Obviously this cannot be in the interest of a debtor if the full measure of sanctions is the inevitable consequence of any form of contract violation. However, it can be in the debtor's interest if it thereby has to bear only part of the costs of full repudiation. On the other hand, it may be strictly to the advantage of creditors to refrain from inflicting dead-weight losses on the debtor, if thereby at least some payments can be obtained. A strategy of outright confrontation can therefore be to the mutual disadvantage of all parties to a debt contract. In this situation, the platform is set for renegotiation.

Renegotiation over obligations from old debt has always been an important component of sovereign debtor-creditor interactions. It is often strategically connected to negotiation over fresh loans. In fact, both may be part and parcel of an overall rescheduling effort. By rescheduling agreements lenders ease a debtor's present pain from full or partial payment of interest or principal due. Lenders achieve this by financing repayment through new loans, or by waiving fulfilment of certain onerous provisions of debt contracts.

Negotiations between sovereign debtors and lenders pose a number of questions. What determines the relative bargaining power of the parties to a sovereign debt contract? What can be the subject of negotiations and what cannot? What is the solution of debt renegotiation? A different set of questions relates to problems connected only with the supply side of international debt. What is the impact of anticipated renegotiation on the supply of loans, what on the risk of lending? Does the possibility of future debt renegotiation aggravate or moderate the adverse selection problem? Is it in the lenders' interest to be capable of negotiating with a sovereign and what is the role thereby of alternative forms of financing? What are the repercussions of debt negotiations in general equilibrium and what is their impact on the stability of the banking system? These and some other questions will have to be addressed in detail. To that end an approach to negotiations will be adopted which is known as non-cooperative bargaining theory.

The ample experience from dispersed incidences or the massed occurrence of debtor countries in arrears has filled the tool-chest of debt managers to the brim. Indexation, forgiveness, financing, debt-equity swaps, buy-backs, and exit bonds are just some of the instruments that enjoy varying popularity amongst practitioners and the parties involved. They differ in importance but have in common that they all are applied, to put it optimistically, with rather modest success. Given the attention they command, it is, however, worthwhile to analyse how they function.

In this context it is often claimed that many of these debt relief instruments cause serious disincentive problems. It is, however, also claimed that these instruments can function only in situations when a debtor already has a disincentive problem. It should therefore not be surprising that the limited success of debt relief instruments can be attributed to these incentive problems. There is, however, an important message emanating from the remainder of this book which says that there is a far more fundamental problem which debt managers have to face when applying such instruments to sovereign debt. Leaving the issues connected with this claim to be taken up shortly, we turn to a set of issues which, in another sense, is broadly related to sovereign debt management.

Institutions like the International Monetary Fund or the World Bank are heavily involved in international debt management. Other institutions on the sovereign debt stage are creditor clubs or creditor consortia which coordinate lender activities. Debtor clubs are also being advocated. Operating somewhat behind the stage are domestic governments and institutions engaged in bank regulation. And so-called 'lenders of last resort' are said to exist clandestinely who are prepared to intervene in the international debt play. All of these are, at least potentially, actors in this play and, to continue the metaphor, it is important to understand the part they play.

To that end, a variety of institutional arrangements will be analysed. They include regulations pertaining to forced write-downs of unenforcable claims and the socialization of losses from international lending. These arrangements require some form of active involvement of certain institutions in the international debt game. However, institutions can influence debtor-creditor interactions without being active. The possible existence of a 'lender of last resort' or the prospect or threat of potential outside intervention by governments can influence the bargaining process between debtors and creditors and can therefore have real effects.

In this section an outlook has been given of the issues that await the reader in the following chapters. There remains a last but important issue to be addressed. This issue differs from those outlined so far in that it is more of a methodological character than those hitherto raised. This issue is taken up here, however, because it threads its way through almost every other issue discussed in this book.

There is a tradition of viewing phenomena of the kind that trouble international debt relations as being inherently out of order, outside the ordinary wheeling and dealing of international economic relations. The label 'crisis' attached to these phenomena vividly stresses this point. More formally, in this view incidents of this kind are viewed as disequilibrium phenomena.

In sharp contrast to this view, in what follows we shall entertain the idea that the symptoms of 'debt crises' are equilibrium phenomena. To that end the analysis is geared towards producing long-run equilibria with sovereign debt outstanding.

Which of these alternative views is more appropriate in describing the international debt situation is, perhaps, anyone's guess. On one hand, this question can be tackled empirically. However, another avenue to ultimately confront it, is to proceed with an equilibrium analysis of sovereign international debt, and then look whether this analysis produces results which correspond to real-world phenomena.

In fact this undertaking proves to be surprisingly successful. It turns out that credit rationing, roll-overs, involuntary lending, reschedulings and debt renegotiations, bank losses, and a resources drain out of debtor economies, to state but some, can all be explained as long-run equilibrium phenomena. It is this message which raises a more fundamental doubt concerning the efficacy of sovereign debt management alluded to above.

An equilibrium analysis of sovereign international debt can be further buttressed. Even if observed incidences of international debt markets 'in disarray' are in fact disequilibrium phenomena it should be of eminent interest to investigate the properties of long-run, steady-state debt relations between debtor and creditor economies. There are several questions that can be addressed in this respect. Is it at all possible to maintain sovereign debt relations between countries without avoiding repudiation in the long run and, if so, what are their properties? If institutional mechanisms fail to make a sovereign ever pay back all debt outstanding, under what conditions is this compatible with the optimality of creditor decisions? Or to put it somewhat differently, would a creditor economy ever begin a credit relationship with a sovereign? Still another variant from this group of questions is to ask whether a sovereign debtor will be allowed to play a 'Ponzi-game'.

III. What the Book Does Not Cover

A 'tour de horizon' over the content of this book has been given in the last section. This section is devoted to an outline of those issues a reader may, perhaps, look forward to, but which for one reason or another are not taken up in this book.

Domestic government debt will not be dealt with. Although one could, perhaps, argue that government debt issued at home is sovereign in some broader sense, this kind of sovereignty in constitutional democracies arises from a constituency waiving its right to enforce repayment; it does not arise from a lack of feasible contract enforcement. Much in the spirit of the rationality assumed in Barro (1974), but somewhat altering his question, we would deny that government bonds are above the law.

Back on the international stage one might wonder, in accordance with a simple symmetry argument, why in our analysis creditors or their governments do not exercise sovereignty in much the same way as debtors and their governments are assumed to. The reader may therefore miss an analysis of creditor sovereignty.

Sovereignty is the freedom not to meet one's obligations from a contract after the other party to the contract already has met hers. The neglect of creditor sovereignty can therefore be motivated by the convention that a loan must be made before any payments from a debtor are due. However, creditor sovereignty could play a role in theory if front-end costs, like fees, had to be borne by debtors before a loan was obtained. It could also play a role in a revolving credit agreement, if old debt is repaid before the new loan is made. In practice, however, the forementioned transactions tend to take place at the same time. It is due to the belief that creditor sovereignty is empirically insignificant that it is neglected in the remainder of this book.

A further and, admittedly, more severe omission pertains to the denomination of international debt. If a country can issue foreign debt in domestic currency it can formally service, yet tacitly repudiate, debt simply by printing money. On the contrary, if debt is denominated in foreign currency debt servicing is always associated with costs in terms of foregone consumption. The denomination of foreign debt is therefore important and both domestic and foreign denomination deserve attention. Alas, in what follows only foreign denomination is considered.

In defence of this omission one can perhaps argue that empirically almost all of the debtor countries are precluded from domestically denominated foreign debt. However, there are important exceptions to this rule. Another reason for omitting domestic denomination is that, including it, it would not have been possible to maintain a single formal framework for the analysis.

Many other issues which are claimed to be important for understanding LDC indebtedness are being dismissed from the analysis. The transfer and revenue generation problems, income distribution and capital flight, to state but a few issues from the realm of development economics, are left out. This should, however, not be understood as a disclaimer concerning their importance for LDC indebtedness. Rather, in deciding on the inclusion or exclusion of an issue the line of demarcation has been essentiality for the general issue at hand, sovereign debt. As the topics mentioned can pose problems under both sovereign and non-sovereign debt, and because debt sovereignty is likely not to sever them, these issues are being dismissed.

IV. A Methodological Remark

At the end of this preview we return to a methodological point raised earlier. As has been argued their, debtor sovereignty creates a situation where debtors and creditors are strategically connected. As has been also stated, the instruments to tackle this problem will be provided by dynamic game theory. The central presumption is, that debtors decide on the fate of a contract under a cool judgement of the relative advantage of violating or honouring the debt agreement.

This concept has been under fire ever since it has been applied to international debt. The critique can be exemplified by the following quotation:

'The new economic analyses of the debt are often led astray by an exaggerated Benthamism as regards rationality and the calculation of costs and benefits. ... There can be no doubt that this represents a development of the concept of *homo economicus* to a level which undermines its usefulness for diagnosis and subscription' (Devlin, 1985, footnote 18).

The point in which such a critique goes awry is that it dismantles the 'Emperor' and leaves him without clothes (Hollis, 1985). Put differently, such a critique fails to come up with any operational alternative. How many layers of rationality should be taken off from 'homo economicus' to restore the concept's usefulness remains in the dark. As a consequence results vary with the degree of rationality applied, and the preference for some reduced concept of rationality runs the risk of being obscured by the attraction of the associated results.

Progress in the realm of behavioural economics could eventually fill this gap with an operational alternative. For the time being there is, however, no alternative in sight to maintaining the concept of full rationality criticized in the quotation. It appears to be the only working hypothesis that has been successfully applied to sovereign debt.

CHAPTER 2

Sovereign Debt and Dynamic Contract Theory

I. Introduction

This chapter links up debtor sovereignty with game theory. Game-theoretic concepts are introduced which are important in understanding what is special about sovereign debt. Rather than giving general definitions of these concepts and then applying them to the issue at hand, they are introduced by way of directly touching on the strategic difficulties associated with sovereign debt. Formal requirements are thus kept to a minimum. Having brought to the fore important general aspects of debtor sovereignty they are applied to the special environment of international debt. The chapter ends with the derivation of a condition which is to replace legal enforcement of international debt contracts in the long run. This condition will be extensively applied in the analysis which follows in subsequent chapters.

II. Unenforceable Contracts, Individual Incentives and Collective Benefit

If two rational individuals meet and engage in a voluntary exchange of goods it must be to their mutual advantage. A debt contract specifies such a voluntary exchange of goods in time. One individual, the lender, must be at least as well off from receiving the future payments associated with this contract as from the best alternative use of the amount lent today. Likewise, another individual, the borrower, must prefer this loan over all alternatives open to him.

A debt contract is not a *quid pro quo* exchange, as at least some of the transfer from the borrower to the lender is to be made strictly after the receipt of the loan. Though it must be in the interest of the potential borrower to become a party to a debt contract it need not at all be in this party's interest to meet its obligations from the contract after the loan is received. This distinction between *ex ante* incentives and *ex post* incentives, where *ex ante* and *ex post* refer to the moment when the loan is made, constitutes the problem of dynamic inconsistency a lender must face before making a loan.

A potential lender will only become a party to a debt contract if the loan remains part of the optimal allocation of resources if all possible consequences of dynamic inconsistency are taken into account. Sovereign and non-sovereign debt vary with respect to the difficulty with which this dynamic incentive problem is overcome.

In the case of non-sovereign debt the resolution of the dynamic inconsistency problem is particularly simple. The disincentives for the debtor to comply with the unpleasant stipulations of the contract, given his ability, are simply irrelevant for the lender. The legal system provides the lender with enforcement instruments which make the payoff to the lender, given solvency, independent of the decisions the debtor takes. In signing a debt contract the borrower gives up the right as well as the ability to inflict losses on the lender other than those which arise from violations of the solvency condition.[1]

If contracts cannot be enforced, dynamic inconsistency poses a more serious problem. A debtor can then violate some or all contractual stipulations, thereby inflicting losses on the lender without having to suffer from a forced transfer to the lender which either exhausts the lender's legal claims or the debtor's resources. The parties to an unenforceable debt contract are thus strategically interconnected. Figure 2.1 illustrates the strategic situation two potential parties to an unenforceable debt contract may have to face.

For simplicity, we presume that each party can pursue one of only two possible strategies. The potential lender chooses rows and the borrower chooses columns. The payoffs associated with the four possible realizations of the game are given by the four pairs of numbers in the box. The first entry lists the payoff to the potential lender and the second entry the payoff

	honor	cheat
lend	1, 1	-1, 2
do not lend	0, 0	0, 0

Figure 2.1 *The prisoners' dilemma.*

to the borrower. Payoffs are defined as the gains the parties receive over what they would receive from their best alternative contracts available.

If the loan is made and the debtor honours the contract, then both receive 1 as a payoff. This would indeed be the outcome if contract enforcement prevented the debtor from cheating. It is, however, apparent from Figure 2.1 that this outcome will not be realized if enforcement mechanisms fail to exist. For if the debtor cheats he can reap a payoff of 2 at the expense of the lender who receives -1 in this case. Whenever the borrower receives a loan it is therefore in his best interest to cheat. It is straightforward that under these circumstances it is best for the potential lender not to make a loan. Under unenforceability of debt the payoff is $(0, 0)$ although under a cooperative mode of behaviour the pareto-dominant payoff $(1, 1)$ could be reached. It is, however, the dynamically inconsistent incentive structure of the borrower which prevents this. Although he prefers cooperation over not receiving the loan, his *ex-post* incentives make him cheat once the loan is made.

The situation depicted in Figure 2.1 is a variant of the single-stage prisoners' dilemma game.[2] The prisoners' dilemma is a notorious example of situations in which individual incentives work against the collective benefit.

Unavailable enforcement technologies can turn a situation in which there is harmony between individual and collective interests into one of conflicting interests. When enforcement mechanisms are unavailable to prevent collectively harmful behaviour there arises the question whether there are substitutes available which can take their place. Fortunately, the prospects for collectively beneficial behaviour in loan agreements, despite a lack of legal enforcement, are brighter than the single-stage prisoners' dilemma would predict.

III. Long-run Debt Relationships and Implicit Contracting

III.1. Repeated prisoners' dilemma games

The single-stage prisoners' dilemma would correctly depict the debtor's inclination to behave irresponsibly in a one-shot sovereign debt relationship. Cheating is unconditionally optimal because the debtor has to balance the immediate gain from cheating against nothing. Debtors, however, are often interested in a long-term credit relationship. A long-term relationship can emerge through repeated contracting between the same parties or through successive contracts between one party and different members of a group of parties.

In a lasting credit relationship the incentive structure can turn against cheating. Because the debtor now has to balance the immediate gain from cheating against possible losses in the long run. Such losses are possible because creditors now can *react* differently to responsible or irresponsible behaviour of a debtor in the past. Such reactions can work like a threat and deter a debtor from cheating. Threats of retaliation thus may support cooperation. Rational, responsible behaviour in a prisoners' dilemma type of game has become widely known in the literature under the labels '(partial) cooperative equilibria for non-cooperative repeated games', or 'deterrence equilibria'.[3,4] The idea behind this concept is quite simple. Retaliation is to prevent deviations from cooperation: 'If you take the deviating action x, I will retaliate with y, which will make you regret x.'

To illustrate the concept consider again the single-stage prisoners' dilemma game depicted in Figure 2.1. But suppose now that the game is repeated indefinitely. The deviating action x then corresponds to cheating by the debtor in any given round of the game. The retaliation, y, represents the actions taken by the single creditor or the group of creditors after the debtor has breached a contract at one stage. To continue with the example, suppose that y represents a credit embargo that lasts forever. That is, the debtor faces the threat that the creditor(s) revert forever to the single-play optimal non-cooperative strategy if he ever cheats. If the debtor discounts future payoffs at the one-period constant factor h^*, $h^* \leqslant 1$, then the present value to the debtor of a permanently responsible behaviour is given by $1/(1 - h^*)$. This present value is the long-run cost of cheating today. It has to be compared with the short-run gain from cheating, which is 2. If $2 \leqslant 1/(1 - h^*)$ then it is optimal for the debtor to honour every contract forever. This is the case if $h^* \geqslant 1/2$. Cooperation between debtors and creditors under conditions of unenforceability can therefore emerge if the relationship is to be long-lasting.

To be eventually part of what effectively determines the behaviour of the debtor, the deterrent, y, need not be explicitly stipulated in a contract. It suffices that y is implicit in the sense that there is a tacit understanding amongst the parties involved that y is part of the overall behaviour of the creditor(s). This is at variance with legally enforceable contracts where collateral, seniority provisions, or the seizure of assets upon default are explicitly stipulated in the debt contract or in the legal codex by which it is backed. To distinguish contracts which are backed only by a set of implicit modes of behaviour from contracts which are legally enforceable the former are called 'implicit contracts'. Implicit contracting is to play a key role in understanding sovereign debt.

It is helpful to distinguish different classes (Crawford, 1987). They differ with respect to the parties involved.

III.2. Internal implicit contracts

Implicit contracting may involve only two parties. The repeated prisoners' dilemma analysed above is an example of this if a debtor time and again contracts with the same creditor. Stipulations, implicit in the contract, are then entirely internal and do not involve third parties. From the point of view of the creditor an internally implicit contract has the advantage that potential punishments can be designed without having to take account of third parties. An example for this would be if the creditor is a monopolist with respect to the debtor at hand. A credit embargo then does not require coordination with other creditors.

III.3. External implicit contracts

A debtor can often turn to different creditors for a loan. An embargo issued by a betrayed creditor is a weak deterrent if a debtor can successfully turn to someone else for a new loan. In this situation an implicit contract may be termed external because it involves outside parties. A credit embargo, for example, has to be supported by all potential lenders to become a deterrent.[5]

IV. Credible Threats

Under conditions of legal enforcement the legal system provides an automatic execution of certain punishments upon a breach of contract. In addition, parties can stipulate punishments in a contract beyond those standardized in the legal codex. Automatic enforcement then pertains to these as well. Punishments under legal enforcement can therefore act as an effective deterrent.

When contracts are not enforceable matters are more complicated. A debtor can be deterred from cheating by the threat of punishment if he is convinced that the punishment will in fact be executed once he has cheated. It is not at all clear, however, that participation in punishment is in the self-interest of everyone called upon to participate. After all a punishment must necessarily imply a withdrawal from cooperation practised so far. Compared to continued cooperation it may inflict deadweight losses on those who execute the threat. Hence, both the delinquent and the hangmen may be victims of the punishment. Therefore, under unenforceability, threats which are implicit in a contract must be credible. With egoistic creditors, credibility requires that it is in each creditor's self-interest to participate in the punishment after a defection has been observed. A debtor then can have no doubts about having to suffer from the execution of a threat if he chooses to defect. The question then arises what constitutes credibility.

IV.1. The perfectness concept

Subgame-perfectness (in the sense of Selten, 1975) of deterrent strategies is acknowledged as a necessary condition for threats to be credible. Cooperation in a repeated game must therefore be supported by (subgame-) perfect deterrent strategies or threats, and the implicit contract must be a (subgame-) perfect Nash equilibrium.

A (subgame-) perfect strategy is a contingency plan prescribing optimal moves for all possible states at all possible stages of a game. Therefore, if threat strategies are (subgame-) perfect, a player has no incentive to *unilaterally* abstain from participation in a costly punishment whoever the defector may be, whenever defection may occur and whatever its nature. A threat which is not perfect cannot be credible.

As a second implication from perfectness it follows that the set of perfect deterrent strategies which form a credible threat are Nash equilibrium strategies. In a Nash equilibrium all strategies are optimal with respect to one another.[6]

At this point an important remark is due. From what was said above it follows that the game-theoretic approach to analysing unenforceable contracts is to view contractual agreements as equilibrium points of a non-cooperative game in time. In this view, contractual agreements are but another example of voluntary exchanges and as such must fulfil certain equilibrium conditions. What makes implicit equilibrium contracts different from equilibrium *quid-pro-quo* exchanges is that the former must take account of a discretionary freedom which can produce a non-equilibrium outcome.

For an illustration of the perfectness concept consider again the repeated prisoners' dilemma in Figure 2.1. Under an internal implicit contract the deterrence strategy requires the sole creditor to lend anew in each repetition of the game for as long as the debtor does not cheat. Contingent on the observation of a defection it calls for a credit embargo for the remainder of time. This strategy is perfect. A debtor who ever decided to cheat would do so in all subsequent periods as in each the same game is played. In this case it is optimal for the creditor never to lend again. Facing a credible termination of the credit relation, and given $h^* \geqslant 1/2$, it is optimal for the debtor to be honest. In turn, facing an honest borrower, it is optimal for the lender to stick to the first part of the deterrent strategy and lend for as long as honesty prevails. Therefore, to cooperate indefinitely is a perfect Nash equilibrium.

Let us continue with the illustration in the context of an external implicit contract. Suppose there exist many lenders and many debtors. Suppose that the single-stage game played by any two members of each group can be described by Figure 2.1. In other words, suppose all lenders and all debtors are identical. Consider a deterrent strategy which requires a creditor to lend whenever he links up with a borrower who has never been dishonest in the past, but never lend to anyone with a history of one or more violations of contract. Obviously, honesty can never again be optimal for a debtor who has cheated in the past and whose fortune it is to receive another loan. This lets it indeed be optimal for each potential lender to abstain from lending to anyone who has cheated in the past. Again, for $h^* \geqslant 1/2$, it is optimal for each debtor to be honest. Cooperation is therefore sustainable as a perfect Nash equilibrium in an external implicit credit relationship.

IV.2. Sufficient conditions

So far perfectness has been shown to be a necessary condition for the credibility of threats. We cannot be certain, however, that perfectness alone is also sufficient. In fact, it can be shown that in general, perfectness is not sufficient (Mohr, 1988a). Important cases can be identified in which sufficient conditions fail to exist. In these cases all threats are incredible. The problem with sufficiency requires some more fundamental considerations, but it can be illustrated in the context of our example.

In games, one has to carefully distinguish between an equilibrium of a game and its solution. We refer to a solution of a game as that evolution (or outcome) of a game which we can expect to materialize as a consequence of rational behaviour of all players. Therefore, the key to finding a solution is to define rationality by a set of axioms which we trust to govern the behaviour of all rational players. In fact, in requiring that cooperation must be a perfect equilibrium we implicitly appeal to this set of axioms.

However, the set contains more elements than those required for the perfectness condition. If an equilibrium is not unique, to find the solution, we need additional axioms which can prescribe what the rational choice of players amongst different equilibria should be. The game depicted in Figure 2.1 is an example of such non-uniqueness.

Besides cooperation from the beginning, the single-stage Nash equilibrium of refusing a loan – and cheating whenever a loan is obtained – also remains an equilibrium point in the repeated prisoners' dilemma. Therefore we need to appeal to further axioms which support cooperation as the solution of the game against its potential contestant. Put differently, we need a principle which governs the players' rationality in such a way that the game starts to unwind cooperatively. In our example, we could appeal, for example, to an axiom which requires each player to choose that equilibrium strategy which corresponds to the equilibrium which is unanimously preferred by everyone.[7]

To be content with such an argument in support of the cooperative equilibrium without additional considerations would mean, however, to paper over a substantial crack. In many situations we should require rationality to be stationary. Under such a stationarity condition the principles which govern the behaviour of players in the first round of a game would apply in all following rounds. This means that we must require the players to repeat the actions taken in the first round of the game whenever the situation is identical to the game at the start. This, however, brings the existence of credible threats into serious jeopardy.

This can be illustrated again by our example in Figure 2.1. The point is that if cheating does not alter the game, in the sense that Figure 2.1 continues to describe the payoffs even after a defection has occurred, after a cheat players are again in the same situation as they were at the beginning of the game. Therefore, if it was rational to cooperate initially, it must be rational to do so again. Evidently, in this case the perfect threat of a credit embargo is incredible. Furthermore, it is straightforward that under these circumstances sufficient conditions for credibility fail to exist.

It is perhaps worthwhile to look at the dilemma we face from a different angle. What we ended up with was the conclusion that threats are incredible if players let bygones be bygones. This is self-evident. But a different and stronger point is made: games can be identified in which conditions which are necessary for a deterrence equilibrium to constitute a solution to a game just require that players let 'bygones' be 'bygones'.[8]

How can the deterrence equilibrium be saved? Several special cases allow for an escape route.[9] One way out of the dilemma would be offered in a game in which the party which is to execute the threat was indifferent between the cooperative and the non-cooperative equilibrium.[10] A different escape route exists in a model in which a defection changes the nature of the game so that cooperation becomes impossible after a defection has occurred. Then a player can have no doubts about the execution of a perfect punishment. In this case, perfectness is a necessary and sufficient condition for the credibility of threats.

Again, this can be illustrated in our example. If, for example, cheating forces the lending party to an internal implicit contract into bankruptcy, cooperation will prevail if $h^* \geqslant 1/2$. It is, however, necessary that a dishonest course of action available to the debtor, which saves the lender from bankruptcy, does not exist.

In external implicit contracts certain legal provisions between potential creditors can achieve such a change in the structure of an external debt relation. Suppose, for example, that seniority provisions guaranteed that the claims remaining from a past violation of a contract are senior to debt issued subsequently. Another creditor, prone to forget a debtor's sins of the past, would know that the proceeds from a new loan would automatically be handed over to the creditor who holds a senior title. A new lender is therefore unavailable if the party holding the title to a senior claim does not waive it. However, it is not optimal to waive a senior claim if it provides the chance of acquiring the payments the debtor eventually makes to anyone. The effect of seniority provisions is therefore to turn an external implicit contract into an internal one once a contract violation has occurred. If the costs of incurring such restrictions on the credit markets are high enough, seniority provisions can sustain cooperation in an external implicit debt contract.

Fortunately, there are several mechanisms and institutional arrangements operating in international debt markets which can function like seniority provisions in changing the nature of the game upon a contract violation. Before turning to a discussion of international debt markets in light of the game-theoretic concepts outlined above we turn to further complications associated with implicit contracts.

IV.3. Ramifications

So far we have restricted our attention to the simple threat of reverting to the single-stage optimal non-cooperative Nash behaviour forever once a defection has been observed. This restriction, however, is not necessary as in general there exists a plethora of threats which can be part of an equilibrium implicit contract. As a consequence, there usually exists a multiplicity of deterrence equilibria to a given repeated game (Lockwood, 1986). There are two directions in which the sophistication of the simple threat, discussed above, can proceed. First, the degree of collusion may be increased through threats which are more severe than reverting to the non-cooperative Nash equilibrium (Abreu, 1983). Second, for a given degree of cooperation, the non-cooperative threat indeed may be an 'overkill', and threats which are less costly to *all* may suffice to ensure a given degree of cooperation (Cave, 1983).

A second ramification pertains to the duration of a relationship. In our example we have presumed that the single-stage game is repeated forever. Such a game is called a super-game. In light of the observation that the lifetime of some economic units is finite it is necessary to investigate finitely repeated games.

Cooperation arises in the super-game because of the perpetual presence of a tomorrow in which defectors have to suffer retaliation. This explains why cooperation cannot emerge in the Figure 2.1 game if it is repeated only a finite number of times. Cheating, and hence not making a loan, is optimal in the last round of the game as then it is indeed a single-stage prisoners' dilemma. By backward induction it is then also optimal not to cooperate in the last but one stage; and so on down to the first round of the game. This contradicts experiments reported in Axelrod (1981). In these experiments cooperation emerged in actual plays of the finitely repeated prisoners' dilemma.

How can cooperation emerge in finitely repeated games? Kreps *et al.* (1982) have shown that cooperation until some time before the end of the game is possible if incomplete information about one or both players' set of possible actions exists. Another possibility for cooperation arises in external implicit contract relations if an infinite overlap of finitely-lived parties creates a situation akin to a super-game (Cremer, 1986). Finally, if the lifetime of a player is uncertain and if the probability of living for another day is always positive, then a player must always assign a positive probability to having to bear the costs of a defection and cooperation can therefore emerge.

For threats to be credible a defection from cooperation must be observable. Implicit contracts which allow for cooperation therefore require that parties do not have undetectable strategies available. This condition is fulfilled in an internal implicit contract relationship if deterministic strategies are played. Defections from randomized cooperative strategies, however, cannot be sensibly regarded as observable in general. In external implicit contracts observability can pose a problem even if choices are deterministic. If the number of parties involved is large, monitoring the behaviour of one party becomes increasingly difficult. Therefore, implicit contracting is more likely to be applicable to small rather than to large groups.[11]

With respect to unenforceable debt contracts, payments made by a debtor are observable. However, a problem can arise if payments due are indexed to a variable under the unobservable control of the debtor. The size of the parties involved in an external credit contract, however, is likely not to pose many difficulties. A careful recording and systematic exchange among banks of information about debtors' behaviour can ensure that past defections are also known to potential new lenders.

V. Implicit International Debt Contracts

V.1. The debtors

Governments, government agencies, firms and in principle even private households can borrow on international credit markets. Should this heterogeneity not be carefully taken into account when international debt is classified as sovereign? Bonds bearing the name of a foreign nation constitute sovereign debt in the sense in which we defined the term. Also, loans made to a foreign government as the most senior decision-making authority in a country qualify as sovereign debt. On the other hand, international debt incurred by subordinate units, be they regional or local authorities, firms, or households, are subject to enforcement in their home countries. For a number of reasons, however, this kind of international debt must be treated as if it were issued by the highest authorities in a country. Thus it, too, is sovereign.

Foreign loans ending in the pockets of the private sector in an indebted country in fact are often debt issued directly by the home government. This is so because rather than having foreign banks making many small loans directly to the domestic private sector, governments sometimes issue foreign debt which then is passed along to the private sector according to the credit demands of domestic firms. Such 'jumbo loans' constitute sovereign debt as far as international economic relations are concerned.

An advantage for the government of issuing debt for its domestic clientele is that it can directly control its use by requiring domestic firms to fulfil certain conditions before qualifying for the loan. One might argue that a disadvantage for banks of making 'jumbo loans' is the fact that the debtor is sovereign whereas under direct lending the debtor is subject to legal enforcement at home. However, this very often proves to be worth very little.

Legal enforcement of private international debt contracts under the law of either country is difficult. If the creditor has the luck to identify assets owned by the private debtor held in the creditor's home country, appealing for enforcement under the law of the lender's home country may be successful. The situation may be similar if assets are held in a third country. However, in very many cases the creditors will have to face the fact that a foreign borrower's main assets are kept at home in the sanctuary of the borrower's domestic legal system.

A creditor may find it impossible to seize assets kept in the borrower's home country. Local expertise and professional assistance, if available at all, may turn out only formally to side with the plaintiff. Kinship and nepotism play important roles in some countries. Even if the plaintiff eventually obtains his rights before the courts he still may have a long way to go before his right to seizure is enforced. Finally, once enforced he may end up with a claim to an empty shell or, more cynically perhaps, one that he may find impossible to retrieve.[12]

These are some of the reasons why making a loan to a sovereign poses no or little disadvantage against making a loan directly to a subject under foreign sovereignty. The fact that banks regularly require a debt guarantee from a foreign private borrower's home government even suggests that advantages must exist in the debtor being a foreign government. Under a government guarantee of an international loan a creditor can turn for repayment to the home government of a foreign private borrower if the borrower fails to meet his obligations.

Surveillance of a government is very likely to be less costly for a foreign bank than surveillance of a multitude of private borrowers, locally dispersed, and operating in different sectors. Furthermore an entire nation's stake in the international economic game is certain to be higher than the stake of any private economic unit within the nation. A government taking account of the interests of at least a number of its subjects can therefore be expected to be a more reliable debtor than any of its subjects.

Before turning to the stake a nation may have in the international market, we conclude that there are good reasons for treating international private debts as though they were issued by a sovereign.[13] In fact, in the theoretical analysis of the remaining chapters we shall presume that all international debt is sovereign and is issued in the name of a nation.

The observation that issuers of international debt essentially are nations implies that the debtors always face a tomorrow where the costs of contract violations today have to be borne. One could object and argue that although the time horizon of a country is infinite or arbitrarily large, the time horizon of a country's highest authority in executive office need not be. In fact, the time horizon of governments sometimes appears to be short. Nevertheless, except for pathological cases, it extends at least for some time into the future. Even for the most unpopular government there may be a small chance of remaining in office. And even if power is lost, parties and interest groups that formed the former government continue to exist and suffer from the costs of punishments due to past violations of international debt contracts.

V.2. Deterrents related to capital markets

Sovereign international debt contracts must be supported by implicit deterrents which ensure that the costs of breaching a debt contract exceed the costs of honouring it. International financial markets are one link through which costs from contract violations can be inflicted on a country.

A country's continued access to international capital markets can depend on the reputation it has built up in the past. Contract violations today then diminish a country's reputation and inflict costs on a country in the form of higher credit costs or a tighter credit line in the future. Historical evidence of international debt contract violations and associated impediments of future access to credit markets suggests the following:[14]

The fact that the history of international debt relations is plagued by many incidences of contract violations suggests that its costs have very often been too low to prevent these violations. Furthermore, costs have appeared to vary considerably in time and across countries. Finally, punishments in the form of restricted access to international credit markets have been conspicuously limited in time. Rather than having to suffer the non-cooperative Nash punishment of an eternal credit embargo, countries have frequently been allowed to borrow again soon after debt contract violations.[15]

The theory of implicit contracting, however, suggests that a prolonged exclusion from new loans may be unnecessary if milder forms of punishment suffice to entail cooperation. Furthermore, implicit contracts may include certain types of excusable default (Grossman and Van Huyck, 1988). According to this view, falling short on one's payment obligations does not constitute a breach of contract if it occurs in a state of the world in which this violation is tacitly excusable.

The history of international debt, however, does not suggest that impediments to a country's free access to credit markets are completely absent from international debt markets. Countries have been regularly kept short of fresh money at least for some time after obligations from old debt have not been met.

This, in part, is due to institutional arrangements. Historically, the legal right of holders of unserviced bonds to block a country's issuance of new bonds abroad has successfully prevented a continued access to international credit markets. In the situation, a country has first to settle the case with old bondholders before new debt can be issued. Such settlements take time. Bondholders are usually large in number and possibly dispersed in several countries. Furthermore, in a well diversified portfolio, each bondholder's stake is likely to be small. Given the costs of participation in bondholder clubs it can be difficult for a country to reach such settlements.

There is a second aspect to the blocking of new bond issues. This aspect relates to the credibility requirement of implicit threats. Small bondholders usually have available other assets which can serve as a perfect substitute to holding bonds issued abroad. In this case, punishing a country by the blocking of new debt issues costs bondholders nothing in terms of future opportunities. More than that, it entails the prospect of obtaining at least some payment in a settlement. The atomistic nature of the demand side of international bond markets ensures therefore that the threat of a credit embargo is credible.

If international debt is bank-financed one may be rightly reluctant to rely for credibility on an atomistic supply side of bank credits. This shortcoming of bank-financing, however, is overcome by certain other institutional arrangements in the creditor countries. These are to ensure credibility of restricted access to credit markets by a forced change of the market structure, unfavourable for a debtor country. This change restricts the supply side of bank loans upon default to the bank or group of banks which already holds unserviced claims.[16]

It was already noted that seniority provisions exclude a debtor from recruiting new lenders. Countries are usually simultaneously debtors of several banks or several bank consortia. It would in principle, therefore, be possible to default on a loan from one lender while maintaining good credit relations with all other lenders who hold claims of equal seniority. This is, however, prevented by cross-default clauses. Under cross-default clauses several loans are in effect parcelled up into a single loan in that lenders agree that payments made on one loan are automatically redistributed to all parties to a cross-default clause agreement. A debtor therefore honours all debtors or defaults on all debts. Therefore, under bank-financing, a country is confronted with the credible threat of losing all opportunities on the international credit markets if it defaults on a single loan. It should be noted, however, that the monopolization of the supply side of international loans upon default does not necessarily imply a complete exclusion from credit markets. The monopolistic bank or group of banks may have a considerable stake in the game played with a country, both in terms of old debt due and in terms of new opportunities. It may therefore be in the banks' interest to continue lending despite contract violations by a debtor. It will be necessary therefore to allow for this possibility in a formal model of international debt.[17]

Further, rather obvious costs of repudiation associated with international capital markets relate to a country's international asset position. Seizure of assets already abroad or investment restrictions arising from pending seizure add to these costs. Although such costs may be important for some countries, it is a characteristic, common to many heavily indebted nations, that such assets are negligible, as is the hope of ever accumulating them.[18]

There are, however, other important sources for costs from international debt contract violations which are unrelated to capital markets. We now turn to them.

V.3. Assaults on sovereignty

The history of international debt features episodic eruptions of international confrontations in the wake of debt contract violations: seizure of goods in transit, withdrawal of military aid and foreign expertise, closing of trade routes, cancellation of preferential trade agreements, naval blockades, occupation of export harbours, even military invasions have occurred after debt contract violations. This list could be continued. For want of something better we call these phenomena 'assaults on the sovereignty' of a country. Such assaults can inflict deadweight costs on a country. The availability of a gunboat-technology in creditor countries to carry out such assaults can therefore entice an indebted country to honour debt it otherwise would not.

To start with the most martial of these assaults, military interventions have been the rare exception, confined to the period before the world economic crisis of 1928–32.[19] Although there are perhaps good reasons for presuming that military interventions intended to punish an indebted country belong strictly to the past, countries may be threatened by less spectacular but nevertheless economically harmful sanctions.

Trade-related sanctions have to be mentioned here first. To prevent a further seizure of export goods, second-best transport-routing may have to be chosen. Besides directly increasing transportation costs, a country thereby may even be excluded from some lucrative foreign markets. The country may have to face the fact that the cancellation of preferential trade agreements may be taken a step further and specific duties levied. On the import side the country may be cut off from essential supplies and thus technological development may suffer since sanctions also affect other sectors of the economy.

The reader may wonder why creditor countries impose sanctions *after* a debtor country has violated a contract. If anything, sanctions reduce the debtor's *ex post* ability to pay. Sanctions, however, can buttress a creditor country's position in negotiations as their suspension can be traded in for receiving at least some payments. Kaempfer and Lowenberg (1988) provide a public choice approach for explaining sanctions. They show that sanctions can serve the interests of pressure groups in the sanctioning country, for example domestic producers who are competing with the importers.[20] Economic sanctions against debtor countries falling behind on their payments can therefore be consistent with interests of, or within, the creditor countries.

V.4. Deadweight losses

In principle, two cases have to be distinguished as to whether costs from punishment inflicted upon a debtor country are deadweight losses for the world community or whether they are, at least in part, repatriated as gains from punishment in the creditor countries. Empirically, perhaps, such gains are negligible, and in any case the literature regularly abstracts from them. It is, however, worthwhile to make clear the importance of possible gains from punishment. Given the credibility of threats, the fact that gunboat-technology provides an opportunity for capturing part of a debtor's ships in transit as a prize is irrelevant for the debtor's behaviour, as for him a ship captured is like a ship sunk.

However, the variant of gunboat-technology which is relevant can be important in determining whether the threat of its application is credible. A small gain accruing to the creditors from the execution of a threat may suffice in tipping the balance in its favour. As in the chapters to come we shall be only concerned with threats which are taken to be credible we shall make the simplifying assumption for much of the remainder of this book that costs from punishments are deadweight losses.

V.5. Resolving the carrot vs stick dichotomy

There is some disagreement in the literature whether the compliance of a sovereign debtor with a contract is to be motivated by the carrot of future access to credit markets alone, or perhaps also by the stick of economic sanctions.[21] In defence of the 'carrot-alone' view one can perhaps argue that the world community lacks a credible gunboat-technology. A more conceptual argument pertains to the distinction between sovereign and non-sovereign debt. As sanctions are inflicted upon the sovereignty of the debtor nations, allowing for them deemphasizes the distinction between the two types of debt. On the other hand, an important point in favour of the 'stick-also' approach is that besides directly causing pecuniary costs, a credit embargo transmits frictions into real economic activity just as sanctions do.

This observation has led to the simplification of not distinguishing any more between carrots and sticks in that the costs of both are expressed in terms of real economic activity alone. Without necessarily contesting both views, we pursue here a neutral approach which nevertheless allows for doing justice to both of them.

In this book we allow for both credit embargoes and sanctions. In that we differ from the 'carrot-only' approach. However, we also depart from the 'stick-also' approach in that we maintain explicit the destinction between the costs inflicted by credit embargoes and those inflicted by sanctions.

This approach features several advantages over its alternatives. In keeping the distinction between the two types of deterrents explicit, we can, with only simple modifications, examine the two cases of 'carrot-only' and 'stick-also'. Interestingly, there are important differences to be observed which are necessarily obscured if the different forms of punishments are aggregated into one. Furthermore, under this approach it is possible to vary the degree of economic sanctions while keeping costs from a credit embargo constant. This allows for viewing sovereign debt as a problem of degree. It is thereby possible to characterize non-sovereign debt and debt under 'carrots-only' as the two polar, limiting cases of sovereign debt.

VI. Long-run Implicit Enforcement Conditions

In this book we investigate the long-run effects of sovereign international debt. To be more precise, we are interested in the long-run equilibrium in a simplified world economy under debtor sovereignty. Of particular interest in this context are the conditions under which a debt relationship without contract violations between a creditor economy and a debtor economy is sustainable as an equilibrium. We have to determine therefore the long-run conditions under which a debtor always wants to honour a debt contract. To that end we make a number of simplifying assumptions.[22]

It is simply presumed that the threats which are to guarantee cooperation are credible. In that we implicitly have recourse to the factors which render credibility possible, discussed in Sections IV and V of this chapter. However, when they turn up, we shall return to some of the finer points of credibility.

As a second simplifying assumption we restrict the intertemporal depth of punishment to its barest minimum in presuming that punishments are restricted to the immediate future. To simplify even further we go to the limit and assume that punishment is instantaneous, so that all costs from a contract violation have to be borne in the same period in which it occurs.[23] This simplification results from the fact that for making some contracts implicitly enforceable the requirement is simply *that*, rather than *when* punishment is feasible. These assumptions are more innocuous than they may appear. We shall later return to this for motivation.

In much of the analysis, but not throughout we take it that debt contracts between creditors and a sovereign debtor are characterized by the following

Assumption 2.1: For all time periods t, international credit given in period $t-1$ matures in period t. The one-period interest rate on international debt, r^{i*}, is exogeneous in period t.[24]

The standard loan contract characterized in Assumption 2.1 has the property that debt accumulation over several periods does not occur if contracts are honoured. The amount borrowed in one period is equal to the total indebtedness of a borrower in the next period. Let b^*_{-1} be the amount a sovereign borrows from abroad in period $t-1$, defined on a unit of measurement, L_{-1}, specific to all quantities in period $t-1$. The payment due from amortization and interest payments in period t, z', is then given by

$$z' = b^*_{-1} \cdot (1 + r^{i*}) \tag{2.1}$$

The payment z' is the cost of honouring the debt contract from period $t-1$. In deciding on a contract violation the sovereign compares these costs with the costs of breaking the contract.

Contract violations can take various forms. For example, in the standard contract of Assumption 2.1 which entails a payment due, z', we can define a continuum of contract violations on the continuum of actual payments made, in the interval $[0, z']$. The lower bound of this interval is overall debt repudiation. A sovereign's choice from this continuum will depend on the consequences each element entails.

If the consequences differ across the set of available violations then the costs of breaching a debt contract are endogenous to the sovereign. In this case it can be optimal for the sovereign neither to honour the contract in full nor to choose outright repudiation (Aizenman, 1989a). For the time being, however, we make the following

Assumption 2.2: The costs of contract violations are independent of the kind of violation.

UNIVERSITY OF BRISTOL LIBRARY

An immediate consequence of this assumption is that outright repudiation is the optimal form of debt contract violation as the sovereign receives no discount on the punishment she suffers from making a positive payment below z'.

It should be noted that Assumption 2.2 does not necessarily imply that the costs from contract violation are exogenous to the sovereign. Although these costs cannot be immediately influenced by the choice of the kind of violation, other actions taken by the sovereign *before* debt is repudiated nevertheless can influence the costs from punishment. Whether such safeguards against punishment are available to the sovereign will depend on the gunboat-technology she faces.

Following the 'stick-also' approach to punishment it is assumed that sanctions are inflicted upon the economic activity of the sovereign. More precisely, it is assumed that the costs from sanctions are proportional to the level of economic activity in the period of repudiation. In choosing this level, the sovereign determines the costs she has to face from repudiation. Let the level of economic activity in period t be given by $y^* > 0$, defined in terms of a unit of measurement, L, specific to all quantities in t. If δ, $\delta \geqslant 0$, denotes the parameter that relates the level of economic activity to the costs of economic sanctions, the latter are given by $\delta \cdot y^*$. Higher values of δ represent more draconian sanctions and imply higher costs from repudiation, given y^*.

For $\delta = 0$ a gunboat-technology is unavailable to the creditors. International debt contracts then are of the 'carrot-only' variant. Upon repudiation, we assume that the sovereign is immediately penalized by a credit embargo. That is, if the sovereign repudiates debt due in period t, she loses the new loan, b^*, defined in terms of the unit of measurement, L, which she would have received had she honoured the debt obligations in t.

In order to determine the condition for the sovereign's incentive to honour debt in period t it remains only to make quantities in the periods $t-1$ and t comparable. Let n, $n \gtreqless 0$, be the constant one-period proportional growth rate of the unit of measurement, so that

$$L = L_{-1} \cdot (1 + n) \ \forall t \tag{2.2}$$

Then, from equations (2.1) and (2.2) a sufficient condition that the sovereign abstains from debt repudiation in period t is given by

$$b^*_{-1} \cdot (1 + r^{i*}) \leqslant b^* \cdot (1 + n) + \delta \cdot y^* \cdot (1 + n) \tag{2.3}$$

The term on the LHS of condition (2.3) is the cost from honouring debt in period t, defined on the unit of measurement L_{-1}. The RHS represents the immediate costs from repudiation also defined on L_{-1}. It is the sum of the costs from the lost access to the credit market and the costs from economic sanctions in period t. If the costs from honouring debt in t do not exceed the immediate costs from repudiation, then a rational sovereign will abstain from repudiation in t.

As it is assumed that costs from contract violations are restricted to the period in which debt is repudiated, the RHS of (2.3) represents all costs associated with repudiation. Therefore, (2.3) is also a necessary condition that debt is honoured in period t. If condition (2.3) is violated then a rational sovereign will repudiate debt. Creditors will have to observe condition (2.3) when making loans in $t-1$. As it emanates from the sovereignty of a debtor we shall call it subsequently the sovereignty restriction on international debt.

As in the chapters that follow our main interest is in analysing international debt in the long-run equilibrium we have to determine the sovereignty restriction for this case. In the framework we shall employ, long-run equilibrium is given as a steady state in which all variables remain constant from period to period. That is, in the long-run equilibrium we have $b_{-1}^* = b^*$ in which case condition (2.3) can be simplified to

$$z \equiv \frac{b^*}{1+n} \cdot (r^{i*} - n) \leqslant \delta \cdot y^* \tag{2.4}$$

The sovereignty restriction (2.4) will be at the heart of the analysis in most of the following chapters. It is therefore worth discussing some of its basic properties and implications at this point.

On the LHS of restriction (2.4) we have, in terms of the period t unit of measurement, the obligations from debt servicing net of the inflow of fresh money due to a continued access to the credit market. Therefore, z is the net transfer from the sovereign to her creditors that is needed to avoid a contract violation. Put differently, z is the net cost to the sovereign of maintaining a good relationship with her creditors. So, what the sovereignty restriction (2.4) says is that the net cost to the sovereign of maintaining the debt relationship must not exceed the costs arising from economic sanctions if repudiation is to be avoided in the long run.

From equation (2.2), the steady-state condition $b_{-1}^* = b^*$ implies that the principal due is permanently rolled over by new loans of equal size if $n = 0$. From restriction (2.4) the net transfer to the creditors, z, then is equal to the interest payments due. If $n > 0$, then, from equation (2.2), $b_{-1}^* = b^*$ implies that in each period the total new loan exceeds the total loan received in the previous period. Growth in terms of lending reduces the sovereign's net costs from maintaining a credit relationship, z.

In the steady state, the effective interest rate on maintaining the credit relationship is $r^{i*} - n$. For $n < 0$, the loan size decreases through time; the effective interest rate on international debt is above the nominal rate, r^{i*}.

From restriction (2.4), the large n is, the less severe economic sanctions can be in order to allow the maintenance of a debt relationship. If $n > r^{i*}$ then $z < 0$, that is the sovereign enjoys a net gain from maintaining a debt relationship. It is plain that a sovereign will never repudiate debt in this case.

Conditions (2.3) and (2.4) help to clarify what the steady-state value is to a sovereign of maintaining access to loans in the future. In condition (2.3) it is recognized that the sovereign loses the loan $b^* \cdot (1+n)$ under repudiation in t. The loan size $b^* \cdot (1+n)$ is obviously the cost of lost access to the credit market in t if repudiation otherwise occurred in $t+1$. However, if restriction (2.3) is fulfilled in $t+1$, repudiation would not occur in $t+1$. The value of obtaining the new loan in t is therefore not given by the size of the loan, as it will be repaid in $t+1$, but, instead, by the size of the surplus after deducting the debt servicing it entails (Hellwig, 1986).

If the steady-state sovereignty restriction (2.4) is observed, repudiation never occurs. The question therefore arises as to whether the steady-state condition (2.4), derived from (2.3), is correctly specified.

The answer is yes. In the steady-state, to determine the value of a loan to a sovereign, the present loan size need not be compared with future obligations stemming from it, it suffices to compare it with current obligations from debt due as they have to be met to obtain the loan. The period value to the sovereign from the steady-state debt relationship is therefore given by $-z = (n - r^{i*}) \cdot b^*/(1+n)$.

For $n < r^{i*}$ this value is negative. Interpreted differently, condition (2.4) states that a sovereign will abstain forever from repudiating debt which has a negative value to her if the value *per period*, in absolute terms, is exceeded by the *total* costs of economic sanctions arising from repudiation today. The sovereignty restriction, therefore, does not compare the total, or present, value of the debt relation with the total, or present, value costs from economic sanctions.

The reason for this asymmetry is simply that in the steady state a necessary and sufficient condition for abstaining forever from repudiation is that it is not optimal to repudiate today. For this to be the case it is only necessary that the running net costs of continuing the relationship for another period, $(r^{i*} - n) \cdot b^*/(1+n)$, do not exceed the total costs from sanctions which arise if repudiation occurs today instead of tomorrow.[25]

The sovereignty restriction (2.4) is derived under the simplifying assumption that economic sanctions are restricted to the period in which a contract is violated. To support the claim that this assumption is innocuous, suppose for the moment that, after a contract violation has occurred, the sovereign is penalized by sanctions extending indefinitely into the future. Let the costs in period $t+j$, defined in terms of the unit of measurement,

L_{+j}, be constant and equal to $\delta' \cdot y^* \;\forall\, j = 0, 1, \ldots, \infty$. If the time horizon of the sovereign is infinite then the value of the stream of sanctions discounted at the rate r^{i*} is given by

$$\delta' \cdot y^* \cdot \frac{1 + r^{i*}}{r^{i*} - n}$$

This alternative gunboat-technology is equivalent to the technology underlying condition (2.4), in the sense of sustaining the same set of sovereign debt contracts, if

$$\delta = \delta' \cdot \frac{1 + r^{i*}}{r^{i*} - n}$$

This is an example of the general observation that threats which sustain a given set of implicit contracts are not unique (e.g. Abreu, 1983). In general, there exists a multitude of equivalent threats and it would be easy to find many other gunboat-technologies which are equivalent to the one assumed in restriction (2.4). So rather than for the single-shot economic sanction $\delta \cdot y^*$ alone, condition (2.4) represents the sovereignty restriction for the entire set of sanctions which are equivalent to an immediate single shot which costs $\delta \cdot y^*$.[26]

A different equivalence pertains to the solvency of the sovereign. Let y^* be the constant resources available for debt service per period, in terms of the unit of measurement L_{+j}, $j = 0, 1, \ldots, \infty$. Then a steady-state debt level, b^*, can be sustained by the debtor's ability to pay if

$$z \leqslant y^* \tag{2.5}$$

that is, if the net payment obligation from debt can be met by the debtor's income. From a comparison of (2.5) with (2.4) it immediately follows that the sovereign's willingness to pay corresponds to her ability to pay if $\delta = 1$, that is, if in the period of repudiation the sovereign loses her entire income through sanctions.

The reader may be somewhat surprised that $\delta = 1$ suffices to make solvency become the bottleneck restriction. After all, economic sanctions are of the immediate single-shot (equivalence) variant while solvency is a concept which draws on an infinite time horizon. In the present model, for example, the steady-state value of the infinite sequence of income, y^*, defined on L_{+j}, $j = 0, 1, \ldots, \infty$, discounted at the rate r^{i*}, is given by $y^* \cdot (1 + r^{i*})/(r^{i*} - n)$, and solvency requires

$$(1 + r^{i*}) \cdot \frac{b^*}{1 + n} \leqslant \frac{1 + r^{i*}}{r^{i*} - n} \cdot y^* \tag{2.6}$$

from which we obtain condition (2.5).

The reason why $\delta = 1$, under the immediate single-shot sanction-technology, suffices to make solvency the binding restriction once again hinges on the steady-state nature of the analysis. In the steady state, solvency requires that the debtor is able to meet the current net transfer to the creditors in each period out of current income available. If, upon repudiation, today's entire income is destroyed, repudiation does not pay today and therefore not in any future period if condition (2.5) is met. Draconian sanctions, completely destroying current income, restricted, however, to the period of contract violation, suffice to make solvency become the binding restriction.

An implication of the above analysis is that the credibility requirements of threats which are to sustain a given degree of cooperation are less demanding than one perhaps would expect. It is an observation frequently made that public opinion soon turns against those who execute a punishment. Credibility, therefore is likely to be a condition which is harder to meet, the longer the duration of the threatened punishment. The above analysis, however, suggests that prolonged punishments are not needed; short, but severe punishments, whose credibility requirements are easier to meet, suffice to sustain even the highest possible degree of cooperation.

The bounds $1 \geqslant \delta \geqslant 0$ define the realm in which debtor sovereignty can exist in the steady state. The parameter δ, within these bounds, can be interpreted as defining the degree of sovereignty the debtor enjoys.

For $\delta \geqslant 1$ solvency is the bottleneck restriction and sovereignty is irrelevant. For $\delta < 1$ solvency is irrelevant and the sovereignty restriction (2.4) is the bottleneck restriction. If a non-sovereign debtor has failed to meet his obligations, he has lost the collateral y^*. If a sovereign violates the contract, she loses $\delta \cdot y^*$. For $\delta \leqslant 1$ a decrease in δ can therefore be interpreted as an increase in the effective sovereignty of a debtor. For $\delta = 0$ sovereignty is complete. Non-sovereignty and sovereignty under 'carrots-only' can therefore be viewed as the polar limiting cases of sovereign debt.

The sovereignty restriction allows important insights into the economic implications of the dichotomy 'carrots-only' vs. 'stick-also'. If economic sanctions are impossible, that is if $\delta = 0$, then restriction (2.4) requires that the net transfer from the sovereign to her creditors must be non-positive at all times. Under a lack of economic sanctions the sovereign therefore never accepts an outflow of resources to the creditors. Debt servicing must be fully financed by renewed borrowing from old or new lenders.

Such a scheme is called Ponzi-financing.[27] As the sovereign never accepts a net outflow of resources, the lenders as a group are never paid back. An important question then is under what conditions rational lenders are prepared to lend to a sovereign if sanctions are impossible. On the other hand, if $\delta > 0$, then the sovereign tolerates at least some outflow of resources. Sovereign debt need not be Ponzi-financed.

There is a further difference between the ‘carrot-only’ and ‘stick-also’ variant of sovereign debt. Given $\delta > 0$ in condition (2.4), the level of economic activity, y^*, determines the maximal payments a sovereign is prepared to make. For $\delta = 0$, payments must be non-positive whatever the level of economic activity. This has important implications.

For $\delta = 0$, the sovereign’s inclination to honour debt depends exclusively on the creditor economy’s ability to provide fresh money at a given interest rate, r^{i*}. If economic sanctions fail to exist, all efforts to manipulate the economic conditions in the debtor economy in order to improve the conditions for payments to the creditors are necessarily in vain (O’Connell and Zeldes, 1988). ‘Carrot-only’ implies therefore that the key to a smooth sovereign debt relationship is to be found in the creditor economies only. On the other hand, under ‘stick-also’, conditions in the debtor economy play a role too.

Debtor sovereignty is only important in determining the long-run steady state if the sovereignty restriction (2.4) is a binding condition. If condition (2.4) is indeed binding, it has to hold with equality. Restriction (2.4) then requires that for $\delta > 0$ the sovereign suffers a permanent outflow of resources equal to the costs from sanctions in each period. On the other hand, if $\delta = 0$, then, in an equilibrium in which condition (2.4) is binding, the net flow of resources between the sovereign and her creditors is zero. Debt is rolled over from period to period.

That has the important implication that in a steady state resources can flow into a debtor economy only if sovereignty is not a binding restriction. This is a result which cannot be overemphasized. Efforts undertaken to provide the debtor economy with a permanent inflow of resources must necessarily fail unless the sovereignty problem is overcome in the sense of making condition (2.4) a non-binding restriction. If this is not achievable, then the provision of fresh, net money cannot be maintained as a steady state.

VII. Conclusions

Let us sum up:[28]

(1) The ultimate debtors in international debt relations are nations represented by their highest authority in executive office. Legal enforcement mechanisms therefore fail to exist. International debt relationships hence must be sustained through implicit contracts in which legal enforcement is replaced by threats of actions unfavourable to the sovereign, undertaken by the creditors upon contract violations.

(2) The exclusion from continued access to international credit markets as well as sanctions which impinge upon the debtor nation’s sovereignty are

punishments which can entice sovereigns to abstain from contract violations. There are a number of institutional arrangements operating in international debt markets which make these threats credible. In general, a multitude of threats exists, each of which is equally successful in sustaining a given level of international debt outstanding.

(3) Debtor sovereignty requires lenders to observe restriction (2.4) in the long-run equilibrium. Different degrees of sovereignty, with the polar limiting cases of full sovereignty ($\delta = 0$) and non-sovereignty ($\delta = 1$), can be characterized in this restriction.

(4) There are important differences in sovereign debt as to whether contracts are sustained by economic sanctions. If sanctions are impossible ($\delta = 0$), then, in any international debt relationship, lenders must allow the sovereign to run a Ponzi-scheme of debt financing. Furthermore, economic conditions in the debtor economy are irrelevant for the debtor's readiness to allow net outflows of resources.

(5) If economic sanctions are possible ($\delta > 0$), then the sovereign accepts a permanent outflow of resources. Economic sanctions imply that the sovereign's readiness to accept net payments to the lenders depends on economic conditions in the debtor economy.

(6) If debtor sovereignty is a binding restriction in an international debt relationship, then in a steady state there is a permanent roll-over of international debt with a zero net flow of resources between debt and creditor economies if sanctions cannot be imposed. Under the threat of economic sanctions a steady state with a binding sovereignty restriction requires a permanent net outflow of resources from the debtor economy. Net inflows into the debtor economy are only sustainable in a steady state if debtor sovereignty is not a binding constraint.

CHAPTER 3

A Two-country Overlapping Generations World Economy

I. The Role of Overlapping Generations

In this chapter we set out to develop the formal model in which sovereign international debt will be analysed. The model features a neoclassical single-commodity, two-country world economy with overlapping generations of the Samuelson (1958) type in the extension of Diamond (1965).

In each period a new generation is born which lives for two periods. All members of a generation are identical. Each member of a newly born generation is endowed with one unit of labour, which it sells on the labour market during the first period of lifetime, its youth. At the end of youth, income is divided into consumption and savings. Saving when young is necessary to finance old age consumption in the second period because generations are assumed to retire from the labour market at the end of the first period. At the end of the second period, after having consumed savings and interest, generations disappear from the economy. There are no bequests.

Due to the permanent supply of two-period-lived generations, in each period there is an overlap of an old and a young generation. The old generation provides the productive capital, which together with labour supplied by the young, is employed in a production process to produce a single good used for consumption and investment.

In a closed economy of this type borrowing and lending is not feasible. Members within each generation are homogeneous; and an intertemporal exchange between a young and an old generation is prevented as the old have no time left for loans to mature.

Enter now the second economy. If the two economies differ in technology or in preferences, then there exist opportunities for mutually advantageous intertemporal trade through borrowing and lending across countries. It is lending between the young generations in the two economies which we set out to analyse.

International lending and borrowing can take place in conceptual frameworks which do not feature overlapping generations.[1] The question arises therefore why we analyse sovereign international debt under this complication.

One answer is that the overlapping generations model allows us to investigate interesting aspects of debtor sovereignty. The overlapping generations model is a general equilibrium model. It thus allows an investigation of the transmission of sovereignty beyond the credit markets alone, into other markets of the creditor and debtor economies. Furthermore, as the analysis takes place at the aggregation level of economies and as debtor sovereignty is a problem between economies, its effect on aggregate output, spending and capital formation can be analysed.

However, to argue simply that the overlapping generations model can be used for an analysis of sovereign debt would not do justice to its importance. A more adequate answer is that the overlapping generations model, or a model which is equivalent in a sense to be specified, is a necessary framework for an adequate analysis of sovereign international debt.

From the sovereignty restriction (2.4) it follows that for $\delta = 0$ international debt must be Ponzi-financed. Allowing for the possibility of Ponzi-financing, one must therefore set out the model so that it can be rational for the lenders to become part of the supply side to a Ponzi game. Each ultimate lender will demand repayment of a loan at some time. For $\delta = 0$, restriction (2.4) requires therefore that the sovereign can hop indefinitely from old ultimate lenders to new ultimate lenders for fresh loans. A rational Ponzi game requires therefore an infinite number of lenders (O'Connell and Zeldes, 1988). In the overlapping generations model, over time, this condition is fulfilled. The overlapping generations model, or a model which is equivalent with respect to the number of lenders, is therefore needed for an analysis of sovereign international debt if the possibility of Ponzi-financing is not to be excluded.

There is a further advantage to the overlapping generations model.

Debtor sovereignty should not be belittled in automatizing the supply of fresh money, as would be done, for example, in a Solow-type of growth model in which the savings rate is exogenous (Solow, 1956).

In the overlapping generations model savings and the supply of fresh money for international loans are endogenously determined. The latter depends on the other opportunities for holding wealth. International debt is therefore under permanent stress from two opposing forces on the supply side of debt; the need for constant repayment to finance old-age consumption of the old members in the lender society; and the need that international loans are permanently attractive enough to the young, to attract the fresh money needed to avoid repudiation. Sustaining international debt without repudiation is therefore not trivial in an overlapping generations context. For all these reasons the overlapping generations model provides a theoretical framework in which necessary and, beyond that, desirable conditions are fulfilled to allow for an analysis adequate to the problems sovereign debt poses.

II. The Model

II.1. General assumptions

In this section we set out the basic assumptions of the model. Throughout this book it will be assumed that all decision-makers in both the creditor and the debtor economy operate under conditions of perfect competition. At variance with what will be presumed at a later stage we make the following

Assumption 3.1: The model is deterministic.

Assumption 3.2: Decision-makers in the debtor country cannot precommit themselves to certain actions.

Assumption 3.2 is the natural presumption in a model of sovereign debt. Debtor sovereignty arises if debt contracts cannot be legally enforced. The natural extension then is that not only debt contracts but also contracts which stipulate certain other actions or some behaviour of the debtor cannot be legally enforced. Then, being a party to such a contract does not precommit a debtor to any action. An implication of the inability to precommit is that rational lenders will expect the debtor to choose a subgame-perfect strategy in the future. That is, the debtor is expected to pursue the promised mode of behaviour only if it is optimal to do so. Lenders will take that into account when making lending decisions. This in turn implies that precommitment, if it is possible, can be in the interest of the debtor. For example, in committing himself to an investment strategy which raises the costs from repudiation when debt is due, a debtor increases his creditworthiness. Thereby, he can raise more debt. The lack of legal enforcement, however, does not necessarily imply that precommitment is impossible. Enforcement can be implicit just as in debt contracts. For now we presume, however, that such implicit enforcement is impossible so that Assumption 3.2 holds.

II.2. Economic growth

Throughout we shall assume a world economy with two countries and overlapping generations. A generation is indexed by the period in which it is born. Let L be the size of generation t in the creditor country. That is, there are L households to the generation born in period t. Let L^* be the corresponding size of generation t in the debtor economy.[2] We shall assume $L = L^*$. Let $n, n \geqslant 0$, be the constant one-period proportional rate of growth of the size of generations. The growth rate n is common to both countries. Equation (2.2) then gives the change in the size of two successive generations. Therefore, we now define the unit of measurement underlying the sovereignty restrictions (2.3) and (2.4) as the number of households in generation $t-1$ and t, respectively. For $n > 0$, quantities which are constant at the level of households are growing at the national level. It is therefore appropriate to define steady-state values per member of the currently young generation. The steady-state condition

$$b^*_{-1} = b^* \ \forall\, t \tag{3.1}$$

then implies that debt per member of the young generation is constant in each period. For $n > 0$, equations (2.2) and (3.1) imply that total debt of the borrowing country, $L \cdot b^*$, is increasing in the steady state.

The term $r^{i*} - n$ in restriction (2.4) has to be interpreted as the interest rate on sovereign debt, net of the growth rate of loans to the sovereign. The sovereignty restriction therefore allows for economic growth in the form of population growth. In the steady state, growth decreases the net transfer to the creditor country. For given costs of economic sanctions, $\delta \cdot y^*$, growth therefore increases the loan size, b^*, which can be sustained at a given interest rate, r^{i*}, without incurring repudiation.

II.3. Preferences

Let c^j and c^o be consumption of a household when young and when old. We make

Assumption 3.3: Preferences are given by the well-behaved utility functions $U(c^j, c^o)$, $U^*(c^{j*}, c^{o*})$, with $U_{c^h} > 0$, $U_{c^h c^h} < 0$, $\lim_{c^h \to 0} U_{c^h} = \infty$, $\lim_{c^h \to \infty} U_{c^h} = 0$, $h = j, o, j^*, o^*$.

Preferences can therefore differ across countries. More specifically, we shall assume the additive separable utility functions

$$\left.\begin{aligned} U(c^j, c^o) &= (1 - \Omega) \cdot \ln c^j + \Omega \cdot \ln c^o \\ U^*(c^{j*}, c^{o*}) &= (1 - \Omega^*) \cdot \ln c^{j*} + \Omega^* \cdot \ln c^{o*} \end{aligned}\right\} \tag{3.2}$$

with $0 < \Omega, \Omega^* < 1$. Utility when old is discounted at the rate $\Omega/(1 - \Omega)$ and $\Omega^*/(1 - \Omega^*)$ respectively. As differences between countries can cause intertemporal trade to occur we allow that time preferences are a source of international borrowing and lending (Buiter, 1981).

Under preferences which satisfy Assumption 3.3, households do not have a bequest motive. With bequests, consumption or utility of later generations would be an argument in the utility functions.

There is a large literature on the role of bequest motives in overlapping generations models. The general conclusion is that results are very sensitive to the existence of an operative bequest motive. Its presence causes a strong economic neutrality of factors which otherwise affect the real economy.[3] Abstracting from bequests is therefore problematic. However, research on dynastic models seems to strongly suggest that allowing for a bequest motive is no less problematic, as results then become very sensitive to '*small*' changes in the specification of the model.[4] Furthermore, recent work suggests that the bequest motive actually *is* inoperative so that the strong neutrality results derived from operative bequest motives do not hold (Bernheim, 1989). Lastly, in more realistic models of dynastic interpersonal links within an economy neutrality is put to the extreme in that public redistribution, distortionary taxes, even relative prices are irrelevant (Bernheim and Bagwell, 1988). One is therefore bound to conclude that the dynastic model is not a good description of the real world.

One might be tempted from all this to abandon altogether the use of overlapping generations.[5] However, taking account of the pros in favour of the overlapping generations model, set out in Section I of this chapter, we come down against this conclusion and abandon the dynastic specification instead.

II.4. Technology

Throughout we assume the Cobb-Douglas technologies

$$\left.\begin{aligned} Y &= K^{\alpha} \cdot L^{\beta} \cdot G^{\lambda} \\ Y^* &= K^{*\alpha^*} \cdot L^{*\beta^*} \end{aligned}\right\} \tag{3.3}$$

Aggregate production of the consumption-cum-investment good in the debtor economy, Y^*, depends on the input of two production factors, capital, K^*, and labour, L^*. In the creditor economy there exists a third production factor of size G.

Apart from the number of factors, technologies can differ with respect to the constant production elasticities of capital, α and α^*, and of labour, β and β^*. The constant production elasticity of the third factor in the creditor economy is λ. We have $\alpha + \beta + \lambda = 1$, $\lambda \geqslant 0$, and $\alpha^* + \beta^* = 1$. International lending and borrowing may therefore be caused by technological differences as well as by preferences (Schmid, 1987).

Let $k \equiv K/L$ and $y \equiv Y/L$. We take it that $G \equiv L$. Then, the production functions (3.3) can be expressed in terms per member of the current young generation

$$\left.\begin{aligned} y &\equiv f(k) = k^{\alpha} \\ y^* &\equiv f^*(k^*) = k^{*\alpha^*} \end{aligned}\right\} \tag{3.4}$$

Under conditions of perfect competition, factor prices are then given by

$$\left.\begin{aligned} r &= f'(k) \\ r^* &= f^{*\prime}(k^*) \end{aligned}\right\} \tag{3.5}$$

$$\left.\begin{aligned} w &= f(k) - r \cdot k - \lambda \cdot f(k) \\ w^* &= f^*(k^*) - r^* \cdot k^* \end{aligned}\right\} \tag{3.6}$$

and

$$\partial Y/\partial G = \lambda \cdot f(k) \tag{3.7}$$

where r is the real interest rate on capital and where w is the wage per unit of labour. In the overlapping generations model, capital in period t, k, is provided by members of generation $t-1$. It is easier to verify from equations (3.4), (3.5), (3.6) and (3.7) that

$$\left.\begin{aligned} \partial r/\partial k &< 0 \\ \partial r^*/\partial k^* &< 0 \end{aligned}\right\} \tag{3.8}$$

$$\left.\begin{aligned} \partial w/\partial k &> 0 \\ \partial w^*/\partial k^* &> 0 \end{aligned}\right\} \tag{3.9}$$

and

$$\partial\,[\partial Y/\partial G]/\partial k > 0 \tag{3.10}$$

The larger the investment in the productive capital stock in the previous period, the larger the wage income and the larger the marginal product of factor G, in the present period.

From conditions (2.4) and (3.4) we obtain for the sovereignty restriction

$$z \equiv \frac{b^*}{1-n} \cdot (r^{i*} - n) \leqslant \delta \cdot f^*(k^*) \tag{3.11}$$

The gunboat-technology makes the costs from economic sanctions proportional to the output per member of the young generation in the borrowing country.[6]

II.5. Banking

It is assumed that banks engaged in international lending are exclusively located in the creditor economy. It is furthermore assumed that ownership of banks is restricted to households in the creditor economy. Although these assumptions seem to be consistent with the observed organization of international financial markets, the reasons for making them are at least, as much as anything, methodological ones. In making these assumptions, the problems associated with bank financing of international debt are identified as sharply as possible as problems of the lending economy. These problems can be classified in two broad categories.

In the first category are all effects of debtor sovereignty on other sectors in the creditor economy, transmitted through the ownership of international banking. Into the second category fall the implications of the institutional framework in which international banks have to operate. One such institutional aspect is the fact that the banks themselves are non-sovereign and hence are subject to legal enforcement of claims against them. The assumption that banks are located in the creditor economy takes this into account.

We take it that banks provide the two classical functions of producing services and of acting as financial intermediaries (Fama, 1980). To the first end, define the production factor G in the creditor economy as bank-specific service capital, which, having the same properties as labour, cannot be transformed into the consumer good.

To fix ideas, take G as the number of banks in the creditor economy, characterizing the size of the banking sector there. As we have set $G \equiv L$, it follows from equation (2.2) that for $n > 0$ the banking sector is growing exogenously at the rate n. In this interpretation of G, equation (3.7) is then the share a representative bank receives in period t as a profit from providing productive bank services to the lending economy. From equation (3.10), this share increases if productive capital per bank, k, increases, employed in production.

Banks are held as assets in the portfolios of households in the creditor country. As bank-specific service capital is non-malleable, owners of the banking system sell it at the end of their second period of life to the next generation in the process of dissaving. As $G \equiv L$, a representative young household buys exactly one bank at the end of youth and sells $1 + n$ banks when old. The banking system thus handed over indefinitely from generation to generation has thus an infinite lifetime itself.

It is well established that there is a degree of freedom in how markets price infinitely-lived assets (Blanchard, 1979; Tirole, 1985). One option would be 'bubble-pricing'. We do, however, exclude 'bubbles' in the pricing of banks and assume, instead, that banks are priced at their 'fundamental', that is, at the discounted sum of the infinite sequence of period-profits. 'Bubbles' involve pricing above the 'fundamental'. Valuation at the 'fundamental' requires

$$r > n \tag{3.12}$$

which in turn excludes 'bubbles'.[7]

Let v^d be the present value of domestic bank services in period t. In the present model, a steady state with $n > 0$ implies that bank profits per period are constant forever. A share in the banking system is thus a consol. In fact, in the steady state shares in the individual banks can be viewed as consols. In this interpretation, the coupon payment per period on steady-state bank services to the creditor economy is given by equation (3.7). The 'fundamental' of a bank's services, $v^d(k)$, is then given by

$$v^d(k) = \frac{1+r}{r-n} \cdot \lambda \cdot f(k) \tag{3.13}$$

If international debt is not bank-financed, providing services to the domestic economy is the only function of banks. Under bank-financing of sovereign debt, international financial intermediation is an additional function the banking system performs. Thus banks are put through the mill of holding unenforceable claims on the active side of the balance sheet while having enforceable obligations on the passive side.

Let r^s be the interest rate banks charge the sovereign for loans due in period t. Although a single bank can refinance a loan in inter-bank markets, the banking system as a whole has to refinance international loans on the domestic market for bank deposits. Let r^d be the deposit rate for bank deposits made by households in the creditor country, due in period t. In the aggregate, all deposits received are to be lent by the banking system. We take it that international lending is the only lending option of banks.[8] Deposits taken by a bank in period $t-1$, $-b_{-1}$, are then equal to international loans made in period $t-1$. Let θ be the profit made in period

t from international financial intermediation of loans due in period t. Then

$$\theta \equiv \frac{-b_{-1}}{1+n} \cdot (r^s - r^d) \gtreqless 0 \tag{3.14}$$

If the spread on financial intermediation in period t, $r^s - r^d$, is positive (negative) then this profit is positive (negative). Let v^i denote the present value of international intermediation in period t. In the steady state, $b_{-1} = b \; \forall t$, and θ is the coupon on the consol 'steady-state financial intermediation'. The steady-state value of financial intermediation is then given by

$$v^i = \frac{1+r}{r-n} \cdot \theta \tag{3.15}$$

Although the separate activities of banks can be valued separately, the title to the profits they entail cannot be purchased separately. Households have to purchase the set. Let v denote the purchasing price of a bank in period t. We have then

$$v = v^d + v^i \tag{3.16}$$

As banks are subject to legal enforcement in the creditor country the solvency restriction

$$v \geqslant 0 \tag{3.17}$$

must be fulfilled in each period.

From equations (3.13), (3.15) and (3.16) the steady-state purchasing price of a bank then is given by

$$v = \frac{1+r}{r-n} \cdot [\lambda \cdot f(k) + \theta] \tag{3.18}$$

As we allow for a negative, zero, or positive spread, $r^s - r^d$, from equations (3.14), (3.15) and (3.16), the value of a bank may be larger, equal or smaller than the value of its domestic activity. If $v^i < 0$, then from the solvency restriction (3.17), profits made in the domestic activity are needed to compensate for losses incurred from the international business. The model allows therefore for the possibility that financial intermediation of sovereign, international debt can cause long-run losses. To investigate this possibility is indeed the reason why we explicitly take account of other, profitable activities of internationally operating banks.[9]

To complete the description of the banking sector it remains to define the terms under which the losses or profits from banking activities are handed over to the owners of the banking system. We shall assume that the purchasing price of banks is cum-dividend. The dividend a bank pays in period

t, $\lambda \cdot f(k) + \theta$, is therefore paid to a member of generation t immediately after becoming the new owners of the bank. The ex-dividend, or net purchasing price of a bank in period t then is $v - \lambda \cdot f(k) - \theta$. From condition (3.17) and equation (3.18) the dividend must be non-negative in the steady state. Letting immortal banks provide an input for production we have endowed the creditor economy with a real store of wealth.

II.6. Circulatory relationships

Let s be savings of a young household in period t. Saving is given by

$$\left.\begin{aligned} s &= w + \lambda \cdot f(k) + \theta - c^j \\ s^* &= w^* - c^{j*} \end{aligned}\right\} \tag{3.19}$$

Investment in reproducible capital in period t determines the capital stock in period $t+1$,

$$\left.\begin{aligned} k_1 &= \frac{1}{1+n} \cdot i \\ k_1^* &= \frac{1}{1+n} \cdot i^* \end{aligned}\right\} \tag{3.20}$$

The wealth of a country in period $t+1$, per member of generation $t+1$, a_1, is determined by the savings of generation t, so that

$$\left.\begin{aligned} a_1 &= \frac{1}{1+n} \cdot s \\ a_1^* &= \frac{1}{1+n} \cdot s^* \end{aligned}\right\} \tag{3.21}$$

International credit is determined by the surplus of savings over the holdings of other assets in the two economies. Per head of generation $t+1$, the size of loans made in period t is given by

$$\left.\begin{aligned} \frac{-b}{1+n} &= a_1 - k_1 - \frac{1}{1+n} \cdot v \\ \frac{-b^*}{1+n} &= a_1^* - k_1^* \end{aligned}\right\} \tag{3.22}$$

Equations (3.22) illustrate that in the debtor economy portfolios are composed of the two assets, real capital and foreign debt, whereas in the creditor country households also hold shares in the domestic banking system besides real capital and foreign claims. *Ceteris paribus*, the existence of a real store of wealth in the creditor economy reduces the supply of international loans, as resources are absorbed in the ownership of the banking system.

Old-age consumption, c^o, is given by

$$\left.\begin{aligned} c^o &= (1+n)\cdot[(1+r_1)\cdot k_1 + v_1] + (1+r_1^i)\cdot(-b) \\ c^{o*} &= (1+n)\cdot(1+r_1^*)\cdot k_1^* - (1+r_1^{i*})\cdot b^* \end{aligned}\right\} \tag{3.23}$$

Note that r^i denotes the interest rate on the international component in the portfolio of a household in the creditor economy. In general, that is, allowing for different forms of financing, the interest rates on the foreign components ($-b$ and b^*) in the portfolios of households in the two countries, r^i and r^{i*}, need not be identical. In contrast to consumption in the debtor country, c^o is increased by the revenue $(1+n)\cdot v_1$ a member of generation t receives from $1+n$ successors for the sale of $1+n$ banks in period $t+1$.

Consumption when young is given by

$$\left.\begin{aligned} c^j &= w + \lambda\cdot f(k) + \theta + b - (1+n)\cdot k_1 - v \\ c^{j*} &= w^* + b^* - (1+n)\cdot k_1^* \end{aligned}\right\} \tag{3.24}$$

Again, the existence of a real store of wealth in the creditor country causes the consumption functions to differ across countries by the net purchasing price $v - \lambda\cdot f(k) - \theta$.

II.7. The sovereign

To complete the model it remains to fix conditions which ensure compatibility of the sovereignty restriction (3.11) with the overlapping generations model at hand. In the model, international debt is ultimately incurred by private households in a country. Debt is due when debtors are old. The carrot of continued access to foreign loans, explicit in restriction (3.11), therefore poses no incentive to the old. Furthermore, from equation (3.6), the claim of old members of the debtor economy against the output produced in period t is given by $f^*(k^*) - w^*$, whereas restriction (3.11) is based on economic sanctions proportional to the entire output, $f^*(k^*)$. If total costs from repudiation are given by restriction (3.11) the difference must be costs suffered by the generation born in the period when repudiation occurs. The young, however, do not participate in the gains from repudiation. There is therefore a conflict between debtors and non-debtors in the debtor country concerning the sovereignty decision.

UNIVERSITY
OF BRISTOL
LIBRARY

To solve this conflict we make an assumption which is to ensure *potential* harmony of interests in the debtor country. In what follows we assume that compensatory payments up to the total costs from debt contract violations *can* be effectuated between presently living generations in the debtor economy.

If such payments can be made directly between generations we can employ the Coase Theorem (Coase, 1960) and sustain condition (3.11) as the sovereignty restriction, irrespective of which generation has the right to execute sovereignty. For illustration, suppose the old members of the debtor society have the exclusive right to repudiate debt. Then, the young are prepared to make side-payments to the old up to the costs they had to incur from contract violations in exchange for the old generation's abstention from repudiating debt. Costs underlying restriction (3.11) then have to be entirely borne by those in charge of the sovereignty decision. Conversely, let the old continue to hold debt obligations but let the young hold the right to repudiate. Side-payments from the old up to their net gains from repudiation entice the young to observe restriction (3.11).

What this argument presumes, however, is that the costs from repudiation completely accrue in the period when repudiation occurs. Gunboat-technologies equivalent to the single-shot sanctions underlying restriction (3.11), but occurring over at least some periods, must be excluded, as trade with yet unborn generations is impossible.

It might appear that the introduction of a government in charge of the sovereignty decision permits sanctions extending over several periods. Although this would allow for a scheme under which the presently old generation is taxed to compensate future generations for the costs from future sanctions triggered today, the converse is not possible in general. The sovereignty decision would then have to be made under possibly incomplete compensation. This would require the introduction of some other explicit value function, which the government applies in making the sovereignty decision.

To avoid the arbitrariness this would involve, we take it, in what follows, that sanctions are of the single-shot variety. We can then maintain restriction (3.11) under direct compensation à la Coase or by forced compensation by a government in charge of the sovereignty decision.

III. Household Optimization

Supply and demand of international loans is to be determined from the savings and portfolio decisions of households. From equations (3.2),

(3.23), and (3.24) the utility maximization problem in period t is given by

$$\max_{k_1, b} U\{w + \lambda \cdot f(k) + \theta + b - (1+n) \cdot k_1, \\ (1+n) \cdot [(1+r_1) \cdot k_1 + v_1] - d_1^* \cdot (1+r_1^i) \cdot b\} \quad (3.25)$$

and

$$\max_{k_1^*, b^*} U^*\{w^* + b^* - (1+n) \cdot k_1^*, (1+n) \cdot (1+r_1^*) \cdot k_1^* - d_1^* \cdot (1+r_1^{i*}) \cdot b^*\}$$

$$\text{s.t. } b^* \leqslant \bar{b}^* \quad (3.26)$$

where

$$d_1^* \equiv \begin{Bmatrix} 0 \\ 1 \end{Bmatrix} \text{ in case of } \begin{cases} \text{repudiation} \\ \text{otherwise} \end{cases}$$

The dummy d_1^* represents the sovereign's repudiation decision in period $t+1$. The optimization problem of a household in the debtor country takes account of a debt limit, $\bar{b}^*$, possibly imposed by the lenders. Such a debt limit has to emerge as an optimization condition from the optimization problem (3.25) in the lending economy. We need not concern ourselves with the non-negativity restrictions on k and k^* as from equations (3.3) some investment is always optimal. Nor need we concern ourselves with the budget constraint, as from Assumption (3.3) consumption when young will always be positive in an optimum. Investment in productive capital cannot therefore be constrained by a young household's budget constraint. Optimal investment in the productive capital stocks in the two countries therefore requires

$$\left.\begin{aligned} \frac{U_{c^j}}{U_{c^o}} &= 1 + r_1 \\ \frac{U^*_{c^{j*}}}{U^*_{c^{o*}}} &= 1 + r_1^* \end{aligned}\right\} \quad (3.27)$$

Marginal utility of consumption when young must be equal to marginal utility of investment in the domestic capital stock.

From Assumption (3.1) and from legal enforcement of claims against all domestic economic units, reproducible domestic capital and shares in the banking sector are perfect substitutes in the creditor country. The return on both assets must therefore be the same. This requires

$$v = \lambda \cdot f(k) + \theta + \frac{1+n}{1+r_1} \cdot v_1 \quad (3.28)$$

Furthermore, domestic enforcement implies that households will only hold bank deposits in an optimal portfolio if

$$r = r^d \tag{3.29}$$

If equation (3.28) holds, then a representative household in the creditor country is prepared to hold any number of shares in the banking system. We need not therefore optimize the number of shares in the banking sector and can simply assume, as is implicitly done in (3.25), that a representative household owns a single bank.[10]

Optimization with respect to the size of international loans, $-b$, requires

$$\frac{U_{c^j}}{U_{c^o}} \leqslant (1 + r_1^i) \cdot d_1^* \tag{3.30}$$

Condition (3.30) cannot be fulfilled for $d_1^* = 0$. As from the sovereignty restriction (2.3) repudiation in the next period can be avoided by lenders by restricting loans, doing so is indeed optimal. Put differently, lenders will always ensure that it is in the sovereign's self-interest to honour all debt contracts, that is

$$d_1^* = 1 \tag{3.31}$$

The debt limit $\bar{b}^*$ in (3.26) is therefore given by the loan size, b^*, for which

$$b^* \cdot (1 + r^{i*}) = b_1^* \cdot (1 + n) + \delta \cdot f^*(k_1^*) \cdot (1 + n) \tag{3.32}$$

Conditions $b^* \leqslant \bar{b}^*$ and (3.30) hold with complementary slackness. An extension of loans is optimal until either the limit b^* or else equality in condition (3.30) is reached. If for $b^* = \bar{b}^*$ condition (3.30) holds as an inequality, an extension of loans at the expense of current consumption would increase a lender's utility if repayment could be guaranteed. Debtor sovereignty forbids this. From the optimization problem (3.26) and from equation (3.31) it follows for the optimal loan demand that

$$\frac{U^*_{c^{j*}}}{U^*_{c^{o*}}} \geqslant 1 + r_1^{i*} \tag{3.33}$$

Condition (3.33) and the limit condition $b^* \leqslant \bar{b}^*$ hold with complementary slackness. If $b^* \leqslant \bar{b}^*$ is a binding constraint, then financing further consumption when young by issuing further debt would increase utility even if debt had to be repaid. Yet, the inability to commit to servicing debt when old prevents borrowers from being able to raise the additional debt.

From condition (3.27) and (3.33) it follows

$$r_1^* \begin{Bmatrix} > \\ = \end{Bmatrix} r_1^{i*} \Leftrightarrow b^* \begin{cases} = \bar{b}^* \\ \varepsilon [0, \bar{b}^*] \end{cases} \tag{3.34}$$

If borrowers face a binding loan constraint, then the interest rate on loans from abroad must be below the marginal productivity of capital in the debtor country. If debtor sovereignty is not a binding constraint, then these rates must be identical.

We have derived the sovereignty restriction, respectively (2.3) and (3.11), by allowing *potential* compensatory payments between generations in the debtor country. Under equation (3.31) compensation would require payments to the old for accepting the burden of debt repayment. The optimization problem (3.26) implicitly presumes that this compensation is not actually paid. Alternatively, the optimization conditions derived from (3.26) would continue to hold if such payments were carried out as lump-sum payments financed by lump-sum taxes on the young.

If the compensation policy required payments which increased with repayment due, the effective interest rate on foreign loans would be below the nominal one, r_1^{i*}. Credit demand would be larger, but the credit limit would be the same. The optimization condition (3.33) would therefore still hold.

From the optimization conditions (3.27), (3.30) and (3.31) we obtain

$$r_1 \begin{Bmatrix} < \\ = \end{Bmatrix} r_1^i \Leftrightarrow b^* \begin{cases} = \bar{b}^* \\ \varepsilon\,[0, \bar{b}^*] \end{cases} \tag{3.35}$$

Condition (3.35) illustrates that international lending and domestic investment are perfect substitutes only for as long as the sovereignty restriction is fulfilled. From conditions (3.34) and (3.35) we obtain

$$r_1 \begin{Bmatrix} < \\ = \end{Bmatrix} r_1^* \Leftrightarrow b^* \begin{cases} = \bar{b}^* \\ \varepsilon\,[0, \bar{b}^*] \end{cases} \tag{3.36}$$

The rational anticipation of the rational sovereignty decision can restrict the international flow of capital so as to prevent real capital in both countries from being equally productive. If sovereignty is not a binding constraint, then the real interest rates in both countries must be the same.

IV. Steady-state World Capital Market Equilibrium

The optimization conditions in the previous section hold in every period. In this section we derive from them a long-run steady-state condition for world capital market equilibrium. We do this for the special utility functions given in equations (3.2).

For the utility functions (3.2) the optimization conditions (3.27) simplify to

$$\left.\begin{aligned} \frac{U_{c^j}}{U_{c^o}} &= \frac{1-\Omega}{\Omega} \cdot \frac{c^o}{c^j} = 1 + r_1 \\ \frac{U^*_{c^{j*}}}{U^*_{c^{o*}}} &= \frac{1-\Omega^*}{\Omega^*} \cdot \frac{c^{o*}}{c^{j*}} = 1 + r_1^* \end{aligned}\right\} \quad (3.37)$$

from which, upon substituting in equations (3.23) and equation (3.28), we obtain

$$\left.\begin{aligned} c^j &= \frac{1-\Omega}{\Omega} \cdot \left\{(1+n) \cdot k_1 - \frac{1+r_1^i}{1+r_1} \cdot b + v - \lambda \cdot f(k) - \theta\right\} \\ c^{j*} &= \frac{1-\Omega^*}{\Omega^*} \cdot \left\{(1+n) \cdot k_1^* - \frac{1+r_1^{i*}}{1+r_1^*} \cdot b^*\right\} \end{aligned}\right\} \quad (3.38)$$

As $s \equiv i + v - b$ and $s^* \equiv i^* - b^*$ we can substitute into these definitions equations (3.19) and (3.20) and solve for $(1+n) \cdot k_1$ and $(1+n) \cdot k_1^*$ to obtain

$$\begin{aligned} (1+n) \cdot k_1 &= w + \lambda \cdot f(k) + \theta - c^j - v + b \\ (1+n) \cdot k_1^* &= w^* - c^{j*} + b^* \end{aligned}$$

Substituting this into (3.38) and collecting terms we obtain

$$\left.\begin{aligned} c^j &= (1-\Omega) \cdot w + \frac{1-\Omega}{1+r_1} \cdot b \cdot (r_1 - r_1^i) \\ c^{j*} &= (1-\Omega^*) \cdot w^* + \frac{1-\Omega^*}{1+r_1^*} \cdot b^* \cdot (r_1^* - r_1^{i*}) \end{aligned}\right\} \quad (3.39)$$

Solving equations (3.37) for c^o and c^{o*} and substituting in equations (3.39) entails

$$\left.\begin{aligned} c^o &= (1+r_1) \cdot \Omega \cdot w + \Omega \cdot b \cdot (r_1 - r_1^i) \\ c^{o*} &= (1+r_1^*) \cdot \Omega^* \cdot w^* + \Omega^* \cdot b^* \cdot (r_1^* - r_1^{i*}) \end{aligned}\right\} \quad (3.40)$$

From (3.19) and (3.39) one obtains for optimal savings

$$\left.\begin{aligned} s &= \Omega \cdot w + \lambda \cdot f(k) + \theta + (1-\Omega) \cdot b \cdot \left[\frac{1+r_1^i}{1+r_1} - 1\right] \\ s^* &= \Omega^* \cdot w^* + (1-\Omega^*) \cdot b^* \cdot \left[\frac{1+r_1^{i*}}{1+r_1^*} - 1\right] \end{aligned}\right\} \quad (3.41)$$

Optimal investment in the domestic capital stock is easily derived from substituting equations (3.41) and (3.28) into $s \equiv i + v - b$ and $s^* \equiv i^* - b^*$

to obtain

$$\left.\begin{aligned} i &= \Omega \cdot w - \frac{1+n}{1+r_1} \cdot v_1 + b \cdot \left[(1-\Omega) \cdot \frac{1+r_1^i}{1+r_1} + \Omega \right] \\ i^* &= \Omega^* \cdot w^* + b^* \cdot \left[(1-\Omega^*) \cdot \frac{1+r_1^{i*}}{1+r_1^*} + \Omega^* \right] \end{aligned}\right\} \tag{3.42}$$

To obtain optimal international credit supply and its use in the debtor country, substitute equations (3.21), (3.28) and (3.41) into equations (3.22) to obtain

$$\left.\begin{aligned} \frac{-b}{1+n} &= \frac{\dfrac{\Omega}{1+n} \cdot w - k_1 - \dfrac{1}{1+r_1} \cdot v_1}{1 + (1-\Omega) \cdot \left[\dfrac{1+r_1^i}{1+r_1} - 1 \right]} \\ \frac{-b^*}{1+n} &= \frac{\dfrac{\Omega^*}{1+n} \cdot w^* - k_1^*}{1 + (1-\Omega^*) \cdot \left[\dfrac{1+r_1^{i*}}{1+r_1^*} - 1 \right]} \end{aligned}\right\} \tag{3.43}$$

In our overlapping generations model the long-run equilibrium can be characterized by constant capital intensities

$$\left.\begin{aligned} k &= k_1 \\ k^* &= k_1^* \end{aligned} \quad \forall t \right\} \tag{3.44}$$

With k and k^* constant, all other variables are constant. From (3.43), international credit supply and its use in the debtor country is then given by

$$\left.\begin{aligned} \frac{-b}{1+n} &= \frac{\dfrac{\Omega}{1+n} \cdot w - k - \dfrac{1}{1+r} \cdot v}{1 + (1-\Omega) \cdot \left[\dfrac{1+r^i}{1+r} - 1 \right]} \\ \frac{-b^*}{1+n} &= \frac{\dfrac{\Omega^*}{1+n} \cdot w^* - k^*}{1 + (1-\Omega^*) \cdot \left[\dfrac{1+r^{i*}}{1+r^*} - 1 \right]} \end{aligned}\right\} \tag{3.45}$$

The numerator in the upper equation in the system (3.45) contains the term $-v/(1+r)$ which, from equations (3.14)–(3.16), itself depends on b. To collect terms, from (3.14)–(3.16), the steady-state value of a bank is given by

$$v = v^d + \frac{1+r}{r-n} \cdot \frac{-b}{1+n} \cdot (r^s - r^d)$$

which after repeatedly collecting terms and making use of the portfolio equilibrium condition (3.29) implies for the upper equation in the system (3.45)

$$\frac{-b}{1+n}=\frac{\dfrac{\Omega}{1+n}\cdot w-k-\dfrac{1}{1+r}\cdot v^{d}}{\dfrac{r^{s}-n}{r-n}+(1-\Omega)\cdot\left[\dfrac{1+r^{i}}{1+r}-1\right]} \tag{3.46}$$

We are now ready to determine the world capital market equilibrium condition for a steady state. In each period world capital market equilibrium requires

$$\frac{-b}{1+n}=\frac{b^{*}}{1+n} \tag{3.47}$$

Upon using the lower equation in the system (3.45) and equation (3.46), world capital market equilibrium can be expressed by

$$H(\cdot)\equiv\left[\frac{\dfrac{\Omega}{1+n}\cdot w-k-\dfrac{1}{1+r}\cdot v^{d}}{\dfrac{r^{s}-n}{r-n}+(1-\Omega)\cdot\left[\dfrac{1+r^{i}}{1+r}-1\right]}\right]+\left[\frac{\dfrac{\Omega^{*}}{1+n}\cdot w^{*}-k^{*}}{1+(1-\Omega^{*})\cdot\left[\dfrac{1+r^{i*}}{1+r^{*}}-1\right]}\right]=0 \tag{3.48}$$

Equation (3.48), together with the sovereignty restriction (3.11) and the portfolio optimization conditions (3.28), (3.29), (3.31), (3.34) and (3.35), constitutes the system in which international borrowing and lending can be analysed. It allows for distinguishing between the different forms of financing: bond-financing as well as international financial intermediation. Furthermore, it allows for an analysis of an alternative to international credit financing under the threat of repudiation: foreign direct investment under the threat of expropriation. To fix ideas, however, we will analyse non-sovereign international borrowing and lending as a starting point from which we embark to develop the implications of sovereignty.

CHAPTER **4**

Non-sovereign International Debt

I. Introduction

In this chapter basic properties of the model introduced in Chapter 3 are developed in $k - k^*$ space. As a frame of reference non-sovereign international debt is analysed. The borrowing and lending steady state is compared with financial autarky and the welfare implications of intertemporal trade are analysed. Conditions are given under which the flow of intertemporal trade corresponds indeed to the arbitrary distinction between the two countries we made in calling the '*'-country the debtor economy and the other country the lending economy.

II. Perfect Capital Markets

In Chapter 3 we set out a model in which debtor sovereignty is the sole potential source of the capital market imperfection. For the analysis in this chapter we dispose of debtor sovereignty in making

Assumption 4.1: International lending and borrowing is constrained only by the debtor's solvency.

In the model we entertain the idea that, if debt is taken to be non-sovereign, capital markets are perfect.[1] From the Modigliani-Miller theorem the form of financing is then irrelevant for the real economy. Hence, without loss of generality we can analyse non-sovereign debt under the presumption that it is bond-financed. Under bond-financing a country raises international debt by borrowing directly from foreign households which hold the bonds in their portfolios as claims against the country.

Under bond financing of international debt

$$v^i \equiv 0 \tag{4.1}$$

so that

$$v = v^d \tag{4.2}$$

With a positive amount of international debt outstanding in the steady state, from equations (3.1), (3.14), (3.15), and (3.29), equation (4.1) is only fulfilled if

$$r^s \equiv r^d = r \tag{4.3}$$

Under Assumption 4.1 the international (steady-state) flow of capital is unconstrained if the debtor is solvent. From Assumption 3.3, in an optional consumption plan $c^{o*} > 0$. It follows therefore from equation (3.23) that the resources available for debt servicing when old, $(1+n)\cdot(1+r_1^*)\cdot k_1^*$, exceed payments due, $(1+r_1^{i*})\cdot b^*$. In the steady state, solvency is not a binding constraint.

Debtors can raise therefore further debt for consumption for as long as the marginal utility of consumption when young exceeds the marginal costs of borrowing. Condition (3.33) must therefore hold with equality. Hence from (3.27) we must have

$$r^* = r^{i*} \tag{4.4}$$

Given solvency, under non-sovereignty foreign loans and investment in the domestic capital stock are perfect substitutes. Portfolio equilibrium in the creditor country requires therefore

$$r = r^i \tag{4.5}$$

It immediately follows from equations (3.27) that in a steady state, condition (3.30) has to hold as an equality.

It is now possible to determine the steady-state condition for world credit market equilibrium under non-sovereignty. For equations (4.3)–(4.5), the general steady-state world credit market equilibrium condition (3.48) simplifies to

$$H^1(k, k^*) \equiv \left[\frac{\Omega}{1+n} \cdot w - k - \frac{1}{1+r} \cdot v^d\right] + \left[\frac{\Omega^*}{1+n} \cdot w^* - k^*\right] = 0 \tag{4.6}$$

From equations (3.5), (3.6), and (3.13) it follows that $H^1(\cdot)$ is an implicit function of k and k^* alone.

To interpret the second term in brackets in equation (4.6) note that from equations (3.21), (3.41), and (4.4) the term $\Omega^* \cdot w^*/(1+n)$ is the wealth per member of the young generation in the '*'-country, out of savings of the currently old generation. If the second term in brackets of equation (4.6) is negative, investment in the domestic capital stock cannot be financed out of domestic savings alone. The country must borrow abroad.

To interpret the first bracketed term in equation (4.6) note that from $\theta \equiv 0$, from equation (4.2), and from the portfolio equilibrium condition (3.28), in the steady state

$$\frac{1}{1+r} \cdot v^d = \frac{1}{1+n} \cdot v^d - \frac{1}{1+n} \cdot \lambda \cdot f(k)$$

That is, the third term in the first bracketed expression in equation (4.6) is the net purchasing price of a share in the banking system per member of the following generation. From $\theta \equiv 0$ and equations (3.41) and (4.5), the term $\Omega \cdot w/(1+n)$ is to be interpreted as wealth in the creditor economy per member of the young generation and net of dividends. The first bracketed term in equation (4.6) is therefore the excess of savings over domestic assets.

The terms in brackets are, therefore, the excess supply of savings in the two countries over domestically held wealth per member of the following generation. World capital market equilibrium requires that the sum of these excess supplies is zero.

From equations (4.4), (4.5), and (3.41) savings in the two countries are independent of interest rates under non-sovereignty. This is due to the linear homogeneity of the production and utility functions. From equations (4.4), (4.5) and (3.42), steady-state investment is given by

$$\left.\begin{aligned} i &= \Omega \cdot w - \frac{1+n}{1+r} \cdot v + b \\ i^* &= \Omega^* \cdot w^* + b^* \end{aligned}\right\} \tag{4.7}$$

International borrowing, b^*, is exclusively used to finance investment in the debtor country. It should be understood that from Assumption 3.2 lenders cannot prevent the dissipation of loans into consumptive activities. Loans are fully invested because with perfect capital markets it is optimal for borrowers to do so. Lenders are therefore not confronted with an incentive problem under which borrowers behave in a way which negatively affects their ability to repay. It will turn out that matters are much more complicated under debtor sovereignty. Then, an array of incentive problems will emerge.

In a perfect capital market the interest rate borrowers have to pay must be equal to the interest rate lenders receive. We therefore have $r^{i*} = r^i$. This implies from equations (4.4) and (4.5) that

$$J(k, k^*) \equiv r - r^* = 0 \tag{4.8}$$

Under non-sovereignty, savings flow across borders until capital is equally productive at the margin in both countries. As from equations (3.5) real interest rates are determined by capital intensities in the two countries, this equilibrium condition can be expressed as an implicit function of k and k^*.

III. The Non-sovereign Debt Steady State

The two-country steady state is determined by the system of equations (4.6) and (4.8). As this system depends only on the capital intensities, k and k^*, we can characterize the steady state in $k - k^*$ space.

At variance with what we shall assume later in this chapter we make

Assumption 4.2: Domestic bank services are productive in the creditor economy, i.e. $\lambda > 0$.

We begin by discussing the shape of the $H^1(k, k^*) = 0$ function in $k - k^*$ space. It can be easily verified that for the production functions (3.4) the different terms in equation (4.6) depend on k and k^* as illustrated in Figure 4.1.

If borrowing and lending is inhibited then the excess supply of savings

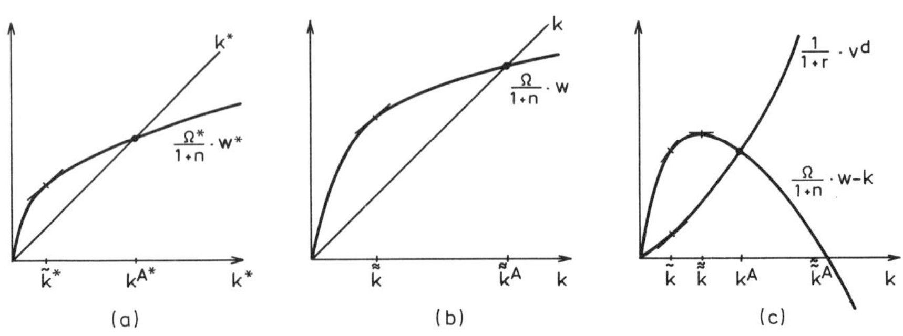

Figure 4.1 *Savings and household portfolios.*

over domestically held wealth must be zero in each country. Each term in brackets in equation (4.6) must be zero. From Figures 4.1(a) and (c), financial autarky therefore requires $k = k^A$ and $k^* = k^{A*}$ in a steady state. International borrowing and lending loosens this condition on capital markets in that only the sum of both excess supplies is required to be zero.

From equation (4.6) and Figure 4.1(a), the '*'-country is a lender on the world credit market for $k^* < k^{A*}$. It is a borrower if $k^* > k^{A*}$. From equation (4.6) and Figure 4.1(c), the other country borrows for $k > k^A$ and lends for $k < k^A$.

The implications of excess supplies, depicted in Figure 4.1, for the world capital market equilibrium condition (4.6) are illustrated in Figure 4.2.

The financial autarky steady state is given by the tuple (k^A, k^{A*}) in A in $k - k^*$ space. From Figure 4.1(a), starting from A and increasing k^* above k^{A*} implies that the '*'-country becomes a borrower. This requires from the other country that it becomes a lender, which in turn, from Figure 4.1(c), requires $k < k^A$. As k is further reduced and hence credit supply is further increased, credit demand must rise, requiring a further increase in k^*. At $k = \tilde{k}$ credit supply and hence k^* attain a maximum. A further reduction in the capital stock k decreases the excess supply of domestic savings over domestically held wealth and hence k^* must decrease. As $k \to 0$, lending comes to a halt so that $H^1(k, k^*) = 0$ can be sustained only for $k^* \to k^{A*}$. For $k^* < k^{A*}$ the '*'-country becomes an international lender. It is straightforward to motivate the branch to the right and below A in a similar manner.

Let k^n be the capital intensity in the creditor country for which $r = n$. As from inequality (3.8) a reduction in k increases r, for $r > n$ we must have

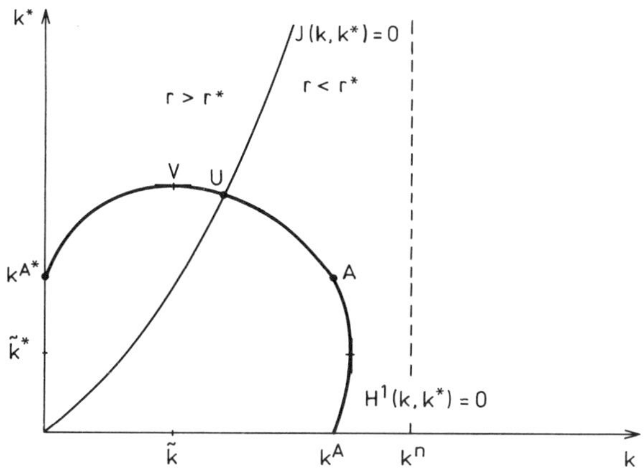

Figure 4.2 *World credit market clearing and the non-sovereignty steady state.*

$k < k^n$. In a steady state with a real store of wealth condition (3.12) must hold. In Figure 4.2 the $H^1(k, k^*) = 0$ function therefore must lie entirely to the left of a vertical through k^n.

To identify the lending and borrowing steady-state under non-sovereignty it remains only to determine the $J(k, k^*) = 0$ function in $k - k^*$ space. From equations (3.8) it immediately follows that $J(k, k^*) = 0$ has the shape depicted in Figure 4.2. An increase in k reduces marginal productivity in that country; and equality of real interest rates across countries requires that k^* must increase as well. To the right and below $J(k, k^*) = 0$, $r < r^*$, and to the left and above $J(k, k^*) = 0$, $r > r^*$.[2]

Let steady-state interest rates under financial autarky be given by $r = r^A$ and $r^* = r^{A*}$ respectively. In Figure 4.2, under autarky

$$r^A < r^{A*} \tag{4.9}$$

This creates opportunities for international, intertemporal trade. Opening up countries, the young in the high-interest country can now improve utility by issuing international debt below the domestic interest rate, r^{A*}, in order to finance additional investment. In the low-interest rate country, the young can improve utility by offering international loans above the domestic interest rate, r^A, instead of investing in the domestic capital stock. Such utility improving opportunities for international, intertemporal trade remain whenever real interest rates differ. An open economy equilibrium must therefore lie on $J(k, k^*) = 0$.

The open economy steady state is given by the intersection of $J(k, k^*) = 0$ and $H^1(k, k^*) = 0$ in U in Figure 4.2. The '*'-country is an international debtor in the steady state. Compared to the autarky steady state, A, in the free-trade steady state the capital intensity in the lending economy is smaller and in the debtor country it is larger.

From the definition in condition (3.11) and from the capital market equilibrium conditions (4.4), (4.5), and (4.8), the steady-state net transfer from the debtor to the creditor country is given by

$$z = \frac{b^*}{1+n} \cdot (r - n) \tag{4.10}$$

As $b^* > 0$ in the steady state, and from inequality (3.12), $z > 0$ in a steady state. z is the balance-of-payments surplus of the creditor country in long-run equilibrium.

z can be expanded into the components of the balance-of-payments. The payments surplus of the creditor country from the export of financial services is given by $b^* \cdot r/(1 + n)$. This trade surplus is to be balanced against net capital exports the creditor country undertakes in the steady state. Net capital exports are given by

$$-\frac{b^*}{1+n}\cdot n = \frac{b^*}{1+n} - \frac{b^*}{1+n}\cdot(1+n)$$

as the balance between gross capital imports from the repayment of principal, $b^*/(1+n)$, and gross capital exports from new loans, b^*.

It should be noted that world capital markets, far from requiring repayment of debt in the long run, permit the debtor country to pile debt on top of debt for ever, at the growing rate per period $n \cdot b^* \cdot L$. It is the infinite sequence of finitely-lived creditor households which makes this consistent with individual household optimization. Although total debt is never repaid, each individual loan is repaid when it is due.

IV. The Direction of International, Intertemporal Trade

We have maintained the convention that the '*'-country is the debtor economy. The steady-state U in Figure 4.2 is consistent with this convention. However, this requires that the intersection of the $J(k, k^*) = 0$ and $H^1(k, k^*) = 0$ functions lies to the left of the autarky point, A. We therefore have to state the precise conditions under which this is indeed the case.

To have the '*'-country be the debtor in the steady state we need $b^* > 0$. From equation (4.6),

$$b^* \begin{Bmatrix} \geqslant \\ \leqslant \end{Bmatrix} 0$$

is consistent with a steady state only if

$$\frac{\Omega}{1+n}\cdot w - \frac{1}{1+r}\cdot v^d - k \begin{Bmatrix} \geqslant \\ \leqslant \end{Bmatrix} 0 \quad \text{and} \quad \frac{\Omega^*}{1+n}\cdot w^* - k^* \begin{Bmatrix} \leqslant \\ \geqslant \end{Bmatrix} 0 \tag{4.11}$$

For the Cobb-Douglas production functions (3.3),

$$\left.\begin{aligned} f(k) &= \frac{r}{\alpha}\cdot k \\ f^*(k^*) &= \frac{r^*}{\alpha^*}\cdot k^* \end{aligned}\right\} \tag{4.12}$$

and

$$\left.\begin{aligned} w &= \beta \cdot f(k) \\ w^* &= \beta^* \cdot f^*(k^*) \end{aligned}\right\} \tag{4.13}$$

Substituting equations (4.13) and (4.12) into condition (4.11) we obtain, after collecting terms,

$$\frac{1+n}{\Omega}\cdot\frac{\alpha}{\beta}\cdot\left[1+\frac{1}{1+r}\cdot\frac{v^d}{k}\right]\begin{Bmatrix}\leqslant\\ \geqslant\end{Bmatrix}r \qquad \text{and} \qquad r^*\begin{Bmatrix}\leqslant\\ \geqslant\end{Bmatrix}\frac{1+n}{\Omega^*}\cdot\frac{\alpha^*}{\beta^*}$$

As in the free-trade steady state equation (4.8) holds, we have $r = r^*$. We obtain therefore as a necessary and sufficient condition for the direction of steady-state intertemporal trade

$$b^*\begin{Bmatrix}\geqslant\\ \leqslant\end{Bmatrix}0 \Leftrightarrow \frac{\alpha}{\Omega\cdot\beta}\cdot\left[1+\frac{1}{1+r}\cdot\frac{v^d}{k}\right]\begin{Bmatrix}\leqslant\\ \geqslant\end{Bmatrix}\frac{\alpha^*}{\Omega^*\cdot\beta^*} \tag{4.14}$$

Condition (4.14) identifies the determinants of the direction of international intertemporal trade as the two potential differences between the countries: time preferences and technologies.

To understand how preferences influence the direction of intertemporal trade, suppose that in an initial situation condition (4.14) holds as an equality. In this case the open economy steady state involves financial autarky. The $J(k, k^*) = 0$ function intersects the $H^1(k, k^*) = 0$ function in A in Figure 4.2. From equations (3.2), higher time preference in one country causes Ω, respectively Ω^*, to decrease. From condition (4.13), higher time preference in a country therefore contributes to the factors which make that country become a debtor under free trade. A higher time preference in the '*'-country decreases savings. Autarky involves therefore a smaller k^{A*}. The autarky point A in Figure 4.2 shifts downward. The $J(k, k^*) = 0$ function comes to lie to the left of A.

To understand the impact of technologies on the direction of intertemporal trade, suppose, for simplicity, $\alpha = \alpha^*$. As from the Cobb-Douglas functions (3.3) $\alpha + \beta + \lambda = \alpha^* + \beta^* = 1$, for $\alpha = \alpha^*$ technologies would be identical if $\lambda = 0$. From (3.13) $v^d = 0$, so the direction of intertemporal trade is exclusively determined by preferences if technologies are identical. From condition (4.12), an increase in the production elasticity of capital in one country, α or α^*, then contributes to make that country a borrower on international credit markets. An increase in α^*, for example, improves the marginal productivity of capital, k^*, and causes $J(k, k^*) = 0$ to turn counterclockwise. Economically, the more productive the capital in a country the higher the incentive to direct savings into that country.

Let us set again $\alpha = \alpha^*$, but let us now enter the real store of wealth, that is, set $\lambda > 0$. Given α, from equation (3.13) and $\alpha + \beta + \lambda = 1$, the introduction of a real store of wealth increases the LHS of condition (4.14). Economically, a real store of wealth absorbs savings and therefore increases interest rates in the country. Given the production elasticity of capital, α, the introduction of a real store of wealth works against the factors which make a country a lender. Given α, if for $\lambda = 0$ the condition for $b^* > 0$ is fulfilled, there exists a range $0 < \lambda < \underline{\lambda}$ for which the introduction of a real store of wealth does not alter the direction of international intertemporal trade. In Figure 4.2, given α, an increase in λ reduces k^A.

In what follows we will maintain the assumption that the conditions for $b^* > 0$ are fulfilled so that $J(k, k^*) = 0$ intersects $H^1(k, k^*) = 0$ to the left of the autarky point A in Figure 4.2. In doing that we assume therefore that the time preference and the productivity of reproducible capital in the lending economy is so much lower than in the borrowing country so as to sustain a production elasticity for bank services, $\lambda > 0$, without altering the direction of international intertemporal trade.

We also presume that the two countries do not differ too much to ensure that the steady-state U lies to the right of V in Figure 4.2. Given α, from equations (3.6) and (3.13) an increase in λ rotates $\Omega \cdot w/(1+n) - k$ downward and $v^d/(1+n)$ upwards around the origin in Figure 4.1(c). Hence, $\tilde{k}$ decreases. A large enough λ, for example, ensures therefore that V lies to the left of $J(k, k^*) = 0$ in Figure 4.2. The reason for making this assumption is that for $k < \tilde{k}$ the world economy features the pathology that further reducing the use of savings for investment into the domestic capital stock in the lending country actually reduces wealth that can be held in the form of international loans.

V. International Debt Without a Real Store of Wealth

To further illustrate the implications of the existence of a real store of wealth we now discuss the case when it is absent. To do this we revoke Assumption 4.2 and make

Assumption 4.3: The production elasticity of reproducible capital, α, remains fixed and the production elasticity of bank services, λ, is set to $\lambda = 0$.

Under Assumptions 4.1 and 4.3 the model simplifies to the one discussed in Schmid (1987).

If α remains fixed and λ is reduced to $\lambda = 0$, from $\alpha + \beta + \lambda = 1$ it then follows that $-\Delta\lambda = \Delta\beta = \lambda$. As the shares in output of the factors L and G, $\beta \cdot f(k)$ and $\lambda \cdot f(k)$, are obtained by households in the form of labour and dividend income, for a given output, household income remains constant. The effect of setting $\lambda = 0$ then is exclusively restricted to the effects of portfolio choice, as household savings do not now need to be absorbed in holdings of a real store of wealth. If α is fixed, it follows from equation (3.4) that the production function underlying the analysis remains unchanged. The interpretation of results obtained for $\lambda = 0$ are then not obscured by a simultaneous change in the per capita production technology.

Under Assumption 4.3 and from equation (3.13), $v^d = 0$, and the world excess supply function for international loans (4.6) simplifies to

$$H^2(k, k^*) \equiv \left[\frac{\Omega}{1+n} \cdot w - k\right] + \left[\frac{\Omega^*}{1+n} \cdot w^* - k^*\right] = 0 \qquad (4.15)$$

From Figures 4.1(b) and (c), autarky in the creditor country now requires $k = \tilde{\tilde{k}}^A > k^A$. The shape of $H^2(k, k^*) = 0$ relative to $H^1(k, k^*) = 0$ is depicted in Figure 4.3.

A comparison of the first terms in brackets in equations (4.6) and (4.15) reveals that for a given k the credit supply of the creditor country must be larger in the case $\lambda = 0$ than in the case $\lambda > 0$. Savings are simply not needed to hold banks as part of a household portfolio. Given k, the credit supply must therefore increase. For a larger credit supply, to clear the international market for loans, credit demand must increase. From Figure 4.1(a) this requires a larger k^*. Similarly, given k^*, from Figure 4.1(b), the world excess supply of loans requires for $\lambda = 0$ an increase of k if $k > \tilde{\tilde{k}}$, and a decrease for $k < \tilde{\tilde{k}}$. The $H^2(k, k^*) = 0$ function lies therefore above and to the right of the $H^1(k, k^*) = 0$ function in Figure 4.3.

Under Assumption 4.3, it follows from equations (3.4) and (3.5) that the position of the $J(k, k^*) = 0$ function in $k - k^*$ space remains the same with or without a real store of wealth. The steady state is therefore given by

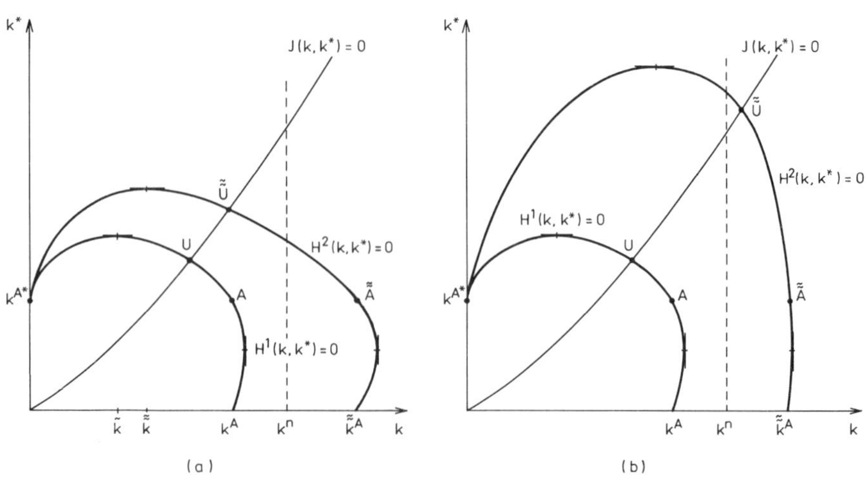

Figure 4.3 *The real store of wealth and the efficiency of steady states.*

point $\tilde{\tilde{U}}$ in Figure 4.3. The absorption of savings in the creditor country for the holding of a real store of wealth implies that in its absence the steady-state capital stock in both countries is larger than under its presence.

An important implication of the absence of a real store of wealth is that condition (3.12) need not hold any longer. As a consequence, and contrary to the $H^1(k, k^*) = 0$ function, the $H^2(k, k^*) = 0$ function need not entirely lie to the left of a vertical line through k''. This is depicted in Figure 4.3(a).

The difference between Figure 4.3(a) and Figure 4.3(b) is that in the former this vertical line is to the right and in the latter to the left of the steady state $\tilde{\tilde{U}}$. In Figure 4.3(a) condition (3.12) continues to hold in the steady state while in Figure 4.3(b) it is reversed to

$$r < n \tag{4.16}$$

A steady state in which $r < n$ is inefficient. To see this, note that in this steady state a household receives $1 + r$ units of the good when old for giving up one unit of consumption when young. As an alternative to private saving being an instrument to fend for old age, consider a social security system which requires each young household to contribute one unit of foregone consumption (Feldstein, 1976). When old, a household then receives $1 + n$ units of the good. For $n > r$ this system strictly dominates saving.

An alternative proof runs as follows. In the steady state the maintenance of the capital stock, k, requires a net investment, i.e. an inflow into firms, equal to $n \cdot K$ in each period. The return on capital is $r \cdot K$. For $n > r$ the net outflow from firms is negative. The economy is over-capitalized.[3]

Efficiency has important implications for the credit relationship between countries. From equation (4.10), the net transfer to the creditor country is positive if the steady state is efficient, it is negative if the steady state is inefficient. In direct analogy to a net inflow into the domestic capital stock, K, the creditor country invests $n \cdot b^*/(1 + n)$ in fresh money and receives less, $r \cdot b^*/(1 + n)$, if condition (4.16) holds.

If $z < 0$ the debtor country runs a permanent balance-of-payments surplus. The debtor country's payments deficit from the import of financial services is smaller than the surplus from net capital imports. It perhaps cannot be overemphasized that efforts to revive a net inflow of resources into debtor countries can only be sustained as a long-run equilibrium in an inefficient, over-capitalized world economy.

It is worth noting that the eternally growing total debt of a country in the steady state is not a phenomenon which is due to debtor sovereignty. Nor is it due to an excessive capital stock which keeps the interest rate below the world growth rate, as total debt is growing at both U and $\tilde{\tilde{U}}$. The sole requirement for allowing a permanent debt position of a country is that the supply side of loans consists of an infinite number of agents.

VI. Welfare

There are several approaches how to analyse the welfare implications of international debt. An ambitious approach would be to apply a social welfare function to the world economy that allows for inter-country welfare comparisons. To avoid the arbitrariness this would involve, one could apply the Pareto-criterion to countries for given welfare functions which hold within each country. In our model, a society consists of two distinct groups of individuals, the young and the old. In general, this could require interpersonal welfare comparisons between households within a country and could therefore again involve a degree of arbitrariness concerning the welfare implications of international debt.

In our analysis, we restrict ourselves to considering steady states. For welfare considerations generations are in an identical situation in a steady-state. Interpersonal welfare comparisons therefore need not be made. Given utility functions for which non-satiation holds, the steady-state welfare then is improved if the number of goods available for consumption in any one period is increased (Phelps, 1961).[4] To see this, let x be the steady-state number of goods available per period for consumption in the lending country. Then from (3.2), household utility can be expressed as

$$U(c^j, c^o) = (1 - \Omega) \cdot \ln c^j + \Omega \cdot \ln[(x - c^j) \cdot (1 + n)]$$

Steady-state utility of a two period lived household in a country with x available for consumption in each period is identical to utility of a single-period-lived household with the above utility function, consuming x.

Measuring welfare by the quantity of goods available for consumption in each period, x and x^*, would allow to identify steady states which are superior or inferior according to the Pareto criterion, applied to each country separately. Of course, even if two steady states could thus be ranked domestically, world-wide they need not be. This task would therefore be rather modest as, *a priori*, we would have to expect that there exist steady states which cannot be compared according to the Pareto criterion even domestically. It will turn out, however, that even this modest goal of analysing the welfare implications of international debt is thwarted in the model at hand. The reason for this is that different debt steady states regularly cannot be ranked according to the size of x and x^*. Facing these problems at this basic level, more ambitious welfare criteria become even more tentative.

To see this, note that x and x^* in our model are given by

$$\left.\begin{aligned} x &= f(k) - n \cdot k + z \\ x^* &= f^*(k^*) - n \cdot k^* - z \end{aligned}\right\} \tag{4.17}$$

The amount of goods available for consumption in each period is given by the sum of a domestic and an international component. The domestic component, x^d, is given by domestic output less goods needed to maintain the domestic capital stock

$$\left.\begin{aligned} x^d &\equiv f(k) - n \cdot k \\ x^{d*} &\equiv f^*(k^*) - n \cdot k^* \end{aligned}\right\} \tag{4.18}$$

The international component, z, is given by the net transfer across countries from a balance-of-payments surplus or deficit.

From equations (3.5), the domestic components depend on capital intensities according to

$$\left.\begin{aligned} dx^d/dk \begin{Bmatrix} \geqslant \\ \leqslant \end{Bmatrix} 0 \quad &\text{if} \quad r \begin{Bmatrix} \geqslant \\ \leqslant \end{Bmatrix} n \\ dx^{d*}/dk^* \begin{Bmatrix} \geqslant \\ \leqslant \end{Bmatrix} 0 \quad &\text{if} \quad r^* \begin{Bmatrix} \geqslant \\ \leqslant \end{Bmatrix} n \end{aligned}\right\} \tag{4.19}$$

Domestic components attain their maximum at the Golden Rule $r = n$, respectively $r^* = n$.

We are now ready to analyse the welfare implications of different steady states. Compare the debt steady state U with the autarky steady state A in Figure 4.2. From (4.19), the domestic component in the creditor country, x^d, is smaller under free trade. Counter to this, however, runs the effect that in autarky $z \equiv 0$, whereas under free trade, from equations (3.12) and (4.10), $z > 0$.

For the debtor country, effects are reversed. Under free trade the domestic, component is improved, whereas the international component worsens welfare.

It cannot therefore be concluded, in general, that free intertemporal trade improves world welfare compared to autarky, or, less ambitiously, that it improves the welfare of a particular country. This need not surprise us. Gains from trade accrue either from specialization or else from a favourable change in the market structure upon opening trade (Kierzkowski, 1987). In our single-commodity, perfect competition model neither is possible.

VII. Conclusions

To sum up:

(1) Under perfect capital markets, loans are used in the debtor country only for investment purposes. Lenders therefore do not have to face an incentive problem even if borrowers cannot be forced to stick to pre-announced investment plans.

(2) Compared to autarky, under free intertemporal trade the steady-state reproducible capital stock is reduced in the low interest rate country and increased in the high interest rate country.

(3) Steady-state capital markets sustain an eternally growing total debt that need never be paid back if the supply side of loans consists of an infinite number of individual lenders.

(4) There is a permanent net flow of resources out of the debtor economy into the lending economy if the debt steady state is efficient. Permanent net inflows of resources into the debtor economy require that the steady state is inefficient.

(5) If specialization and a change in market structure do not occur, the opening of intertemporal trade between countries need not improve welfare in the world nor in any particular country.

CHAPTER 5

Bond-financed Sovereign Debt

I. Introduction

Debtor sovereignty introduces an imperfection into international capital markets. In imperfect capital markets the Modigliani-Miller Theorem fails to hold. We have to distinguish therefore amongst the various forms of financing of international debt. In this chapter we analyse bond-financing of sovereign debt.[1]

We derive the capital market equilibrium conditions for the short and the long run and determine the world excess supply function in $k - k^*$ space. We then introduce the sovereignty restriction into the graphical analysis and distinguish between the cases of 'carrot-only' and 'stick-also'. Steady states are determined and the impact of a variation of the degree of sovereignty is analysed. Autarky and the non-sovereignty steady state are identified as the limiting cases in between which steady states differing with respect to the degree of sovereignty are placed. As under exclusive bond-financing banks have no role in international lending we take this opportunity and continue to investigate the role of the existence of a real store of wealth. It will become apparent that its existence has important implications for sovereign international debt.

II. Imperfect Capital Markets

To introduce debtor sovereignty we abandon Assumption 4.1 and make

Assumption 5.1: Debt is issued by a sovereign. In a steady state she honours contracts only if condition (3.11) is fulfilled.

There are several forms of financing available by which a country can raise capital abroad. Bond- and bank-credit financing and direct investment are perhaps the most important forms of financing. Although these forms do occur simultaneously we will discuss them separately. In that we make

Assumption 5.2: All foreign capital is bond-financed.

Under bond financing, equations (4.1)–(4.3) hold. However, under Assumption 5.1, it is not ensured that capital can flow across borders until the interest rate on the international component in the portfolio of a debtor household is equal to the return on other assets. This follows from equation (3.31) according to which lenders will constrain the credit supply so as to ensure that the sovereignty restriction (3.11) is observed. Instead of equation (4.4), condition (3.34) holds which in steady-state formulation is

$$r^*\begin{Bmatrix} > \\ = \end{Bmatrix} r^{i*} \Leftrightarrow b^*\begin{cases} = \underline{b}^* \\ \varepsilon\,[0, \underline{b}^*] \end{cases} \tag{5.1}$$

Under bond-financing, borrowers and ultimate lenders contract directly with each other, that is under circumvention of intermediation. The interest on debt issued must therefore be the same as the interest on loans held in the ultimate lender's portfolios, that is

$$r^i = r^{i*} \tag{5.2}$$

In the lending country, from (3.35) $r^i = r$ if the sovereignty restriction does not bind. However, it is readily seen that the interest rates on all assets in a lender's portfolio must be the same even if restriction (3.11) is binding. For if $r^i > r$, competition amongst lenders for a larger share in the given size of total loans, $\underline{b}^*$, will reduce the interest rate on bonds, r^i. This reduces the LHS of condition (3.11) and total loans can increase. The process comes to a halt when demand for additional loans has vanished or when bonds yield the same interest as other assets in the lenders' portfolios. Therefore

$$r = r^i \tag{5.3}$$

in a bond steady state.

From equation (3.48) the world capital market equilibrium condition, given equations (4.1)–(4.3) and (5.1)–(5.3), is

$$H^3(k, k^*) \equiv \left[\frac{\Omega}{1+n} \cdot w - k - \frac{1}{1+r} \cdot v^d\right] + \left[\frac{\frac{\Omega^*}{1+n} \cdot w^* - k^*}{1 + (1-\Omega^*) \cdot \left[\frac{1+r}{1+r^*} - 1\right]}\right] = 0 \quad (5.4)$$

under Assumption 4.2. In contrast, under Assumption 4.3 the capital market equilibrium condition is given by

$$H^4(k, k^*) \equiv \left[\frac{\Omega}{1+n} \cdot w - k\right] + \left[\frac{\frac{\Omega^*}{1+n} \cdot w^* - k^*}{1 + (1-\Omega^*) \cdot \left[\frac{1+r}{1+r^*} - 1\right]}\right] = 0 \quad (5.5)$$

The $H^3(k, k^*) = 0$ and the $H^4(k, k^*) = 0$ functions are depicted in Figure 5.1.

From a comparison of $H^3(k, k^*) = 0$ and $H^4(k, k^*) = 0$ with $H^1(k, k^*) = 0$ and $H^2(k, k^*) = 0$, respectively, it follows that sovereignty solely changes the denominator in the second bracketed term which represents the indebted economy. It is straightforward that $H^3(k, k^*) = H^1(k, k^*)$ in the autarky point A, and $H^4(k, k^*) = H^2(k, k^*)$ in $\tilde{\tilde{A}}$.

Below the $J(k, k^*) = 0$ function $r < r^*$. Therefore, as $1 > \Omega^* > 0$, we

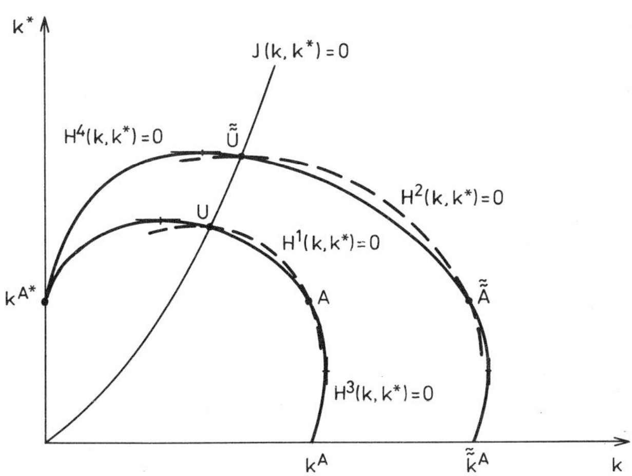

Figure 5.1 *World credit market clearing under sovereignty and bond-financing.*

have

$$1 > 1 + (1 - \Omega^*) \cdot \left[\frac{1+r}{1+r^*} - 1\right] > 0$$

below $J(k, k^*) = 0$. Therefore, given $k^* > k^{A*}$, below $J(k, k^*) = 0$ the second term in brackets in equations (5.4) and (5.5) is larger in absolute terms than in equations (4.6) and (4.15) respectively. Inserting equations (5.2) and (5.3) into the (lower) equation (3.45) and differentiating with respect to k^* it can be verified that

$$d[-b^*/(1+n)]/dk^* < 0$$

for $k^* > k^{A*}$, respectively $k^* > \tilde{\tilde{k}}^{A*}$. Given k, k^* must therefore be smaller under debtor sovereignty than under non-sovereignty for world credit markets to clear. Therefore, $H^3(k, k^*) = 0$ is located below $H^1(k, k^*) = 0$ and $H^4(k, k^*) = 0$ below $H^2(k, k^*) = 0$, if $k^* > k^{A*}$ and $r > r^*$.

On $J(k, k^*) = 0$

$$1 + (1 - \Omega^*) \cdot \left[\frac{1+r}{1+r^*} - 1\right] = 1$$

Therefore, the $H^3(k, k^*) = 0$ and $H^1(k, k^*) = 0$ functions intersect again on $J(k, k^*) = 0$. The same is true for the $H^4(k, k^*) = 0$ and $H^2(k, k^*) = 0$ functions.

The decline in the sustainable world capital stock per young household in a country, $k + k^*$, in the area between the autarky and the non-sovereignty steady states is readily explained. If households in the indebted economy can issue bonds at the foreign interest rate, r, instead of at the higher domestic rate, r^*, then old-age consumption is higher. Intertemporal consumption optimization then requires a smoothing of consumption across periods; that is, some of the additional consumption when old is to be transferred into additional consumption when young. Savings in the debtor country decline and the world economy can only sustain a smaller world capital stock.

III. The Sovereignty Restriction

In this section we determine the properties of the sovereignty restriction (3.11) in $k - k^*$ space. Of particular interest to us will be cases when restriction (3.11) is a binding constraint. To that end let

$$R(\cdot) \equiv \frac{b^*}{1+n} \cdot (r^{i*} - n) - \delta \cdot f^*(k^*) = 0 \tag{5.6}$$

Equation (5.6) is the upper bound of restriction (3.11). Insert equations (5.2) and (5.3) into equation (5.6), substitute from equation (3.47) $-b$ for b^* and note that $-b/(1+n)$ is given by the first term in brackets in equations (5.4) and (5.5), respectively. Under Assumption 4.2, it follows then from equation (5.6)

$$R^1(k,k^*,\delta) \equiv (r-n)\cdot\left[\frac{\Omega}{1+n}\cdot w - k - \frac{1}{1+r}\cdot v^d\right] - \delta\cdot f^*(k^*) = 0 \quad (5.7)$$

and under Assumption 4.3

$$R^2(k,k^*,\delta) \equiv (r-n)\cdot\left[\frac{\Omega}{1+n}\cdot w - k\right] - \delta\cdot f^*(k^*) = 0 \qquad (5.8)$$

Equation (5.7), or equation (5.8) respectively, represents the sovereignty restriction as an implicit function of k and k^*. The sovereignty restriction in $k-k^*$ space is depicted in Figure 5.2.

To determine the properties of $R^1(k,k^*,\delta)=0$ in $k-k^*$ space note that the relevant case requires $b^* \geqslant 0$. This in turn requires $k \leqslant k^A$ so that the first term in equation (5.7) is positive. Furthermore, under Assumption 4.2 $r-n>0$.

Suppose the indebted country need not suffer from economic sanctions after repudiation, that is, suppose $\delta = 0$. Then for all $k^* \geqslant k^{A*}$ equation (5.7) is fulfilled only if the first term is zero, that is if $k = k^A$. Therefore, under an absence of economic sanctions the sovereignty restriction (5.7) is parallel to the k^*-axis at $k = k^A$. This case is depicted in Figure 5.2(a).

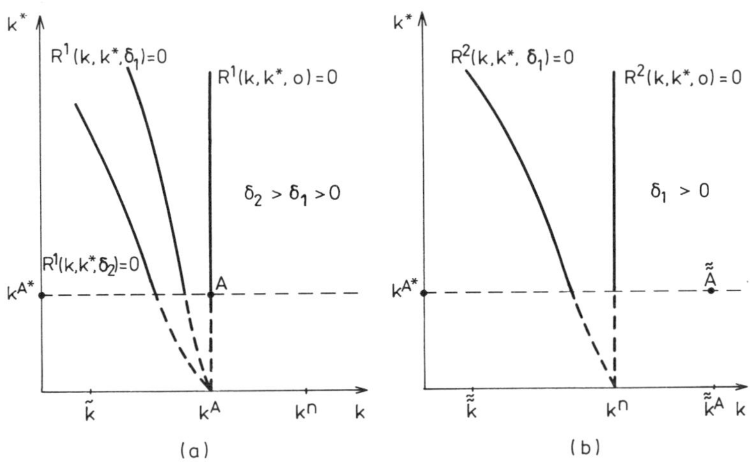

Figure 5.2 *The sovereignty restriction under debt-financing.*

Suppose $\delta > 0$. Then for $k^* \geqslant k^{A*}$ we have $\delta \cdot f^*(k^*) > 0$ and the first term in equation (5.7) must be positive, that is, $k < k^A$. From $\partial r/\partial k < 0$ and from Figure 4.1(c) it follows that the first term in equation (5.7) is increasing if k is decreased for all $k \geqslant \tilde{k}$. As $f^{*\prime}(k^*) > 0$, k^* must increase if k is decreased in $[\tilde{k}, k^A]$. Therefore $R^1(k, k^*) = 0$ is decreasing in $[\tilde{k}, k^A]$. Economically, a smaller k is associated with a larger debt service obligation for the debtors. To maintain the sovereign's indifference between honouring debt and repudiation, economic sanctions must be higher. This in turn requires a larger output in the debtor economy.

In Figure 5.2(a), points to the right of $R^1(k, k^*, \delta) = 0$ represent (k, k^*) tuples for which the sovereignty restriction (3.11) holds as an inequality. In this area the sovereign strictly prefers honouring debt compared to repudiation. To the left of $R^1(k, k^*, \delta) = 0$, given the net obligation from debt, z, economic sanctions are too low. The sovereign strictly prefers repudiation over servicing debt.

An increase in the parameter δ increases economic sanctions for a given k^*. Given $\delta = \delta_2$, $\delta_2 > \delta_1$, the sovereign honours debt she would repudiate if $\delta = \delta_1$. Hence an increase in δ causes the $R^1(k, k^*, \delta) = 0$ function to turn counterclockwise in Figure 5.2(a).

The properties of $R^2(k, k^*, \delta) = 0$ in $k - k^*$ space are depicted in Figure 5.2(b). There is a single, important difference between the $R^1(k, k^*, \delta) = 0$ function and the $R^2(k, k^*, \delta) = 0$ function in $k - k^*$ space. As depicted in Figure 4.3(b), if a real store of wealth does not exist $k^n < \tilde{\tilde{k}}^A$ is possible. In $[k^n, \tilde{\tilde{k}}^A]$, $z < 0$ if $b^* > 0$, and the sovereign will always strictly prefer debt servicing. For $k^n < \tilde{\tilde{k}}^A$ equation (5.8) can only be fulfilled if $k \leqslant k^n$. If $k^n < \tilde{\tilde{k}}^A$ the $R^2(k, k^*, \delta) = 0$ function therefore intersects the k-axis at k^n. If $k^n > \tilde{\tilde{k}}^A$, a case which is not depicted in Figure 5.2, the intersection is at $k = \tilde{\tilde{k}}^A$.

It will prove helpful to investigate the size of the international transfer, z, along the $R(\cdot) = 0$ functions. As z is equal to the first term on the LHS of equation (5.6), we obtain

$$z_{|R(\cdot)=0} = \delta \cdot f^*(k^*) \tag{5.9}$$

and

$$\frac{dz}{dk}_{|R(\cdot)=0} < 0 \tag{5.10}$$

as $dk^*/dk < 0$ along $R(\cdot) = 0$ in the interval $[\tilde{k}, k^A]$, and $[\tilde{\tilde{k}}, \tilde{\tilde{k}}^A]$ respectively.

IV. Steady States with a Real Store of Wealth

In this section we suppose that Assumption 4.2 holds. In this case the steady state under debtor sovereignty can be determined by bringing together the $H^3(k, k^*) = 0$ function depicted in Figure 5.1 and the $R^1(k, k^*, \delta) = 0$ function depicted in Figure 5.2(a). This is done in Figure 5.3.

As in the case of non-sovereignty, a steady state cannot lie to the left of the $J(k, k^*) = 0$ function. This must be so because both supply of and demand for international debt vanishes there. Furthermore, a steady state must lie on $H^3(k, k^*) = 0$. Contrary to the case of non-sovereignty, however, under debtor sovereignty a steady state cannot be situated to the left of $R^1(k, k^*, \delta) = 0$ as then repudiation would occur. Three different types of sovereignty steady states can occur.

In Figure 5.3(a) the case is depicted where the gunboat-technology, represented by the parameter δ_2, imposes sanctions on the country which are so severe that $R^1(k, k^*) = 0$ intersects $H^3(k, k^*) = 0$ to the left of the non-sovereignty steady state U. In this case loans can be increased until real interest rates are the same worldwide without violating the sovereignty restriction. The sovereignty steady state is unconstrained and identical to the non-sovereignty steady state, U.[2]

If δ is small enough, then $R^1(k, k^*) = 0$ intersects $H^3(k, k^*) = 0$ to the right of U. This case is depicted in Figure 5.3(b), where $\delta_2 > \delta_1 > 0$. Sanctions are so weak that the sovereignty restriction (3.11) is binding before the international flow of capital can equalize real interest rates. The constrained sovereignty steady state is located at B in Figure 5.3(b). At B

$$r < r^* \tag{5.11}$$

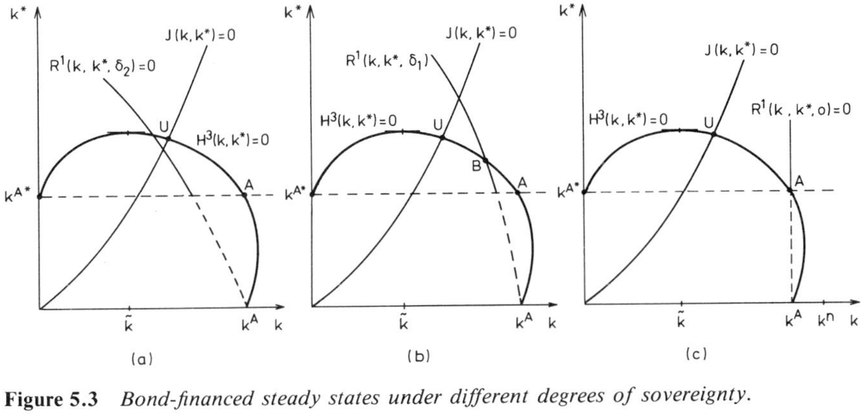

Figure 5.3 *Bond-financed steady states under different degrees of sovereignty.*

and

$$b^* > 0 \tag{5.12}$$

In the constrained steady state, debtors wish to raise more debt, but they are rationed. Furthermore, competition amongst debtors for a larger share in the given total debt outstanding cannot raise the interest rate on bonds as this too would violate the solvency restriction.

Figure 5.3(c) depicts the case $\delta = 0$. As $r > n$, any debt outstanding would involve a net outflow of resources from the debtor country. For $\delta = 0$ this net transfer cannot be sustained by the threat of economic sanctions. Neither borrowing nor lending is feasible. If a credit embargo is the sole deterrent from repudiation the sovereignty steady state under bond-financing is given by the autarky steady state, A, if there exists a real store of wealth.

Figure 5.3 visualizes that the effects of debtor sovereignty are a matter of degree, sandwiched between the extremes of absolute sovereignty and complete non-sovereignty. Starting at $\delta = 0$, and continuously increasing δ in the interval $[0, 1]$ turns $R^1(k, k^*, \delta) = 0$ continuously counterclockwise. The sovereignty steady state moves continuously from A to U. In this sense the theory of non-sovereign debt and the theory of sovereign debt are not competing. Rather, the theory of sovereign debt is more general. It specializes as an important limiting case to the theory of non-sovereign debt.

In the remainder of this section we shall analyse the properties of the constrained steady state in greater detail.

Inserting equations (5.2) and (5.3) into equation (3.42) one obtains for the steady-state investment

$$\left.\begin{aligned} i &= \Omega \cdot w - \frac{1+n}{1+r} \cdot v + b \\ i^* &= \Omega^* \cdot w^* + b^* \cdot \left[(1 - \Omega^*) \cdot \frac{1+r^*}{1+r} + \Omega^* \right] \end{aligned}\right\} \tag{5.13}$$

As in a constrained steady state condition (5.11) holds, in a steady state such as B

$$(1 - \Omega^*) \cdot \frac{1+r^*}{1+r} + \Omega^* < 1$$

Comparing equations (5.13), with the non-sovereign steady-state investment (4.7) it follows that for given (k, k^*) investment in the debtor country is smaller under sovereignty than under non-sovereignty. In particular, whereas under non-sovereignty, debt raised is fully invested this is not true in the constrained sovereignty steady state. Here, in each period part of the loan dissipates away from investment.

If loans were fully invested, output, and hence economic sanctions upon repudiation would be higher. Full investment of loans received would therefore improve the creditworthiness of the debtor country. This causes an incentive problem which is completely absent under non-sovereignty. Debtors cannot successfully improve their creditworthiness by promising to use loans exclusively for investment. Rational creditors know that full investment will not be optimal once the loan is received. Therefore such a promise is simply not credible.[3]

There is a straightforward economic interpretation why in the constrained steady state loans are not fully invested. Compared to the unconstrained case where $r = r^*$, debtors issue debt in the constrained steady state at a rate below the return on domestic investment. *Ceteris paribus* this increases consumption when old. Intertemporal utility maximization requires that part of this additional old-age consumption is shifted into youth. This is achieved by dissipating some of the loan away from investment into consumptive activities.

Let us now turn to the welfare effects of a marginal change in the sovereignty of the debtor country. In Figure 5.3(b) a marginal increase in δ moves the steady state B along $H^3(k, k^*) = 0$ in the direction of U. From (4.19) the associated decline in k decreases the domestic component of disposable income in the creditor country. The domestic component of disposable income increases in the debtor country as k^* increases.

In each country, however, the international component of welfare works against the domestic component. This is readily seen from the observation that a movement on $H^3(k, k^*) = 0$ in the north-western direction increases k^*. As the constrained steady state must lie on $R^1(k, k^*, \delta) = 0$, equation (5.9) must hold. As $f^{*\prime}(k^*) > 0$ a larger k^* is therefore associated with a larger net transfer from the debtor economy to the creditor economy. The international component of disposable income improves in the creditor country and it is worsened in the debtor country by a marginal decrease in sovereignty. Welfare effects in each country of a marginal change in δ are therefore ambiguous.

For these reasons it is also impossible to derive general results concerning welfare comparisons between the constrained steady state and either the unconstrained steady state, U, or autarky, A.

V. Reputational Equilibria

If economic sanctions pose no credible threat, that is, if $\delta = 0$, then a steady state with sovereign debt outstanding can be interpreted as a reputational equilibrium. To see this, suppose that instead of a *quid-pro-quo* exchange of new loans for the repayment of old debt and interest due, repayment strictly precedes the receipt of new credit. Nevertheless, condition (3.11), for $\delta = 0$, continues to represent the sovereignty restriction. Now the interpretation is simply that in servicing debt the sovereign maintains her reputation to continue to do so in the future. This reputation is lost if old debt due is repudiated.

From the constraint (3.11) a reputational equilibrium must be characterized by

$$z \leqslant 0 \tag{5.14}$$

Reputational equilibria can therefore never involve net transfers out of the debtor economy.

In Bulow and Rogoff (1989a) a general condition for reputational equilibria in a stochastic environment is given which, under the assumptions we maintain here, simplifies to condition (5.14).[4,5] This general condition is derived under two assumptions. First, the debtor country operates under perfect competition on the world capital markets. Second, it has at least one alternative portfolio choice to maintaining international debt, where this alternative is indexed to the same variables as debt. Such alternatives could be 'cash-in-advance contracts' such as buying insurance abroad. The conclusion derived is that under these conditions reputational equilibria fail to exist, or put differently, the country can never issue debt abroad.

This is exactly the conclusion we obtained from the analysis in Figure 5.3(c) where we assume $\delta = 0$. In fact, in our model context the two conditions underlying the general conclusion are fulfilled in any constrained reputational equilibrium. In a constrained reputational equilibrium equation (5.12) holds and

$$z = 0 \tag{5.15}$$

That is, a constrained reputational equilibrium is in our model context a pure roll-over. Debt servicing is exactly offset by new loans. The gross outflow of resources is equal to the gross inflow.

In this situation the debtor country has a perfect portfolio alternative to international debt. Forsaking the gross inflow of new loans it can repudiate debt and collect the payments from international debt due from the old – and redistribute them as domestic government loans to the young under the same terms available on bonds issued abroad. The interest rate in the debtor country would be the same as if it continued with the reputational equilibrium. The country can therefore take the interest rate as given, just as if it acted under perfect competition. This operation would leave both living generations as well off as in the reputational equilibrium. In fact, all subsequent generations can be made as well off if the domestic government loan scheme is maintained.

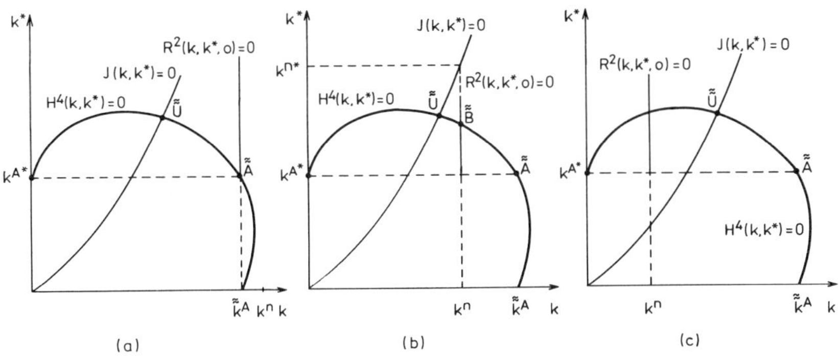

Figure 5.4 *Bond-financed steady states under the lack of gunboat-technologies.*

It would, however, be premature to attribute generality to the conclusion derived from Figure 5.3(c). To see this, abandon Assumption 4.2. Suppose instead that Assumption 4.3 is valid. Figure 5.4 depicts the sovereignty steady states under the absence of economic sanctions and under the absence of a real store of wealth.

Under Assumption 4.3 equations (5.5) and (5.8) are relevant. Figure 5.4(a) depicts the case when the growth rate, n, is so low that $\tilde{\tilde{k}}^A < k^n$. In this case the vertical $R^2(k, k^*, 0) = 0$ function must intersect the k-axis at $k = \tilde{\tilde{k}}^A$. Just as in Figure 5.3(c), a reputational equilibrium does not exist.

Consider, however, the case $k^n < \tilde{\tilde{k}}^A$. From Figure 5.2 the $R^2(k, k^*, 0) = 0$ function now intersects the k-axis in $k = k^n$.

In Figure 5.4(b), the case is illustrated where the $R^2(k, k^*, 0) = 0$ function intersects $H^4(k, k^*) = 0$ between $\tilde{\tilde{U}}$ and $\tilde{\tilde{A}}$. On $H^4(k, k^*) = 0$, to the right of $\tilde{\tilde{B}}$ debtors are unconstrained yet have an incentive to raise more debt. Debt associated with points to the left of $\tilde{\tilde{B}}$ are unavailable. The reputational steady state is therefore given by $\tilde{\tilde{B}}$. In $\tilde{\tilde{B}}$ equations (5.11), (5.12) and (5.15) hold. Furthermore,

$$r = n \tag{5.16}$$

Therefore a reputational equilibrium exists in the case depicted in Figure 5.4(b). Furthermore, it has the property that in the creditor country the Golden-Rule capital stock is attained. Note that the Golden Rule is obtained from a positive analysis. However, the Golden Rule does not emerge from a normative analysis.

To see that the Golden Rule is not optimal for the creditor economy, consider a marginal movement on $H^4(k, k^*) = 0$ at $\tilde{\tilde{B}}$ in the direction of $\tilde{\tilde{U}}$. From (4.19) the domestic component of disposable income, x^d, does not change. However, the international component, z, increases as both debt and the interest rate increase. The Golden-Rule roll-over steady state $\tilde{\tilde{B}}$ is therefore suboptimal for the creditor country. Dominant steady states would require $\delta > 0$. Some 'stick-also' equilibria are therefore strictly preferred to the reputational equilibrium.

Figure 5.4(c) depicts the case in which the growth rate is so large so that $R^2(k, k^*, 0) = 0$ intersects the $H^4(k, k^*) = 0$ function to the left of $\tilde{\tilde{U}}$. In this case the unconstrained reputational equilibrium is in $\tilde{\tilde{U}}$. As in $\tilde{\tilde{U}}$ $r = r^* < n$, the steady state is inefficient. As $r - n < 0$, $z < 0$. The reputational equilibrium requires a permanent net transfer from the creditor country into the debtor country.

There is an important difference between the cases illustrated in Figures 5.4(b) and (c). As in the latter $z < 0$, the debtor country cannot attain the same welfare under the domestic tax and government loan scheme depicted earlier. In Figure 5.4(c) the debtor country has therefore no portfolio alternative to international debt available.

We are left to explain why in the case depicted in Figure 5.4(b) a reputational equilibrium does exist under circumstances under which it cannot exist in Bulow and Rogoff (1989a). The reason is that in our model we allowed that the debtor country can run a rational Ponzi game. And in fact, in the reputational equilibrium of Figure 5.4(b) the debtor country does run a Ponzi type of financing.

Under conditions of perfect competition portfolio alternatives to international debt are available. However, the fact that the debtor country can forever raise fresh loans from new lenders to repay old debt means that this portfolio alternative never needs to be chosen. Under these circumstances, individual lenders can trust that the debtor country will not quit the debt relationship while they are a party to it. Reputational equilibria are thus sustainable. If debtors can run a rational Ponzi type of financing the availability of portfolio alternatives at competitive terms is neither necessary nor sufficient to prevent the existence of reputational debt equilibria. Rather it is the condition that growth rates are sufficiently high which is crucial. Furthermore, from condition (5.14), if a reputational debt equilibrium exists, it must be financed by a rational Ponzi game.

There are further interesting aspects to reputational debt equilibria. Given the potential for international intertemporal trade, the existence of reputational equilibria does *not* depend on economic conditions in the debtor country. The sole requirement is that the interest rate in the creditor country is not above the growth rate in that country. The intuition for this is that all that is needed for a reputational debt relationship to persist is the creditors' aggregate ability to serve the claims they have out of their own pockets. Obviously, this ability depends solely on conditions in the creditor country.

Remaining in the creditor country, a constrained reputational debt equilibrium works like a social security scheme which requires each young household to pay b^*, and each old household to receive $(1+n)\cdot b^*$. In the debtor country a constrained reputational debt equilibrium works like a domestic redistribution from old to young. These similarities help to interpret the welfare effects of constrained reputational debt equilibria.

From Figure 5.4(b) the autarky steady state in the creditor country is inefficient whereas it is efficient in the debtor country. From equations (5.15) and (4.17) disposable income in a constrained reputational equilibrium depends solely on the domestic components, x^d and x^{d*}. From condition (4.19), in both countries domestic components in the reputational equilibrium $\tilde{\tilde{B}}$ are larger than in autarky $\tilde{\tilde{A}}$. Welfare in each country and therefore worldwide is higher in any constrained reputational equilibrium than in the autarky steady state. International reputational debt reduces the overcapitalization in the creditor country and increases capital in the undercapitalized debtor country.[6]

VI. Conclusions

Let us sum up:

(1) Bond-financed sovereign debt reduces the world capital stock which is sustainable by a clearing of the world bond market.

(2) If debtor sovereignty is a binding constraint there exists an incentive problem in that it is optimal for debtors to use part of the debt raised for consumption instead of investment.

(3) The non-sovereignty steady state and autarky are the limiting cases of sovereign debt steady states.

(4) If there exists a real store of wealth bond-financed debt steady states fail to exist if a credit embargo is the sole deterrent from repudiation. If a steady state exists it involves net transfers out of the debtor country. If the steady state is constrained, marginal productivity of capital differs across countries.

(5) Reputational debt equilibria can exist if a real store of wealth fails to exist. A growth rate in excess of the autarky interest rate in the creditor country is sufficient for the existence of reputational equilibria. Reputational equilibria require a Ponzi game type of debt financing.

(6) The constrained reputational equilibrium is characterized by Golden-Rule conditions in the creditor country and a pure roll-over of international debt. In a constrained reputational equilibrium welfare in both countries is strictly larger than under autarky.

CHAPTER 6

Sovereign Debt and Financial Intermediation

I. Introduction

Instead of issuing bonds abroad and engaging in a direct credit relationship with foreign households a country can borrow from foreign private banks.[1] Under bank credit financing economic relations between a debtor country and foreign private households are indirect only. There are two such indirect links.

First, in as far as households abroad hold shares in banks, engaged in international lending, their wealth depends on the success or failure of the credit relationship between a sovereign and the banks they own.[2]

The second link connects a sovereign and foreign households via the refinancing of bank loans on the market for bank deposits. An internationally operating bank system acts as a financial intermediary between the ultimate borrower, a sovereign, and the ultimate lenders, private households in the lending countries. If financial intermediaries are subject to bankruptcy laws in the creditor countries the solvency of banks and the utility of depositors can depend on the sovereign's discretionary behaviour.[3] This can pose a potential threat to the stability of the banking system.[4]

Financial intermediation is merely a 'veil' over a real economy if capital markets are perfect. Under imperfect capital market conditions, however, financial intermediation can play a part in the real economy (see for example Fama, 1985). Besides the wealth and solvency issues described above there are two further basic differences between bank and bond financing of international debt.

Individual bondholders terminate a credit relationship with a foreign country before the lending country as a whole terminates the relationship. A banking system in charge of international financial intermediation has a time horizon beyond that of individual depositors. Furthermore, banks have a stake in an international debt relationship left from lending in the past. The decision problem for a bank having a standing debt relationship with a sovereign can therefore be different from that of a household deciding about engaging in international bond-financing. We begin the analysis of bank-financing with a discussion of this issue.

II. Longevity, Standing Relations and Rational Opportunism of Banks

Whenever a country continuously issues bond-financed debt abroad there will exist households in the creditor countries which already hold international bonds. These households then have to decide whether to expand their engagement in financing international debt. What is characteristic, however, for the supply side of bond-financed international loans is that individual lenders at one time or another do quit the market for good. In aggregate the long-run persistence of bond-financed international debt therefore depends on the recurrent emergence of new households prepared to *become* a new party to an international debt relationship. This requirement holds irrespective of whether bonds are traded only on a primary or also on a secondary market. This long-run requirement of bond-financing is quite naturally captured in an overlapping generations model.

Under bank-financing this is different. Individual banks may quit international financial intermediation, other banks may decide whether to enter the market. However, on aggregate the banking system does not, in the long run, decide whether to begin a credit relationship.

Under perfect competition, banks maximize their value for their current owners. As banks are traded on the capital market the time horizon of banks extends beyond the time horizon of their owners into the infinite future. As time progresses banks hold claims from past loans to a sovereign. In the long run banks therefore merely decide whether or not to *continue* a standing debt relationship with a sovereign. This decision will depend on its implications for the current and future discounted stream of profits.

What makes this decision particularly troublesome is that claims currently due against the debtor are unenforceable. The bank may therefore fear that it can preserve the value of claims due only if it continues the standing relationship by lending anew. The bank is locked in. To bail out principal and interest due the bank may exhibit an opportunism it otherwise would not.[5] A bank may therefore find itself in a situation where it wants to continue a debt relationship it would not become a party to in the first place.

Under bank credit lending, international debt is idiosyncratic (Williamson, 1985). International lending can become involuntary.[6] Under bond financing this is impossible in the long run.

The idiosyncratic nature of international financial intermediation can be shown to exist in our model. To do this revoke Assumption 5.2 and make

Assumption 6.1: All foreign capital is bank credit-financed.

For idiosyncrasy to exist, a bank's stake in a debt relationship cannot be infinitesimal. If it were, opportunism would be too. Nor can the stake a sovereign has in a relationship with a particular bank be infinitesimal if Assumption 2.2 holds and costs of repudiation are those underlying the sovereignty restriction (3.11). If it were, it always would be optimal to service an infinitesimal claim.[7] To ensure that this precondition for idiosyncrasy is met we make

Assumption 6.2: No strategic interdependencies exist between different debt contracts.

What Assumption 6.2 does is to change a single debt relationship between a debtor country and a creditor country into L independent debt relationships between the debtor country and L foreign banks. Under Assumption 6.2 if a sovereign repudiates one contract this has no effect on other contracts. In particular, all other banks do not impose a credit embargo. It also implies that economic sanctions associated with the breach of a particular contract must be independent from what happens to other contracts. A further important implication is that individual banks cannot free-ride on a collective effort to preserve the value of all loans.[8]

Under Assumption 6.2 the sovereignty restriction (3.11) relates exclusively to an individual contract. As banks and contracts are identical, however, it again holds for the aggregate debt relationship between the countries.

Lending is involuntary only if the return on new loans is below normal. Under competitive terms this involves losses which need to be compensated for by profits made elsewhere. We therefore revoke Assumption 4.3 and revert to Assumption 4.2.

If a loan from a particular bank is repudiated, its value is nil. The present discounted value of that bank's future international activity, however, need not be, if, after a period of abstinence, the bank reenters the market for international financial intermediation. We shall abstract from this complication in making

Assumption 6.3: After suffering from repudiation, $v^i = 0$.

For example, this would be the case if, after a repudiation, a bank abstained for ever from the market for international financial intermediation. We can now formally analyse the banks' opportunism when continuing a debt relationship.

It is evident that opportunism can occur only if the sovereignty restriction (3.11) is binding. Otherwise the loan size could be reduced without having to fear repudiation. Furthermore, for opportunism to occur we need $v^i < 0$, that is, from equations (3.14) and (3.15) we need $r^s < r^d$. From equation (3.16) opportunism then is an issue if $v < v^d$, that is, if the value of the bank would be higher under abstinence from international financial intermediation. The question then is under what conditions a rational bank is willing to continue an unprofitable international activity.

Under rational opportunism a bank compares the contribution to the wealth of shareholders of continuing a standing debt relationship with the contribution to shareholder wealth of terminating the relationship. In a steady state, continuation formally requires

$$\frac{b^*}{1+n} \cdot (1 + r^s) \geqslant -\frac{1+n}{1+r} \cdot v^i \tag{6.1}$$

On the LHS of condition (6.1) is the increase in current dividend paid to current owners of the bank from a continuation of the debt relationship. This increase is identical to the repayment of old debt due enticed by fresh lending.

On the RHS of condition (6.1) is the change in the discounted price of a bank from a sale to the next generation in the next period, if the debt relationship is continued instead of being terminated. As $v^i < 0$ for opportunism to occur, the current owners must suffer from having to sell the bank at a discount if the unprofitable international operation is continued. This discount has to be borne by current owners because the bank has to refinance the maintenance of the credit relationship at a rate r^d, above the interest rate on loans, r^s.

Therefore, condition (6.1) compares the short-term gains in terms of higher dividends with the long-term losses in terms of a depressed share price from the maintenance of an unprofitable debt relationship. Put still differently, the LHS of condition (6.1) represents the costs from terminating the relationship whereas the RHS represents the costs from continuing it. Condition (6.1) says that it is rational for a bank to exhibit opportunism if the termination of the debt relationship is costlier than its continuation.

Inserting the capital market equilibrium conditions (3.29) and (3.47) into the steady-state equation (3.14), inserting this into equation (3.15) and substituting in condition (6.1) it follows

$$\frac{b^*}{1+n}\cdot(1+r^s) \geqslant -\frac{1+n}{r-n}\cdot\frac{b^*}{1+n}\cdot[(1+r^s)-(1+r)]$$

Collecting terms we obtain as a condition for rational opportunism of banks

$$r^s \geqslant n \tag{6.2}$$

Condition (6.2) is readily interpreted. To obtain in a steady state a repayment $(1+r^s)\cdot b^*/(1+n)$, a bank must raise deposits and lend anew b^*. The net transfer to a bank from this operation is non-negative only if condition (6.2) is fulfilled. Together with equation (3.29) it entails

$$r = r^d \geqslant r^s \geqslant n \tag{6.3}$$

which determines the parameter constellation under which a competitive bank exhibits rational opportunism in a steady state and under which involuntary lending can occur.[9,10] Condition (6.3) succinctly captures the idea that

'... the new credits are simply part of the overall administration of old debt and their appearance is due to the need to avoid capital losses rather than to the attractiveness of the price of the operation' (Devlin, 1985).

We now turn to investigate the implications of rational opportunism for the world capital markets.

III. Capital Markets

Under financial intermediation the international component in the portfolios of households in the lending country is the deposit made in the banking system, which is needed for refinancing international bank loans. Therefore

$$r^i = r^d \tag{6.4}$$

Furthermore the interest rate on the international component in the portfolios of households in the debtor country is given by the interest rates foreign banks charge on loans. Therefore

$$r^{i*} = r^s \tag{6.5}$$

Given equations (6.4) and (6.5), and using the portfolio equilibrium condition (3.29), the condition for the clearing of the world credit market (3.48) simplifies to

$$H^5(k, k^*, r^s) \equiv \left[\frac{\dfrac{\Omega}{1+n}\cdot w - k - \dfrac{1}{1+r}\cdot v^d}{\dfrac{r^s - n}{r - n}}\right] + \left[\frac{\dfrac{\Omega^*}{1+n}\cdot w^* - k^*}{1 + (1-\Omega^*)\cdot\left[\dfrac{1+r^s}{1+r^*} - 1\right]}\right] = 0 \tag{6.6}$$

The world credit market clearing condition under financial intermediation is therefore an implicit function of k, k^*, and r^s.

If $r^s > r^d$ banks would make profits from financial intermediation. If the sovereignty restriction (3.11) did not bind for $r^s > r^d$, banks would raise more deposits and increase loans. If condition (3.11) was binding for $r^s > r^d$ competition amongst banks for a larger share in total loans would reduce r^s, allowing for an increase in total loans. Capital market equilibrium therefore requires

$$r^s \leqslant r^d = r \tag{6.7}$$

For a comparison of equations (6.6) and (5.4) it follows that the $H^3(k, k^*) = 0$ function and the $H^5(k, k^*, r^s) = 0$ function are identical if $r^s = r^d$. Intuitively, for $r^s = r^d$ financial intermediation is like a veil over the economy having no real impact. To determine the position of $H^5(k, k^*, r^s) = 0$ in $k - k^*$ space for $r^s < r^d = r$ reformulate equation (6.6) to yield

$$\left[\frac{\dfrac{\Omega}{1+n}\cdot w - k - \dfrac{1}{1+r}\cdot v^d}{\dfrac{\Omega^*}{1+n}\cdot w^* - k^*}\right] + \left[\frac{\dfrac{r^s - n}{r - n}}{1 + (1-\Omega^*)\cdot\left[\dfrac{1+r^s}{1+r^*} - 1\right]}\right] = 0 \tag{6.8}$$

It is easy to verify that the derivative with respect of r^s of the second, positive term in equation (6.8) is given by

$$\frac{\frac{1}{r-n}\cdot\left\{1+\frac{1-\Omega^*}{1+r^*}\cdot(n-r^*)\right\}}{\left\{1+(1-\Omega^*)\cdot\left[\frac{1+r^s}{1+r^*}-1\right]\right\}^2}$$

This derivative is positive as $1 > (1-\Omega^*)\cdot r^*/(1+r^*)$. A parametrical reduction of r^s below $r^d = r$ therefore reduces the second term in equation (6.8). To reestablish equality in equation (6.8) the first, negative, term must increase. Given k, the first, negative, term increases if k^* is increased for $k^* > k^{A*}$. The $H^5(k, k^*, r^s) = 0$ function therefore lies above the $H^3(k, k^*) = 0$ function in $k - k^*$ space for $k^* < k^{A*}$ if $r^s < r^d = r$. From equation (6.6) the numerator in the first term is zero for $k = 0$ and for $k = k^A$. Therefore $H^5(k, k^*, r^s) = H^3(k, k^*)$ for all r^s if $k = k^A$ or $k = 0$. Figure 6.1 depicts the properties of $H^5(k, k^*, r^s) = 0$ for different values of r^s.

For $k = k^A$, $r = r^A$. A reduction of k below k^A increases r. Let $r^s = r^A$. It then follows that for $k < k^A$, $r^s < r$. Therefore the $H^5(k, k^*, r^A) = 0$ function lies above the $H^3(k, k^*) = 0$ function. A parametrical reduction in r^s shifts $H^5(k, k^*) = 0$ upwards. The $H^5(k, k^*, r_1^s) = 0$ function therefore lies above the $H^5(k, k^*, r^A) = 0$ function if $r_1^s < r^A$. A further reduction of r^s shifts $H^5(k, k^*, r^s) = 0$ further upwards.

Opportunism of banks can be indexed by the parameter r^s in $k - k^*$ space. The more lenient banks are, that is the lower r^s, the further outward is the steady-state world capital possibility frontier shifted. Opportunism

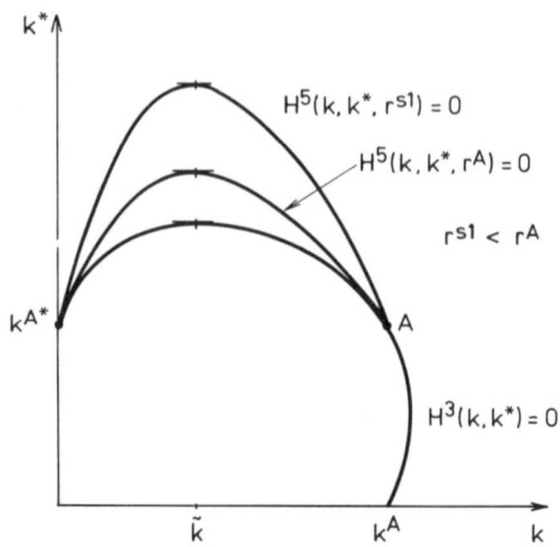

Figure 6.1 *World credit market clearing under financial intermediation.*

hence increases the possible world capital stock. There is a ready economic explanation for this.

The value of international operations, v^i, is not an argument in equation (6.6). However, the value of international operations is implicit in the denominator of the first term in equation (6.6); the term which represents the supply side of international debt. Given debt outstanding, a reduction of r^s increases the losses of banks from financial intermediation. This increases the discount on the banking system. Out of given savings less resources are therefore absorbed for holding banks as a real store of wealth in the portfolios of the young. Given the capital stock, k, the supply of bank deposits and hence of international loans must therefore be larger. This additional supply of loans triggers additional investment in the debtor country.

We have identified here two channels through which the opportunism of banks is transmitted into real economic activity in the debtor country. The first is the direct link by which banks maintain a credit relationship which is unprofitable. The second link draws on the connectedness of markets in the creditor country in a general equilibrium. It is transmitted through asset prices and portfolio choices in the creditor country into international credit markets and from there into consumption, savings, and investment in the debtor country.

There is a further, interesting implication of opportunism. Opportunism of banks aggravates the incentive problem creditors face under sovereign debt. To see this, substitute r^s from equation (6.5) into the condition for optimal investment (the lower equation in (3.42)) to obtain in the steady state

$$i^* = \Omega^* \cdot w^* + b^* \cdot \left[(1 - \Omega^*) \cdot \frac{1 + r^s}{1 + r^*} + \Omega^* \right] \tag{6.9}$$

Opportunism only occurs if the sovereignty restriction (3.11) is binding. From the analysis in Chapter 5 we know that then $r^* > r$. As for opportunism to occur $r^s < r^d = r$, from (6.9) the fraction of loans which is invested and not immediately consumed is further decreased under involuntary lending. Economically, the reason for this is that borrowers get an extra discount on loans under opportunism. The extra consumption at old age which this implies is partly transferred into consumption when young.

IV. Financial Intermediation and Solvency

Banks may make losses from their international activities. In the long run banks must compensate for these losses with profits from other activities.

Solvency of banks in the steady state requires $v \geqslant 0$, which is from equation (3.18) given if the dividend per period is non-negative, that is if

$$\lambda \cdot f(k) + \theta \geqslant 0 \tag{6.10}$$

Of particular interest are cases under which solvency is a binding constraint.

Note that from the upper equation in (3.22) in a steady state

$$\frac{-b}{1+n} = a - k \tag{6.11}$$

if $v = 0$. Inserting from inequality (3.14) the steady-state definition for θ in (6.10), $v = 0$ if

$$\lambda \cdot f(k) + \frac{-b}{1+n} \cdot (r^s - r) = 0$$

where we have substituted in equation (3.29). Substituting in equation (6.11) and collecting terms we obtain

$$r^s = r - \frac{\lambda \cdot f(k)}{a-k} \equiv \underline{r}^s$$

as the zero-profit condition. Inserting equations (6.4) and (3.29) in the upper equation in (3.41) it follows that $s = \Omega \cdot w + \lambda \cdot f(k) + \theta$. Noting that $v = 0$ if $\lambda \cdot f(k) + \theta = 0$ it follows from the upper equation in (3.21) that in a steady state

$$a = \frac{\Omega}{1+n} \cdot w \tag{6.12}$$

Substituting this into the definition of $\underline{r}^s$, we obtain as the zero-profit condition, that is for the minimal value of r^s,

$$\underline{r}^s = r - \frac{\lambda \cdot f(k)}{\dfrac{\Omega}{1+n} \cdot w - k} \tag{6.13}$$

It is easy to verify that

$$d\underline{r}^s / dk < 0 \tag{6.14}$$

in $[\tilde{\tilde{k}}, k^A)$.

We have now two lower bounds on the interest rate, r^s. From the rational opportunism condition (6.2), $r^s \geqslant n$ to ensure that banks want to continue an unprofitable international debt relationship, and from equation (6.13), $r^s \geqslant \underline{r}^s$ to ensure that banks can continue the debt relationship. The binding constraint is $\max[n, \underline{r}^s]$.

To determine $\max[n, \underline{r}^s]$, insert (6.12) in

$$\underline{r}^s \begin{Bmatrix} > \\ = \\ < \end{Bmatrix} n$$

to obtain after collecting terms

$$\frac{\Omega}{1+n} \cdot w - k \begin{Bmatrix} > \\ = \\ < \end{Bmatrix} \frac{\lambda \cdot f(k)}{r-n}$$

From equation (3.14) it follows that the RHS is equal to $v^d/(1+r)$. It therefore follows

$$\underline{r}^s \begin{Bmatrix} > \\ = \\ < \end{Bmatrix} n \Leftrightarrow \frac{\Omega}{1+n} \cdot w - k - \frac{1}{1+r} \cdot v^d \begin{Bmatrix} > \\ = \\ < \end{Bmatrix} 0$$

This is familiar. From Figure 4.1(c) it follows that

$$\underline{r}^s \geqslant n \;\forall\, k \leqslant k^A \tag{6.15}$$

As a steady state must involve $k \leqslant k^A$ we conclude that solvency is the binding restriction in any debt steady state.

To determine the zero-profit function in $k - k^*$ space insert equation (6.12) in equation (6.11) to obtain

$$\frac{-b}{1+n} = \frac{\Omega}{1+n} \cdot w - k \tag{6.16}$$

Inserting equation (6.16) and the lower equation in (3.45) in the credit market clearing condition (3.47) we obtain upon setting $r^{i*} \equiv \underline{r}^s$ the zero-profit function in $k - k^*$ space

$$\underline{H}(k, k^*, \underline{r}^s) \equiv \left[\frac{\Omega}{1+n} \cdot w - k\right] + \left[\frac{\dfrac{\Omega^*}{1+n} \cdot w^* - k^*}{1 + (1-\Omega^*) \cdot \left[\dfrac{1+\underline{r}^s}{1+r^*} - 1\right]}\right] = 0 \tag{6.17}$$

The properties of equation (6.17) are depicted in Figure 6.2.

From equation (6.13) $\underline{r}^s \leqslant r$ for $k \leqslant 0$. Therefore for $k > 0$ the denominator in the second term in equation (6.17) is smaller than the denominator in the second term in equation (5.5). Therefore the negative, second term in equation (6.17) is smaller than the negative, second term in equation (5.5). Given k, k^* must therefore be smaller in $\underline{H}(k, k^*, \underline{r}^s) = 0$ than in $H^4(k, k^*) = 0$. The zero-profit function is below the $H^4(k, k^*) = 0$ function in Figure 6.2. It is easily seen that these functions intersect for $k^* = k^{A*}$.

Economically, if profits are zero, it is as if a real store of wealth does

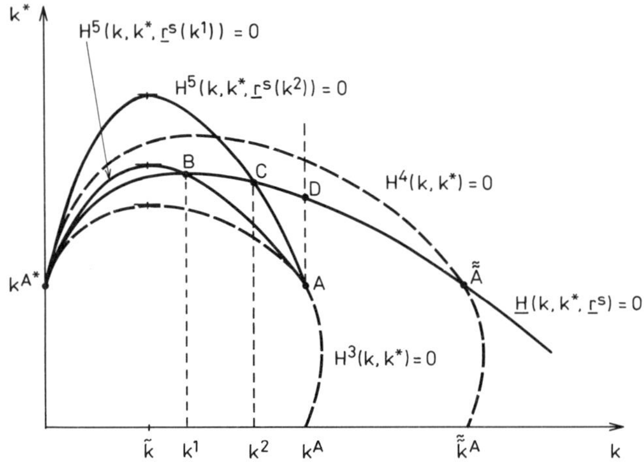

Figure 6.2 *The solvency restriction.*

not exist. As zero profits require a discount on the interest rate on international loans, the only difference between the world economy with a zero profit real store of wealth and the economy without a real store of wealth is that this discount increases consumption in the debtor country and therefore reduces the sustainable capital stock, k^*.

Solvency is given in Figure 6.2 on and below the $\underline{H}(k, k^*, \underline{r}^s) = 0$ function. Combinations of $k - k^*$ above the zero-profit function cannot be a steady state as banks cannot compensate losses from the international activities by profits from domestic activities. Above the zero-profit function the foreign capital stock, k^*, requires a loan size which is too high.

To determine the properties of the zero-profit function with respect to $H^5(k, k^*, r^s) = 0$ note that $H^5(k, k^*, r^s) = \underline{H}(k, k^*, \underline{r}^s)$ if $r^s = \underline{r}^s$.[11] For $k = k^1$ it follows from equation (6.13) $\underline{r}^s = \underline{r}^s(k^1)$. Therefore the $H^5(k, k^*, \underline{r}^s(k^1)) = 0$ function intersects the $\underline{H}(k, k^*, \underline{r}^s) = 0$ function at B. From (6.14) $\underline{r}^s(k^2) < \underline{r}^s(k^1)$. From Figure 6.2 the $H^5(k, k^*, \underline{r}^s(k^2)) = 0$ function therefore lies above the $H^5(k, k^*, \underline{r}^s(k^1)) = 0$ function and intersects the zero-profit function at C.

V. The Sovereignty Restriction Under Financial Intermediation

Before we can analyse steady states under financial intermediation it only remains to determine the implications of financial intermediation for the sovereignty restriction (3.11). From the market-clearing conditions (3.47) and (6.6) it follows that

$$\frac{b^*}{1+n} = \frac{\frac{\Omega}{1+n}\cdot w - k - \frac{1}{1+r}\cdot v^d}{\frac{r^s - n}{r - n}} \tag{6.18}$$

Substituting this and r^s from equation (6.5) into equation (5.6) yields

$$R(\cdot) = (r^s - n)\cdot \frac{\frac{\Omega}{1+n}\cdot w - k - \frac{1}{1+r}\cdot v^d}{\frac{r^s - n}{r - n}} - \delta \cdot f^*(k^*) = 0$$

from which upon collecting terms we immediately obtain equation (5.7). The sovereignty restriction, represented in $k - k^*$ space by the $R(\cdot) = 0$ function is therefore the same under both bond-financing and financial intermediation.

If the spread on intermediation, $r^s - r^d$, is zero it is obvious that the sovereignty restriction must be the same under both forms of financing. However, under involuntary lending $r^s < r^d$. The net transfer obligation, z, is therefore, *ceteris paribus*, smaller if $r^s < r^d$, allowing for additional leeway in sovereign debt relations. The sovereignty restriction therefore depends on r^s. Equation (5.7), however, is independent of r^s.

To understand this it must be borne in mind that the above analysis, *ceteris paribus*, is in need of a supplement in general equilibrium. A reduction in r^s below r^d reduces the value of banks. In the creditor economy less savings need to be absorbed in holding the real store of wealth. For a given savings and capital stock, k, credit supply and hence international debt outstanding is larger if $r^s < r^d$. Formally this follows from the optimal credit supply (6.18) which is larger the smaller r^s. Larger debt outstanding puts additional pressure on the sovereignty problem. This second general equilibrium effect of a change in r^s works against the direct effect, *ceteris paribus*. For the special functional forms we entertain, these effects exactly offset one another.

VI. Steady States in the Presence of a Threat of Economic Sanctions

Bringing together Figures 6.1, 6.2 and 5.2(a) it is easy to determine steady states under financial intermediation. Contrary to bond-financing there is

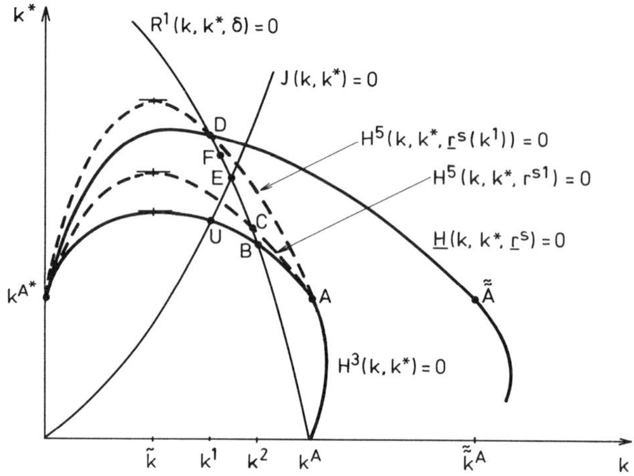

Figure 6.3 *Steady states under financial intermediation when a gunboat-technology exists.*

a multiplicity of bank-financing steady states associated with the degree of freedom of setting r^s in $[\underline{r}^s, r]$.[12] Figure 6.3 depicts constrained bank steady states under financial intermediation.

There is a continuum of sovereignty-constrained steady states in $[k^1, k^2]$ associated with points on the $R^1(k, k^*, \delta) = 0$ function between B and D. The steady state B is associated with a zero spread on financial intermediation, with $r^s = r(k^2)$. It is the constrained steady state under bond-financing depicted in Figure 5.3(b). This is the sole sovereignty-constrained bank-financing steady state with voluntary lending. All other bank steady states involve involuntary lending.

A continuous reduction of r^s below $r(k^2)$ shifts the $H^5(k, k^*, r^s) = 0$ function continuously upward. The constrained bank steady state therefore moves continuously upwards on $R^1(k, k^*, r^s) = 0$. For example, if $r^s = r^{s1} < r(k^2)$ then the bank steady state is at C. Steady states above B are associated with involuntary lending.[13]

Constrained bank steady states are bounded above by the zero-profit condition. For $r^s < \underline{r}^s(k^1)$ the $H^5(k, k^*, \delta) = 0$ function intersects the $R^1(k, k^*, \delta) = 0$ function above the zero-profit function $\underline{H}(k, k^*, \underline{r}^s) = 0$. As banks would then make losses, bank steady states are bounded to lie in the interval $[k^1, k^2]$.

Figure 6.3 depicts the case where the zero-profit function intersects the $R^1(k, k^*, \delta) = 0$ function to the left of $J(k, k^*) = 0$. This implies that steady states between E and D involve $r > r^*$. The real interest rates are reversed. Under financial intermediation this is possible because involuntary lending involves $r^s < r$. It is therefore possible to have

$r^d = r > r^* \geqslant \underline{r}^s(k^1)$. If $r^* < \underline{r}^s(k^1)$ then credit demand ends at F, say, before the zero-profit line is reached.

It is possible that the intersection of the $R^1(k, k^*, \delta) = 0$ function and the zero-profit function is to the right of $J(k, k^*) = 0$. In fact for δ small enough the $R^1(k, k^*, \delta) = 0$ function becomes so steep that this intersection lies to the right of $J(k, k^*) = 0$. In this case the lower bound on r^s is always given by $\underline{r}^s(k^1)$.

Let us compare the different bank-financing steady states with one another. The larger the opportunism of a bank is, that is the smaller r^s is, the smaller the capital stock in the creditor country, k, and the larger the capital stock in the debtor country, k^*. From (4.18) and (4.19), the domestic component of disposable income therefore diminishes in the creditor country, if opportunism becomes stronger. Contrary to the creditor country, the domestic component in the debtor country increases.

Nevertheless, it does not follow that the creditor country suffers welfare losses and the debtor country enjoys welfare gains from involuntary lending. This is due to the fact that the foreign component of disposable income, z, is larger the larger the spread $r - r^s$. To see this, note that a smaller r^s is associated with a smaller k, as $R^1(k, k^*, \delta) = 0$ is decreasing in k. From (5.10) it then follows that the net transfer from the debtor country is larger the larger the opportunism, that is the larger the spread $r - r^s$. Although opportunism is bad for banks in the sense that it depresses their value, it need not be bad for the creditor economy in the sense of necessarily diminishing welfare. Similarly, the debtor country need not necessarily gain in welfare terms from involuntary lending.

Economically, once again the explanation for the indeterminacy in the welfare effects of involuntary lending is to be found in the transmission of wealth effects in general equilibrium. Opportunism frees savings which are then used to expand the foreign component in the portfolios of households in the creditor country. Opportunism thus increases rather than decreases the claims against the debtor economy.

Figure 6.3 depicts sovereignty-constrained steady states under financial intermediation. Of course, under bank-financing a steady state could also be unconstrained. In Figure 6.3 if δ is large enough the $R^1(k, k^*, \delta) = 0$ function intersects the $H^3(k, k^*) = 0$ function to the left of U. In this case, as under bond-financing, the steady state is unconstrained and is characterized by U in Figure 6.3.

VII. Reputational Equilibria

If economic sanctions are impossible then $\delta = 0$ and $R^1(k, k^*, 0) = 0$ is a parallel to the k^*-axis through k^A. It follows therefore that the autarky

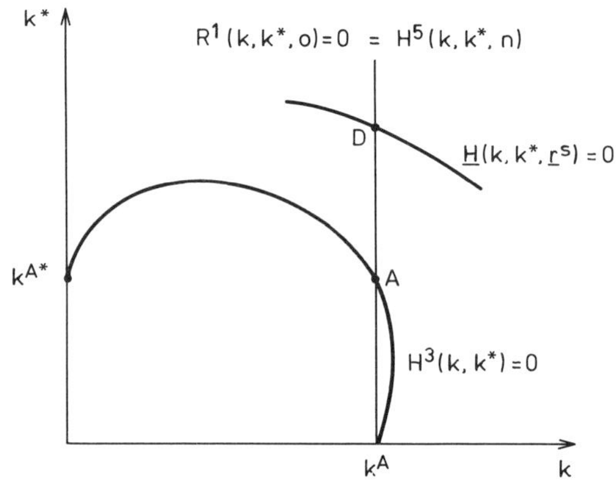

Figure 6.4 *Steady states under financial intermediation and a lack of gunboat-technologies.*

steady state A in Figure 6.4 is a constrained steady state under financial intermediation. However, contrary to bond-financing, this does not imply that reputational debt equilibria do not exist. In fact all points on $R^1(k, k^*, 0) = 0$ between A and D in Figure 6.4 are associated with a reputational equilibrium.

To see this note that for $\delta = 0$ and from equation (6.5) the sovereignty restriction (5.6) requires

$$r^s = n \tag{6.19}$$

From equation (3.45) it follows for $r^i = r$

$$\frac{-b}{1+n} = \frac{\Omega}{1+n} \cdot w - k - \frac{1}{1+r} \cdot v \tag{6.20}$$

From equations (3.14), (3.15) and (3.16) it follows for $r^s = n$

$$v = v^d - (1+r) \cdot \frac{-b}{1+n}$$

That is, for $r^s = n$ the discount on the value of a bank is equal to the deposit service obligation $(1+r) \cdot (-b)/(1+n)$. Substituting this for v in equation (6.20) we obtain

$$\frac{-b}{1+n} = \frac{\Omega}{1+n} \cdot w - k - \frac{1}{1+r} \cdot v^d + \frac{1}{1+r} \cdot (1+r) \cdot \frac{-b}{1+n}$$

Collecting terms, the loan size, $-b$, cancels out in this equation and we obtain

$$0 = \frac{\Omega}{1+n} \cdot w - k - \frac{1}{1+r} \cdot v^d \; \forall \; -b \tag{6.21}$$

From Figure 4.1(c) equation (6.21) therefore requires that $k = k^A$ for all loan sizes, $-b$. Hence it follows that the autarky steady-state capital stock in the creditor country, k^A, is consistent with any positive loan size, $-b$.

To establish that world credit markets clear for $-b > 0$ it is simply required that these loans are absorbed in the debtor country. In terms of Figure 4.1(a) this requires that $k^* > k^{A*}$. Furthermore k^* must be larger, the larger the loan size, $-b$. Points further to the north on $R^1(k, k^*, 0) = 0$ in Figure 6.4 are therefore associated with a larger debt outstanding.

The consistency of such reputational equilibria with the world capital market-clearing condition can be directly seen from equation (6.6). For $r^s \to n$ the denominator in the first term vanishes. World capital market clearing requires, therefore, that the numerator vanishes too. This in fact is what is required in equation (6.21). For $r^s = n$, $H^5(k, k^*, r^s) = 0$ is a vertical line through A.

We have established the existence of reputational equilibria under financial intermediation. All reputational equilibria require a situation as if the creditor country were actually in financial autarky. To understand what happens economically in the creditor country in a reputational equilibrium we next determine the economic value of debt relations to the creditor country.

VIII. The Economic Value of Debt Relations

In the debtor country the steady-state value of the debt relationship is simply given by the net inflow of resources, $-z$. In the creditor country, however, matters are more complicated because under financial intermediation the net inflow of resources depends on r^s which in turn determines the value of banks. Under bank-financing evaluating a debt relationship for the creditor country must involve an evaluation of all underlying portfolio transactions associated with a bank steady state.

To do this one has to bear in mind that this may require a distinction between the generations alive in any period. Let z^j be the value of a steady-state debt relationship to a young household in the creditor country. Then

$$z^j = -v^i + b + \theta \tag{6.22}$$

The first term on the RHS of equation (6.22) represents the 'gains' from the credit relationship due to the fact that households are able to purchase the banking system at a discount if $v^i < 0$. The remaining terms $b + \theta \leqslant 0$ represents 'costs' due to the requirement that savings are absorbed for maintaining the relationship by fresh loans and due to the smaller dividends banks pay if $\theta < 0$. Inserting in equation (6.22) the steady-state value for θ and v^i from equation (3.14) and (3.15) it follows upon collecting terms

$$z^j = b \cdot \frac{r^s - n}{r - n} \tag{6.23}$$

For a positive loan, that is if $b < 0$ the value to the young of the debt relationship is negative if $r^s > n$. It is equal to b if $r^s = r$, that is under bond-financing or voluntary bank lending.

The value to an old household, z^o, is given by

$$z^o = [(1 + r) \cdot -b + (1 + n) \cdot v^i] / (1 + n) \tag{6.24}$$

The value to the old is positively affected by the payments received from withdrawing bank deposits. It is negatively affected by the discount on the sale of banks they suffer if $v^i < 0$. Upon inserting steady-state values for equations (3.14) and (3.15) into (6.24) and collecting terms we obtain

$$z^o = \frac{1 + r}{1 + n} \cdot \frac{r^s - n}{r - n} \cdot -b \tag{6.25}$$

We can now determine the value of the debt relationship to the creditor country. If compensatory payments between generations are allowed this value is given by $z^j + z^o$. From equations (6.23) and (6.25) it follows that

$$z^j + z^o = (r^s - n) \cdot \frac{-b}{1 + n} \tag{6.26}$$

From the definition in (2.4), from the clearing condition $-b = b^*$ and from $r^i = r^s$ we obtain from (6.26)

$$z^j + z^o = z \tag{6.27}$$

That is, under compensatory payments between generations in the creditor country the value of the debt relationship is given by the net transfer the country receives in the steady state. We can now interpret the reputational equilibria in Figure 6.4.

From equations (6.23) and (6.25) $z^j = z^o = 0$ if $r^s = n$, which from (6.19) is required in a reputational equilibrium. If $r^s = n$, the capital markets in the creditor country price the banking system so that both young and old households are in the same situation as if banks did not engage in any international activity and as if individual portfolios did not contain any international component. It is straightforward that equilibrium in the creditor country then requires a capital stock, k, for which savings are entirely absorbed for domestic investment. If $k = k^A$ this is fulfilled.

For $r^s = n$, $z^j + z^o = z = 0$. There is no transfer of resources across countries. Reputational equilibria are roll-over steady states. With a permanent roll-over of old debt due the debtor country can sustain a capital stock which is larger than the autarky stock, k^{A*}. In the creditor country, on the other hand, a perpetual roll-over is valued by capital markets as if the debt relationship did not exist.

There is an interesting implication to this. Compared to autarky, a debt stalemate between banks and a debtor country involving involuntary lending and a perpetual roll-over of debt causes neither welfare gains nor welfare losses in the creditor country. Capital markets value such stalemates in such a way that economic policy intervention is not needed. Furthermore reputational equilibria Pareto-dominate the autarky steady state as $k^* > k^{A*}$. Involuntary lending therefore improves world welfare if economic sanctions are impossible.

IX. A Stylized 'History' of Bank Lending

The present model succinctly explains why an unprofitable debt relationship between foreign banks and debtor countries persists. The model does not, however, explain why banks ever got involved in such an engagement. As our formal analysis is exclusively restricted to steady states, we cannot answer this question formally. However, at this point we will briefly depart from the formal analysis and try to address this issue.

One answer to the question why banks engage in an activity which in the long run involves losses is that banks acted irrationally in entering the market for sovereign debt in the first place. Although we do not want to claim that irrationality has played no role in the structural change international debt has gone through upon the emergence of bank-financing after World War II, we try to entertain a different explanation.

Suppose a bank-financed reputational debt equilibrium is stable. Furthermore, suppose banks were rational before deciding to enter the market for sovereign debt. Then the 'history' of bank lending involves at least three phases. The properties of these phases can be determined by backward induction.

The final phase is the steady state. Suppose it involves involuntary lending. A rational bank, anticipating this, is prepared to enter the market only if, at an earlier stage, it can make profits. It is, however, understood that profits can only be made in a phase in which the sovereignty restriction (2.3) is binding. Otherwise a bank could enter the market in that phase, make profits, and leave the market again. From that period onwards in which the sovereignty restriction becomes binding, banks are caught in an idiosyncratic relationship and cannot leave the market unless they accept that old loans are lost. The first phase then is when debt still is so low that sovereignty is not a binding restriction. In the first phase of international bank lending, banks cannot make profits.

If the 'history' of bank-financed debt evolves in these three phases, it can be rational for banks to enter the market. Profits in the second phase must simply be high enough to compensate the losses expected in the final stage.

What perhaps is interesting is that the optimal intertemporal plan for a bank suffers from a problem of time-inconsistency. Although *ex ante* it is optimal to enter the market for international sovereign debt, *ex post* a bank regrets this decision. Yet the incentive to protect the value of old debt outstanding is strong enough to stay on.

X. Conclusions

Let us sum up:

(1) If lending is voluntary then the steady state under bank-financing is the same as the steady state under bond-financing.

(2) Bank steady states can involve involuntary lending in the sense that banks are willing to maintain a debt relationship under which they suffer losses from financial intermediation.

(3) Under involuntary lending the sustainable world capital stock is larger than under bond-financing. Involuntary lending steady states involve a smaller capital stock in the creditor country and a larger capital stock in the debtor country if economic sanctions are possible.

(4) Involuntary lending aggravates the incentive problem in that it increases the proportion of loans which is consumed rather than invested.

(5) Under bank-financing there exist reputational equilibria even in the presence of a real store of wealth. In all reputational equilibria capital markets value the debt relationship so that for the creditor economy there is no difference from the autarky steady state.

(6) Involuntary lending does not necessarily worsen welfare in the creditor country, nor need it improve welfare in the debtor country.

(7) If economic sanctions are impossible then involuntary lending steady states improve world welfare compared to financial autarky.

(8) If banking steady states are stable then an optimal intertemporal plan for a bank is time-inconsistent in that a bank which rationally decides to enter the market for international financial intermediation regrets this decision *ex post*.

CHAPTER 7

Aspects of Credit Supply

I. Introduction

In Chapter 5 and Chapter 6 we investigated beyond the credit markets into the general equilibrium implications of sovereign debt. In this and the following chapter we shall look into credit markets in some greater detail. To do this we restrict ourselves to a partial equilibrium analysis. In the next chapter the demand side to sovereign debt is analysed, whereas here we focus on the supply side to sovereign debt.

We shall introduce risk associated with debt repudiation and we will determine the equilibrium credit supply schedule a sovereign faces. We further investigate conditions under which a sovereign is effectively excluded from the loan market. Individual lenders can control the size of loans they make but not necessarily the total indebtedness of a sovereign. If the repudiation decision depends on total debt, then the ability or inability to control total debt must be of some importance for credit market equilibrium. We address this issue in this chapter. Finally we investigate the incentives of sovereigns to invest in the containment of sanctions pending and the adverse selection problem lenders may thereby have to face.

In this chapter we shall maintain Assumptions 2.2, 3.2, 4.2, and 5.1. Some other assumptions introduced so far will be replaced as we proceed.

II. Repudiation Risk and the Credit Supply Schedule

Under certainty rational lenders have an incentive to ration a sovereign so that repudiation never occurs. The interest rate a sovereign has to pay is therefore the risk-free rate. The sole implication of sovereignty for the supply schedule of loans a debtor faces is then a cut in the credit limit. In the general equilibrium model of Chapters 5 and 6 this loss of creditworthiness is in fact the underlying reason that a constrained steady state is achieved instead of the unconstrained steady state.

In reality a sovereign debt relationship faces a number of uncertainties. Lending can then face the problem that the state of nature on which the fate of a loan depends is realized only after a loan decision has been made.

Such risk could be associated with factors which are an argument in the gunboat-technology the sovereign faces. Uncertain levels of exports or of general economic activity fall under this category. Into a different class of risks fall uncertainties with respect to the punishment-technology itself. In some states of nature, unfavourable for lenders, sanctions may be impossible or a credit embargo infeasible. Still other sources of risk may be directly associated with credit contracts. Total debt outstanding may not be known when a new loan decision is made or the interest rate may depend on the state of nature.

What all these risks have in common is that repudiation can now actually take place in a credit equilibrium. Although for some moderate levels of lending repudiation may be avoided for all states of nature, credit markets in general do not impose such a tight credit limit. In this section we investigate the consequences of risk for the credit supply schedule a sovereign faces.[1] To that end we revoke Assumption 3.1 and make

Assumption 7.1: The gunboat-technology parameter δ is i.i.d. The density function is given by $g(\delta)$ with $0 \leqslant \underline{\delta} \leqslant \delta \leqslant \overline{\delta} \leqslant 1$. The state of the world is a function of δ only and is realized after a loan is made.

Hence we presume that the sole source of uncertainty stems from the technology which allows for economic sanctions. In analysing implications of risk we abstract therefore from reputational debt equilibria. Risk in economic activity and risk associated with stipulations of a contract may be common to both sovereign and non-sovereign debtors. Restricting risk to the punishment technology allows therefore to bring to the fore aspects of risk which are singular to the problem of sovereignty.

To simplify the analysis we make

Assumption 7.2: Lenders are risk-neutral.

Assumption 7.2 can be maintained if Assumption 3.3, under which decision-makers are averse to risk, is revoked in as far as lenders are concerned. Alternatively, we could maintain Assumption 3.3 also for lenders and presume that they hold loans in a perfectly diversified portfolio.

In this chapter we depart from the presumption in Assumption 2.1 that lenders take the market interest rate as exogeneously given and determine solely the loan's size in a debt contract. Instead we make

Assumption 7.3: Lenders can set the loan size and the interest rate which is constant for all states of nature in a loan contract, (b^*, r^{i*}), which they offer.

In this analysis, we do not distinguish between different forms of financing. From the analysis in Chapters 5 and 6 bank-financing and bond-financing differ only in the presence of involuntary lending. Abstracting from the form of financing we therefore investigate the voluntary supply schedule of sovereign debt.

Given the punishments underlying the sovereignty restriction (3.11), the condition for honouring a contract (b^*, r^{i*}) is

$$z(b^*, r^{i*}) \leqslant \delta \cdot f^*(k^*) \tag{7.1}$$

The contract (b^*, r^{i*}) determines the gross payment obligation of the debtor. If the debtor's access to future credit markets is exogenous to the individual lender, then (b^*, r^{i*}) also determines the borrower's net payment obligation z. Condition (7.1) therefore represents the sovereignty restriction as a function of the decision variables of the lenders (b^*, r^{i*}).

Let $\tilde{\delta}$ be the state of nature in which the borrower, whose sovereignty decision is described in condition (7.1), is indifferent between honouring and repudiating a contract (b^*, r^{i*}). $\tilde{\delta}$ then satisfies

$$z(b^*, r^{i*}) = \tilde{\delta} \cdot f^*(k^*). \tag{7.2}$$

The critical state of nature is therefore a function of variables specific to the debtor, k^*, and of the net payment obligation, z. For $\delta > \tilde{\delta}$ the sovereign honours the contract. For $\delta < \tilde{\delta}$ the contract (b^*, r^{i*}) is repudiated. Furthermore,

$$d\tilde{\delta}(z, k^*)/dz > 0 \tag{7.3}$$

Let Φ be the probability that a borrower whose repudiation decision is described by condition (7.1) honours a contract. Under Assumption 7.1, Φ is a function of z and k^* and is given by

$$\Phi(z, k^*) = \int_{\tilde{\delta}(\cdot)}^{\bar{\delta}} g(\delta)\, d\delta \tag{7.4}$$

where from (7.3)

$$\partial\Phi(z, k^*)/\partial z < 0 \tag{7.5}$$

The larger the net payment obligation associated with a debt contract the smaller is the probability that the contract is honoured.

Under risk-neutrality lenders maximize the expected yield of a contract they offer. Let r be the risk-free interest rate. Under perfect competition and risk-neutrality of lenders capital market equilibrium requires

$$\Phi(z, k^*) \cdot (1 + r^{i*}) = (1 + r) \tag{7.6}$$

The expected return on the risky loan to the sovereign must be equal to the risk-free rate. Under certainty rational lenders constrain the loan supply so as always to ensure that repudiation never occurs. The credit market equilibrium condition (7.6) does not require $\Phi(z, k^*) = 1$. Repudiation can therefore be an equilibrium phenomenon.

In the context of Chapter 6, $r^{i*} = r^s$ and $r = r^d$. The equilibrium condition (7.6) therefore requires $r^s > r^d$ if sovereign debt is risky.[2] Furthermore, it implies that the credit market equilibrium need not be a pure interest equilibrium as z is a function of the loan size, b^*. We can now determine the loan supply schedule a sovereign faces. It is depicted by the graph $S - S$ in Figure 7.1.

For $b^* = 0$, $z = 0$ and therefore $\tilde{\delta} = \underline{\delta}$, so that from Assumption 7.1 and equation (7.4) $\Phi(z, k^*) = 1$. From the credit market equilibrium condition (7.6) the sovereign then is charged the risk-free interest rate r. Figure 7.1 depicts the case where $\underline{\delta} > 0$ so that some lending $b^* \leqslant b^{*1}$,

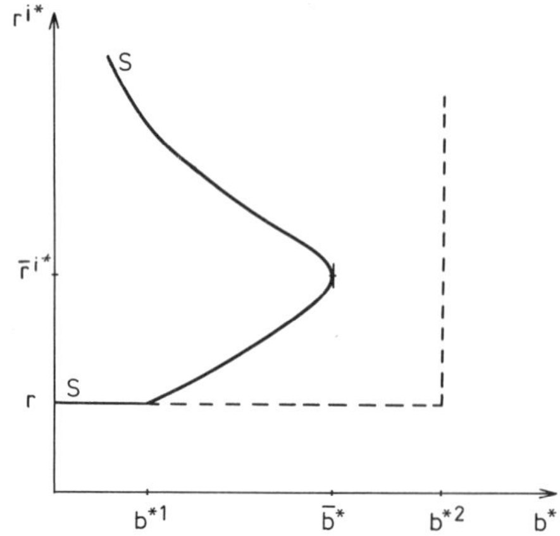

Figure 7.1 *The supply of sovereign debt.*

where

$$z(b^{*^1}, r) = \underline{\delta} \cdot f^*(k^*),$$

ensures repayment of principal and interest for all states of nature. From equation (7.6) $r^{i*} = r$ and the loan supply function is horizontal for $k^* < k^{*^1}$.

For $k > k^{*^1}$, $\Phi(z, k^*) < 1$ and therefore credit market equilibrium requires $r^{i*} > r$. Furthermore, a larger loan increases z and hence from the derivative (7.5) the probability of repayment declines. Capital market equilibrium therefore requires a higher interest rate. The loan supply schedule an individual sovereign faces is therefore increasing in b^* in an interval $[b^{*^1}, \bar{b}^*]$.

As b^* and r^{i*} are further increased, z increases so that an equilibrium contract $(\bar{b}^*, \bar{r}^{i*})$ exists for which $\tilde{\delta} = \bar{\delta}$. The contract $(\bar{b}^*, \bar{r}^{i*})$ is honoured with probability $\Phi(z, k^*) = g(\bar{\delta})$. Loans in excess of $\bar{b}^*$ will be repudiated with probability 1 unless $r^{i*} < \bar{r}^{i*}$. A competitive lender, however, will require $r^{i*} \geqslant \bar{r}^{i*}$. Hence $\bar{b}^*$ is the credit limit a sovereign faces. To maintain the repayment probability $\Phi(z, k^*) = g(\bar{\delta})$ interest rates in excess of $\bar{r}^{i*}$ must be associated with a loan size below $\bar{b}^*$. The higher r^{i*}, the smaller b^*. The loan supply schedule is therefore backward bending.

If capital markets are perfect, a debtor country can borrow at a constant rate up to the credit limit, b^{*^2}, which is determined by the borrower's solvency. We have established here that debtor sovereignty gives rise to a number of capital market imperfections. Besides a shortening of the credit line, a country faces an upward sloping supply schedule, which for high enough interest rates is backward bending. By offering higher interest rates a country cannot raise debt in excess of $\bar{b}^*$.

III. Income and Exclusion from Credit Markets

If debtor countries differ in some aspects which matter for the efficacy of economic sanctions, then these countries face different conditions on the supply side of international debt. For illustration, suppose that two countries I and II are identical except for the level of economic activity, indexed by k_{I}^* and k_{II}^*. International credit market equilibrium requires

$$\Phi(z_{\mathrm{I}}, k_{\mathrm{I}}^*) \cdot (1 + r_{\mathrm{I}}^{i*}) = \Phi(z_{\mathrm{II}}, k_{\mathrm{II}}^*) \cdot (1 + r_{\mathrm{II}}^{i*}) = 1 + r$$

Suppose $k_{\mathrm{I}}^* < k_{\mathrm{II}}^*$. From equation (7.2) and $f^{*\prime}(k^*) > 0$ it then follows that $\tilde{\delta}_{\mathrm{I}} > \tilde{\delta}_{\mathrm{II}}$. Given $z_{\mathrm{I}} = z_{\mathrm{II}}$, from equation (7.4) the repayment probability for country I is then lower than the repayment probability for country II. To establish credit market equilibrium country I must be charged a higher interest rate than country II for a given loan of size b^*. 'Poor' countries, therefore, face higher credit costs than 'rich' countries if the level of economic sanctions is an increasing function of the level of economic activity. More generally, allowing also for differences in the gunboat-technology, it follows that countries which face hard punishments have access to international loan markets on better terms.

It is possible that the poorest countries are completely excluded from international loan markets. For example, in the present model country I has no access to loan markets if

$$\lim_{z_I \to 0} \Phi(z_I, k_I^*) \cdot (1 + r_I^{i*}) < \Phi(z_{II}, k_{II}^*) \cdot (1 + r_{II}^{i*}) \ \forall r_I^{i*} < r_I^A$$

Economically, country I is so poor and hence repayment of debt is so unlikely that lenders require an interest rate in excess of the autarky rate, r_I^A even for the smallest loan. Again, a generalization of this conclusion for different punishment technologies is straightforward.

The supply schedule sovereigns face gives rise to a number of incentives which will be taken up in greater detail in Chapter 8. At this point, however, it already transpires that harsh economic sanctions need not necessarily be to the disadvantage of a debtor country. If repudiation occurs, costs are higher. However, this makes repayment more likely and allows the country to raise debt on better terms.

IV. Asymmetric Information, Credit Market Equilibrium and the Control of Total Indebtedness

In determining a credit equilibrium, markets draw on information about the characteristics of debtors. It cannot always be taken for granted that all relevant information is available to lenders. This is certainly not singular to sovereign debt. However, under debtor sovereignty in particular, information problems are likely to be present.

Although it might rightly be disputed that many parameters relevant to a country's lenders are harder to observe than those associated with non-sovereign debt, the problem is rather one of verification than a problem of observation. By definition, sovereigns cannot be contractually committed with respect to their behaviour. Debtors' discretion can therefore be responsible that the state of nature when the debt is due differs from the state when a particular loan was made.

An important point in case is total indebtedness. Collateral and seniority provisions, for example, effectively limit and make verifiable total indebtedness of a non-sovereign debtor. There exists symmetric infor-

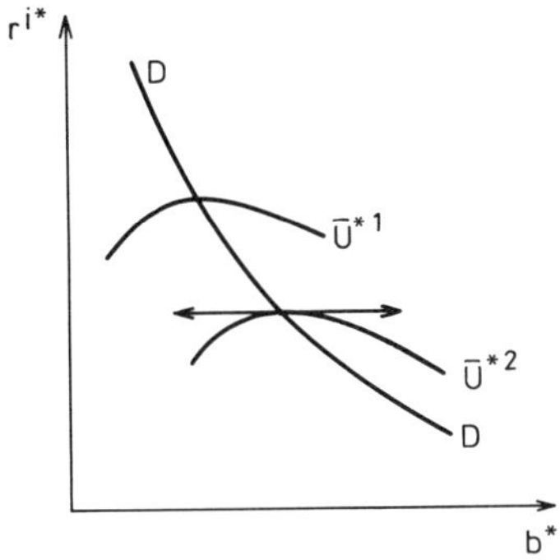

Figure 7.2 *The demand for loans.*

mation about total indebtedness between debtor and lenders. As collateral and seniority provisions are absent from sovereign debt relationships, lenders may find it impossible to verify total indebtedness at the date of repayment when making a loan. In this case there exists asymmetric information between lenders and a sovereign. In the remainder of this section we investigate the implications of symmetric and asymmetric information about the total indebtedness of a borrower.[3]

Suppose the debtor's demand schedule is given by the graph $D-D$ in Figure 7.2.[4] Indifference curves, $\bar{U}^*$, have the shape depicted. $\bar{U}^{*^1}$ represents a lower expected utility level than $\bar{U}^{*^2}$, as, *ceteris paribus*, a higher interest rate reduces expected utility of the debtor. Indifference curves attain a maximum on the demand schedule $D-D$. Furthermore, indifference curves are concave as a discrete movement away from $D-D$ in the direction of the arrows reduces the debtor's utility by definition of the demand schedule.

When analysing the case of symmetric information we can implicitly have recourse to Assumption 6.2. If individual loan contracts are strategically independent then total indebtedness accruing from all loans to a sovereign is irrelevant for an individual lender. All that matters is the size of the individual loan, which is known to the lender.

If asymmetric information about total indebtedness is to matter, individual loans cannot be strategically independent. When we determine the loan equilibrium under information asymmetries we therefore revoke Assumption 6.2 and make

Assumption 7.4: The decision to honour or violate an individual debt contract depends on the total indebtedness of a sovereign rather than on the size of the individual loan.

Under Assumption 7.4 the repayment probability and hence the interest rate to compensate for risk depends on total indebtedness. However, if individual lenders possess no information about total indebtedness then the equilibrium must be an interest rate equilibrium. In an interest rate equilibrium the market is cleared by the interest rate alone.

On the other hand, under symmetric information lenders can effectively control the total indebtedness of the sovereign and the equilibrium need not be an interest rate equilibrium. With these preliminaries in mind we can now determine the credit market equilibrium for an individual sovereign by bringing together in Figure 7.3 the graphs depicted in Figures 7.1 and 7.2.

Under asymmetric information lenders cannot control total indebtedness and the equilibrium must therefore lie on the demand schedule $D-D$, otherwise the interest rate alone could not clear the market. As at B the sovereign's utility is higher than at A, the credit market equilibrium under asymmetric information is at B in Figure 7.3. Total indebtedness is b^{*^3}.

Under symmetric information the sovereign can be rationed effectively by lenders and the equilibrium need not lie on the demand schedule. As the supply schedule depicts all contracts (b^*, r^{i*}) offered by lenders, the sovereign will pick the contract (b^{*^2}, r^{i*^2}) as it provides the highest utility level to the debtor. The credit market equilibrium under symmetric information is therefore at C in Figure 7.3.

Comparing the equilibria at B and C we note that C is on a higher utility indifference level than B. It therefore follows that sovereign debtors *ex ante* have an interest in providing the information that allows lenders to control total indebtedness.

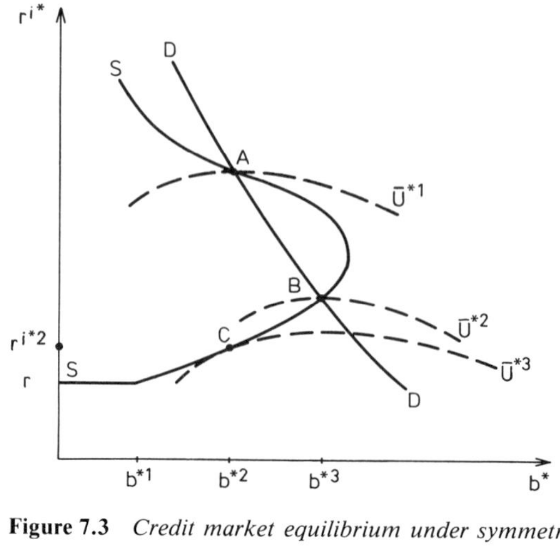

Figure 7.3 *Credit market equilibrium under symmetric and asymmetric information.*

The result obtained also suggests that credit rationing need not be to the disadvantage of borrowers. Economically, if sovereigns can be rationed, debt servicing obligations decrease. The associated increase in the probability of debt repayment is rewarded by credit markets, in that the sovereign is permitted to raise debt on more favourable terms. In the present model this utility-improving cost effect exceeds the negative size effect of credit rationing.

The model also sheds some light on the structural change international debt has undergone since the Second World War. If it is in the interest of debtor countries to raise debt under conditions of symmetric information then they will take their case to those lenders who are best able to monitor and control total indebtedness. The emergence of bank credit-financing and its preponderance over bond-financing after the war suggests therefore that banks are better able to monitor and control debtor countries than individual bondholders.[5,6]

V. Investment in the Containment of Economic Sanctions

If sovereign debtors preserve a degree of freedom in their decisions after a loan is made, rational lenders will take this into account when making a loan. In further understanding the role of repudiation risk for lenders we therefore have to investigate its implications for the rational behaviour of sovereigns.

Of particular interest in this respect is that the existence of repudiation risk implies that the costs from violating contracts have to be borne with positive probability. Sovereigns may therefore have an incentive to allocate resources for the containment of these costs. To close the argument, such containment of repudiation costs increases the risk associated with a particular loan. The loan supply critically depends therefore on an anticipation of such investment incentives.

In practice such containment activities could include the protection of assets abroad through repatriation or hiding them in numbered accounts or off-shore. On the macro level examples include import substitution oriented policies.

In the present model we will summarize such activities to insulate the debtor economy against the perils of sanctions by a variable, Ψ, under control of the sovereign. In particular we take it that

$$y^* = f^*(k^*, \Psi) \tag{7.7}$$

with $\partial f^*(k^*, \Psi)/\partial\Psi > 0$ and $\Psi \in [\underline{\Psi}, \bar{\Psi}]$.

The sovereignty restriction (7.1) now has to be replaced by

$$z(b^*, r^{i*}) \leqslant \delta \cdot f^*(k^*, \Psi) \tag{7.8}$$

and the critical state of the world, $\tilde{\delta}(z, k^*, \Psi)$, satisfies

$$z(b^*, r^{i*}) = \tilde{\delta} \cdot f^*(k^*, \Psi) \tag{7.9}$$

As $\partial f^* / \partial \Psi > 0$ it follows that

$$\partial \tilde{\delta}(z, k^*, \Psi)/\partial \Psi < 0 \tag{7.10}$$

and hence from equation (7.4)

$$\partial \Phi(z, k^*, \Psi)/\partial \Psi = -g(\tilde{\delta}) \cdot \partial \tilde{\delta}(\cdot)/\partial \Psi > 0 \tag{7.11}$$

Economically, Ψ may be interpreted as an efficiency parameter set by the debtor government after a loan is obtained. Given the investment decisions of the private sector, k^*, the debtor government can reduce the costs of economic sanctions by setting $\Psi < \bar{\Psi}$.

$\Psi = \bar{\Psi}$ may be interpreted as the efficient project or technology choice. An inefficient project or technology choice, that is $\Psi < \bar{\Psi}$, has two effects. First, as $\partial f^*(k^*, \Psi)/\partial \Psi > 0$ domestic output is reduced. This represents the opportunity costs of the containment of economic sanctions. Second, lower sanctions raise the critical state of the world, $\tilde{\delta}$, and hence the probability that sanctions have to be incurred.

To determine the optimal project choice, Ψ, we take it that the debtor government is risk-neutral. Under risk-neutrality the decision problem is given by

$$\min_{\Psi} \; [f^*(k^*, \bar{\Psi}) - f^*(k^*, \Psi)] + \Phi(z, k^*, \Psi) \cdot z(b^*, r^{i*})$$
$$+ \int_{\underline{\delta}}^{\tilde{\delta}(\cdot)} g(\delta) \cdot \delta \cdot f^*(k^*, \Psi) \cdot d\delta \qquad \text{s.t. } \bar{\Psi} - \Psi \geqslant 0. \tag{7.12}$$

The country minimizes the sum of the costs from the efficiency loss (the term in square brackets), the expected repayment obligation (the second term), and the expected costs from economic sanctions (the integral term).

Taking the derivative with respect to Ψ and using equations (7.9) and (7.11) we obtain as the condition for the optimal efficiency level

$$\Gamma(z, k^*, \Psi) \equiv -\partial f^*(k^*, \Psi)/\partial \Psi + \int_{\underline{\delta}}^{\tilde{\delta}(\cdot)} g(\delta) \cdot \delta \cdot \partial f^*(k^*, \Psi)/\partial \Psi \cdot d\delta \leqslant 0 \tag{7.13}$$

where $\Gamma(z, k^*, \Psi) \leqslant 0$ and $\bar{\Psi} - \Psi \geqslant 0$ hold with complementary slackness.

The first term on the LHS of inequality (7.13) is the marginal efficiency gain from an increase in Ψ. The second term on the LHS is the associated marginal increase in expected costs from economic sanctions. If for all $\Psi \in [\underline{\Psi}, \bar{\Psi}]$ the efficiency gain exceeds the marginal expected increase in the costs from punishment then it is optimal for the country to choose the efficient project $\Psi = \bar{\Psi}$. If condition (7.13) holds with equality for $\Psi < \bar{\Psi}$ then it is optimal to choose an inefficient project.

If economic sanctions are independent of Ψ then the second term on the LHS is zero. As $\partial f^*(k^*, \Psi)/\partial\Psi > 0$, it then follows from (7.13) that it is always optimal to choose efficient projects or technologies.

The second-order optimality condition requires

$$\partial\Gamma(z, k^*, \Psi)/\partial\Psi > 0 \tag{7.14}$$

In the remainder of this section we investigate the properties of an interior optimum. In an interior optimum

$$\Gamma(z, k^*, \Psi) = 0 \tag{7.15}$$

Of particular interest for lenders is the sensitivity of the optimal investment in the containment of economic sanctions with respect to the debt contract offered by them. What matters to debtors is the net repayment, z, associated with a contract (b^*, r^{i*}). From the optimality condition (7.15) we obtain for the optimal reaction

$$\frac{d\Psi}{dz}\Big|_{\Gamma(\cdot)=0} = -\frac{\partial\Gamma(z, k^*, \Psi)/\partial z}{\partial\Gamma(z, k^*, \Psi)/\partial\Psi} \tag{7.16}$$

From the definition of $\Gamma(z, k^*, \Psi)$ in (7.13),

$$\partial\Gamma(z, k^*, \Psi)/\partial z = g(\tilde{\delta}) \cdot \delta \cdot \partial f^*(k^*, \Psi)/\partial\Psi \cdot \partial\tilde{\delta}(z, k^*, \Psi)/\partial z > 0 \tag{7.17}$$

As $\partial f^*(k^*, \Psi)/\partial\Psi > 0$, and from the derivative (7.3), it follows that $\partial\Gamma(z, k^*, \Psi)/\partial z > 0$. This and the second-order optimality condition (7.14) imply that the optimal reaction in equation (7.16) is given by

$$\partial\Psi/\partial z\,|_{\Gamma(\cdot)=0} < 0 \tag{7.18}$$

This creates an adverse selection problem for lenders.[7] By offering a loan contract with a higher repayment obligation, z, lenders create an incentive for the debtor country to choose projects or technologies of lower quality. As a consequence output declines and hence also the costs from economic sanctions. Besides directly increasing the probability of repudiation, there is an indirect effect due to adverse selection working in the same direction. In the remainder of this chapter we investigate the consequences of adverse selection for the loan supply.

VI. Adverse Selection and Credit Supply

Under risk-neutrality and voluntary lending, creditors maximize the expected return from a loan. Taking future access of the sovereign to the loan markets as given, the expected return is maximal if the expected net payment obligation is maximized. The lenders' optimization problem is given by

$$\max_{z} \ \Phi(z, k^*, \Psi) \cdot z \tag{7.19}$$

subject to $\Gamma(z, k^*, \Psi) \leqslant 0$, where $\Gamma(\cdot)$ is defined in (7.13). Taking the derivative with respect to z from the Lagrangian associated with the optimization problem (7.19) we obtain

$$\Phi(z, k^*, \Psi) + z \cdot \partial\Phi(z, k^*, \Psi)/\partial z + \xi \cdot \partial\Gamma(z, k^*, \Psi)/\partial z = 0 \tag{7.20}$$

Furthermore, from the complementary slackness conditions

$$\xi \cdot \Gamma(z, k^*, \Psi) = 0 \tag{7.21}$$

The first two terms on the LHS in the first-order optimality condition (7.20) represent the direct effect on the expected return from a marginal increase in z. The third term on the LHS results from the potential adverse selection problem. ξ is the Lagrangian multiplier associated with problem (7.19).

Let $\tilde{z}$ be the optimal repayment obligation if the adverse selection problem is absent. $\tilde{z}$ is the solution to

$$\Phi(z, k^*, \Psi) + z \cdot \partial\Phi(z, k^*, \Psi)/\partial z = 0 \tag{7.22}$$

If $\Gamma(z, k^*, \Psi) < 0$, then from the optimality condition (7.21), $\xi = 0$. Hence $z = \tilde{z}$ is the optimal repayment obligation. Economically, if $\Gamma(z, k^*, \Psi) < 0$, then the debtor country chooses efficient projects, $\bar{\Psi}$, even for a marginally higher repayment obligation. On the margin, lenders do not face an adverse selection problem and therefore set $z = \tilde{z}$.

Adverse selection is pending if $\xi \neq 0$. From the optimality condition (7.21) $\Gamma(z, k^*, \Psi) = 0$, that means, the constraint in the optimization problem (7.19) is binding. From the debtor's optimal reaction (7.18) and from (7.11), the contribution of adverse selection to the achievable maximal expected return on a loan is negative. Therefore $\xi < 0$ if adverse selection is a binding constraint. As from equation (7.17) $\partial\Gamma(z, k^*, \Psi)/\partial z > 0$ it follows that the third term in the optimality condition (7.20) is negative if $\xi < 0$. Hence in an optimum, constrained by adverse selection,

$$\Phi(z, k^*, \Psi) + z \cdot \partial\Phi(z, k^*, \Psi)/\partial z > 0$$

That is, the increase in expected return due to a marginal increase in the repayment obligation is larger than the expected decrease in the expected return from an associated increase in the probability of repudiation. In the absence of adverse selection the expected return would therefore increase by a further increase in z. We can hence conclude that the optimal repayment obligation under adverse selection is smaller than if adverse selection were absent from sovereign debt. In Figure 7.1, adverse selection, therefore, shifts the loan supply schedule downwards.

There are a number of implications that follow from the analysis. First, the expected return on lending is smaller under adverse selection. This follows because the equilibrium repayment obligation is smaller and because projects are inefficient. Lenders have thus an incentive to neutralize adverse selection.

A simple method to neutralize adverse selection is to let the debtor country suffer from lump-sum sanctions. In our model if sanctions are independent of $f^*(k^*, \Psi)$, then the debtor country will choose efficient projects and technologies. The problem with this approach is that it is not an easy task to manipulate the gunboat-technology. There may exist some lump-sum components to economic sanctions. However, most components seem to be endogenous to variables which are under at least partial control of debtor countries. Creditor countries could also try to credibly forsake endogenous sanctions. However, if sovereignty is a binding constraint in international debt, overall there are not enough of them. This in mind, adverse selection may prove the smaller problem.

An alternative approach to tackle the adverse selection problem from scratch would be to constrain lending so as to ensure that contracts are honoured with certainty. In this case the country never has to bear the costs of repudiation, hence investment in the containment of these costs cannot be in its interest. However, the optimality condition (7.20) suggests that this approach is in general not in the interest of lenders.

VII. Conclusions

To sum up:

(1) If risk associated with the repudiation decision exists, then debtor sovereignty gives rise to a number of capital market imperfections. Besides a reduction in creditworthiness a sovereign then faces an upward sloping supply function of loans. If sanctions positively depend on economic activity, 'rich' countries can raise debt at lower costs than 'poor' countries and the 'poorest' countries are altogether excluded from international loans.

(2) If lenders can control total indebtedness of borrowers then the credit market equilibrium can involve effective credit rationing. Credit rationing, however, need not be to the disadvantage of debtors compared to the equilibrium when total indebtedness cannot be controlled so that credit markets are cleared by the interest rate alone.

(3) Under risk of repudiation debtors have an incentive to invest in the containment of economic sanctions. This can result in the selection of inefficient projects and technologies. Furthermore, it creates an adverse selection problem lenders have to face.

(4) Under adverse selection credit market equilibrium involves a lower repayment obligation for debtors compared to the case when adverse selection is absent.

(5) With adverse selection pending there is an advantage to lump-sum sanctions over sanctions depending on variables under the control of the debtor country.

CHAPTER **8**

Aspects of Credit Demand

I. Introduction

In this chapter we investigate credit demand in more depth. One central aspect will be the role of repudiation risk in determining the demand for international loans. Presumably, repudiation risk gives an incentive to raise more debt, as it does not necessarily have to be repaid. However, from the analysis in Chapter 7, this is at the cost of a larger risk premium on the interest rate, creating an incentive to restrain borrowing. The role of risk for the level of loan demand is therefore *a priori* indeterminate. The issue increases in complexity if we differentiate between the purposes of borrowing. As the costs of borrowing do not necessarily have to be borne, borrowing both for consumption and for investment ought to increase. The impact of repudiation risk on the intertemporal consumption profile is, therefore, undetermined at first glance. Hence, it is worthwhile to tackle these issues formally.

One must expect that the impact of repudiation risk on credit demand critically depends on who raises debt and who has to suffer from economic sanctions. If potential costs from repudiation do not have to be borne exclusively by those who issue debt then the debtor country suffers from an externality which can distort credit demand. We therefore investigate this and other externalities specific to sovereign debt.

If borrowers face a binding credit constraint they may have an incentive to invest in furthering their creditworthiness. Given an institutional environment under which debtor countries can make a binding investment commitment, this incentive may increase investment. We shall analyse the implications of commitment possibilities for credit markets, but also for the general equilibrium in the world economy. Under risk of repudiation, once again, we expect the effect of investment into creditworthiness to be ambiguous as a debtor now faces the possibility that additional costs of repudiation associated with an investment in creditworthiness may actually have to be incurred. We shall tackle all these problems in the context of a variant of our model to be specified in Section II.

II. Household Optimization Under Commitment and Risk

We shall maintain Assumptions 2.2, 5.1, 7.2, 7.3, and 7.4 throughout this chapter. When we allow for risk we take it that Assumption 7.1 holds. Again, the gunboat-technology parameter δ is the sole source of risk. To constrain the complexity of the analysis in this chapter, and because we already have investigated the problem of adverse selection, we take it that the debtor country always chooses efficient projects and technologies, that is we set $\Psi \equiv \bar{\Psi}$. To allow for investment into creditworthiness we revoke Assumption 3.2 and make instead

Assumption 8.1: Decision-makers in the borrowing country can commit themselves to an investment plan.

Under Assumption 8.1 borrowers can raise debt subject to a precommitted investment plan. Under Assumption 5.1 investment in the domestic capital stock, k^*, raises a country's creditworthiness both in terms of the maximally sustainable debt, $\bar{b}^*$, and in terms of the probability of repayment, $\Phi(z, k^*)$. From the credit market equilibrium condition (7.6) the latter implies that the interest rate on sovereign debt, r^{i*}, is lower if precommitted investment is higher. We can therefore set

$$r_1^{i*} = r_1^{i*}(b^*, k_1^*) \tag{8.1}$$

with $\partial r_1^{i*}/\partial k_1^* < 0$.

In this section we set out the model so that it also allows for an analysis of externalities associated with sovereign debt. It is therefore necessary to specifically define who in the debtor country gains the benefits and who incurs the various costs associated with international debt.

In conformity with Assumption 5.1 we take it that the government is in charge of the repudiation decision. However, demand for debt is exerted by the private sector which therefore fully enjoys the direct benefit from raising debt. In principle, the government could socialize the costs of servicing debt. We shall, however, abstract from this and presume, following the tradition of non-sovereign private debt, that a household which has raised debt is fully in charge of the associated interest and repayment costs if the home government decides against repudiation. To allow for the possibility of externalities associated with the sovereignty decision, we leave it open, however, who has to bear the costs of repudiation.

For the two-period-lived debtor households of the overlapping generations model, old-age consumption is therefore a function of the repudiation decision of the home government. Under certainty and rational behaviour of lenders, repudiation actually never occurs and repudiation externalities cannot be present. However, under risk of repudiation, old-age consumption in the debtor country is risky and repudiation externalities can be present. We allow for this by letting

$$c^{o*} = \begin{cases} \tilde{c}^{o*} = (1+n)\cdot(1+r_1^*)\cdot k_1^* - [1+r_1^{i*}(b^*, k_1^*)]\cdot b^* & \text{otherwise} \\ \tilde{\tilde{c}}^{o*} & \text{in case of repudiation} \end{cases} \tag{8.2}$$

For the case when repudiation does not occur, old-age consumption, $\tilde{c}^{o*}$, is derived from the lower equation in (3.23), allowing for commitment as represented by equation (8.1). Old-age consumption under repudiation, $\tilde{\tilde{c}}^{o*}$, will be further specified when we investigate the repudiation externally.

The optimization problem of a household in the debtor country is now given by

$$\begin{aligned} \max_{k^*, b^*} \; & EU^*(c^{j*}, c^{o*}) \\ = & \int_{\tilde{\delta}(\cdot)}^{\bar{\delta}} g(\delta)\cdot U^*\{w^* + b^* - (1+n)\cdot k_1^*, \\ & (1+n)\cdot(1+r_1^*)\cdot k_1^* - [1+r^{i*}(b^*, k_1^*)]\cdot b^*\}\, d\delta \\ & + \int_{\underline{\delta}}^{\tilde{\delta}(\cdot)} g(\delta)\cdot U^*[w^* + b^* - (1+n)\cdot k_1^*, \tilde{\tilde{c}}^{o*}]\, d\delta \\ \text{s.t.} \quad & (1+n)\cdot b_1^* + \bar{\delta}\cdot f^*(k_1^*)\cdot(1+n) - [1+r^{i*}(b^*, k_1^*)]\cdot b^* \geqslant 0 \end{aligned} \tag{8.3}$$

From the repayment probability (7.4) the first integral term on the RHS of the decision problem (8.3) is the expected household utility under debt repayment. The second integral term is the expected household utility under debt repudiation. The optimization problem takes account of the two possible effects of investment commitment. The interest effect is represented by the endogenous interest rate $r^{i*}(b^*, k_1^*)$. The impact of commitment on the maximally available loan size, $\bar{b}^*$, is represented by the constraint in the optimization problem. This constraint is the risk version of the sovereignty constraint (2.3) taking account of the fact that the best state of nature for lenders available is given by $\delta = \bar{\delta}$.

Let ξ be the shadow price of the constraint in the optimization problem (8.3). Necessarily

$$\xi \geqslant 0 \tag{8.4}$$

as a larger credit limit $\bar{b}^*$ cannot decrease the utility maximum of a debtor household.

Let $U^*_{\tilde{c}^{j*}}$ and $U^*_{\tilde{\tilde{c}}^{j*}}$ be the marginal utility of youth consumption if debt is honoured, respectively repudiated. The first order optimality condition of problem (8.3) with respect to credit demand, b^*, is given by

$$\begin{aligned}
&\int_{\tilde{\delta}(\cdot)}^{\bar{\delta}} g(\delta)\cdot\{U^*_{\tilde{c}^{j*}} - U^*_{\tilde{c}^{o*}}\cdot[1 + r_1^{i*}(b^*, k_1^*) + b^*\cdot\partial r_1^{i*}/\partial b^*]\}\,d\delta \\
&\quad - g[\tilde{\delta}(b^*, k_1^*)]\cdot U^*(c^{j*}, \tilde{c}^{o*}, \tilde{\delta}(b^*, k_1^*))\cdot\partial\tilde{\delta}(b^*, k_1^*)/\partial b^* \\
&\quad + g[\tilde{\delta}(b^*, k_1^*)]\cdot U^*(c^{j*}, \tilde{c}^{o*}, \tilde{\delta}(b^*, k_1^*))\cdot\partial\tilde{\delta}(b^*, k_1^*)/\partial b^* \\
&\quad + \int_{\underline{\delta}}^{\tilde{\delta}(\cdot)} g(\delta)\cdot\{U^*_{\tilde{\tilde{c}}^{j*}} + U_{\tilde{\tilde{c}}^{o*}}\cdot\partial\tilde{\tilde{c}}^{o*}/\partial b^*\}\,d\delta \\
&\quad - \xi\cdot[1 + r_1^{i*}(b^*, k_1^*) + b^*\cdot\partial r_1^{i*}/\partial b^*] = 0
\end{aligned} \tag{8.5}$$

The first-order optimality condition of problem (8.3) with respect to investment, k_1^*, is given by

$$\begin{aligned}
&\int_{\tilde{\delta}\beta(\cdot)}^{\bar{\delta}} g(\delta)\cdot\{-(1+n)\cdot U^*_{\tilde{c}^{j*}} + U^*_{\tilde{c}^{o*}}\cdot[(1+n)\cdot(1 + r_1^*) - b^*\cdot\partial r_1^{i*}/\partial k_1^*]\}\,d\delta \\
&\quad - g[\tilde{\delta}(b^*, k_1^*)]\cdot U^*(c^{j*}, \tilde{c}^{o*}, \tilde{\delta}(b^*, k_1^*))\cdot\partial\tilde{\delta}(b^*, k_1^*)/\partial k_1^* \\
&\quad + g[\tilde{\delta}(b^*, k_1^*)]\cdot U^*(c^{j*}, \tilde{\tilde{c}}^{o*}, \tilde{\delta}(b^*, k_1^*))\cdot\partial\tilde{\delta}(b^*, k_1^*)/\partial k_1^* \\
&\quad + \int_{\underline{\delta}}^{\tilde{\delta}(\cdot)} g(\delta)\cdot\{-(1+n)\cdot U^*_{\tilde{\tilde{c}}^{j*}} + U^*_{\tilde{\tilde{c}}^{o*}}\cdot\partial\tilde{\tilde{c}}^{o*}/\partial k_1^*\}\,d\delta \\
&\quad - \xi\cdot[(1+n)\cdot\bar{\delta}\cdot f^*(k_1^*) - b^*\cdot\partial r^{i*}/\partial k_1^*] = 0
\end{aligned} \tag{8.6}$$

Furthermore, from the complementary slackness conditions

$$\xi \cdot \{(1+n) \cdot b_1^* + \bar{\delta} \cdot f^*(k_1^*) \cdot (1+n) - [1 + r^{i*}(b^*, k_1^*)] \cdot b^*\} = 0 \qquad (8.7)$$

Rather than analysing the system of optimality conditions (8.4)–(8.7) in this general form, we shall first simplify this system to analyse commitment under conditions of certainty. We then allow for risk in a second step. However, we take it that repudiation costs are fully internalized. In a last step we then can tackle the problem of repudiation externalities.

III. Commitment Under Conditions of Certainty

Commitment is a problem which is not unique to sovereign debt markets. It can arise whenever borrowers face a binding credit constraint. There is, however, one issue related to commitment which attains special importance in the case of sovereign debt.[1]

A precondition for commitment is the existence of an institutional environment in which promises to pursue certain plans can be made credible. Within the reach of domestic law contracts are an instrument which enable commitment. Almost by definition, such instruments are unavailable in the realm of sovereign debt. There are, however, a number of factors which facilitate commitment even in an international environment.

If investment is of the 'point-of-no-return' type, a project has to be completed once it has attained a critical stage. Once this stage is reached creditors can lend on the basis of the remaining investment programme. Projects with a large initial 'cash-sink-hole' can have such a 'point-of-no-return' property. Large-scale projects are a case in point.[2] International institutions also play some role in the provision of commitment services.[3]

Under certainty lenders ensure that debt is always honoured. The interest rate is equal to the risk-free rate. In particular $\partial r^{i*}/\partial k_1^* = \partial r^{i*}/\partial b^* = 0$. Furthermore, $\partial\tilde{\delta}/\partial k_1^* \equiv \partial\tilde{\delta}/\partial b^* \equiv 0$. Taking this into account the optimality conditions (8.5)–(8.7) simplify to

$$\frac{U^*_{c^{j*}}}{U^*_{c^{o*}} + \xi} = 1 + r_1^{i*} \qquad (8.8)$$

$$\frac{U^*_{c^{j*}}}{U^*_{c^{o*}}} = (1 + r_1^*) + \frac{\xi}{U^*_{c^{o*}}} \cdot \delta \cdot f^{*\prime}(k_1^*) \qquad (8.9)$$

and

$$\xi \cdot [b_1^* \cdot (1+n) + \delta \cdot f^*(k_1^*) \cdot (1+n) - b^* \cdot (1 + r_1^{i*})] = 0 \qquad (8.10)$$

Solving the first-order optimality conditions (8.8) and (8.9) for ξ, we obtain

$$\xi = \frac{U^*_{c^{o*}} \cdot (r_1^* - r_1^{i*})}{(1 + r_1^{i*}) - \delta \cdot f^{*\prime}(k_1^*)} \geqslant 0 \qquad (8.11)$$

In an unconstrained optimum $\xi = 0$. From the optimality conditions (8.8) and (8.9) we obtain $r_1^* = r_1^{i*}$. This is in fact the optimality condition we obtained in Chapter 4 in a non-sovereign debt steady state (compare equation (4.4)). The ability to commit therefore is irrelevant.

The intuition behind this is that when the sovereignty constraint is not binding, the available loan, $\bar{b}^*$, is larger than the desired loan. Investment in creditworthiness then cannot be optimal. An implication of this is that commitment facilities are economically valuable only if sovereignty is a binding constraint.

In a sovereignty-constrained equilibrium the term in square brackets in the complementary slackness condition (8.10) is equal to zero. Therefore, in a constrained equilibrium $\xi \geqslant 0$. From condition (8.11), if $r_1^* < r_1^{i*}$ then

$$(1 + r_1^{i*}) - \delta \cdot f^{*\prime}(k_1^*) < 0$$

in order to sustain $\xi \geqslant 0$. However, $f^{*\prime}(k_1^*) = r_1^*$ and as $\delta < 1$ to have a constrained equilibrium, this inequality is violated if $r_1^* < r_1^{i*}$. Therefore, for $\xi \geqslant 0$

$$r_1^* \geqslant r_1^{i*} \qquad (8.12)$$

For $r_1^* > r_1^{i*}$ the equilibrium is constrained by the credit limit $\bar{b}^*$. In this case $\xi > 0$ which, from equation (8.11), requires

$$(1 + r^{i*}) - \delta \cdot f^{*\prime}(k_1^*) > 0 \qquad (8.13)$$

Condition (8.13) provides a valuable insight into investment commitment. It requires that a marginal investment, fully financed by borrowing, increases the incentive to repudiate debt by more than the incentive to repay. As in a constrained equilibrium, the sovereign is indifferent between honouring and repudiating debt, condition (8.13) implies that debtors cannot fully finance investment by raising debt. That is, in an equilibrium an investment in raising creditworthiness must be financed in part by forgoing consumption. Economically, the reason for this is that when $r_1^* > r_1^{i*}$, fully debt-financed investment would increase old-age consumption. It would therefore be suboptimal not to invest further in creditworthiness.

To determine the investment incentive under commitment, insert ξ from equation (8.11) and $f^{*\prime}(k_1^*) = r_1^*$ into the condition for optimal investment (8.9). This entails

$$\frac{U^*_{c^{y*}}}{U^*_{c^{o*}}} = (1 + r_1^*) + \frac{(r_1^* - r_1^{i*}) \cdot \delta \cdot r_1^*}{(1 + r_1^{i*}) - \delta \cdot r_1^*} \equiv 1/\varsigma^1(k_1^*, r_1^{i*}) \qquad (8.14)$$

Without commitment, optimal investment is given by the lower equation in (3.27). From conditions (8.12) and (8.13), in a constrained equilibrium the second term on the RHS of equation (8.14) is positive. The consumption profile is therefore biased towards old-age consumption. Investment is larger compared to the case without commitment possibilities. As investment cannot be fully debt-financed in a constrained equilibrium, youth consumption must decline.

In an equilibrium, constrained by debtor sovereignty, savings, investment and output in the debtor country increase if the country is given the opportunity to commit herself to investment projects.[4] As investment is larger under commitment, the credit limit, $\bar{b}^*$, is extended. Commitment helps therefore mitigate the costs arising from debtor sovereignty.

IV. Commitment in General Equilibrium

We analyse in this section the consequences of commitment possibilities for general equilibrium. To do that we must again presume that utility functions are given by equations (3.2). Furthermore, we continue to presume that risk is absent.

Following the procedure pursued in Section V of Chapter 3, taking account of the optimality condition (8.14), instead of the lower equation in (3.27), we obtain

$$c^{j*} = \varsigma^2(k_1^*, r_1^{i*}) \cdot \left[(1-\Omega^*)\cdot w^* + \frac{1-\Omega^*}{1+r_1^*}\cdot b^* \cdot (r_1^* - r_1^{i*})\right] \tag{8.15}$$

where

$$\varsigma^2(k_1^*, r_1^{i*}) \equiv \frac{(1+r_1^*)\cdot \varsigma^1(k_1^*, r_1^{i*})}{\Omega^* + (1-\Omega^*)\cdot \varsigma^1(k_1^*, r_1^{i*})\cdot (1+r_1^*)} \tag{8.16}$$

It is easily verified that $\varsigma^2(k_1^*, r_1^{i*}) \leqslant 1$ for $r_1^* \geqslant r_1^{i*}$ with complementary slackness. From a comparison with the lower equation in (3.39) we can therefore verify for the special utility functions (3.2) what we obtained for general utility functions in Section III. If the debtor country can commit herself to an investment plan, then consumption when young is smaller in a constrained equilibrium than without commitment possibilities.

For youth consumption given by equation (8.15) continuing with the procedure pursued in Section V of Chapter 3 we obtain

$$s^* = [1-(1-\Omega^*)\cdot \varsigma^2(k_1^*, r_1^{i*})]\cdot w^* + (1-\Omega^*)\cdot \varsigma^2(k_1^*, r_1^{i*})\cdot b^* \cdot \left[\frac{1+r_1^{i*}}{1+r_1^*} - 1\right] \tag{8.17}$$

and

$$\frac{-b^*}{1+n}=\frac{\dfrac{1}{\Omega^*+(1-\Omega^*)\cdot\zeta^1(k_1^*,r_1^{i*})\cdot(1+r_1^*)}\cdot\dfrac{\Omega^*}{1+n}\cdot w^*-k_1^*}{1+\zeta^2(k_1^*,r_1^{i*})\cdot(1-\Omega^*)\cdot\left[\dfrac{1+r_1^{i*}}{1+r_1^*}-1\right]} \tag{8.18}$$

The corresponding equation for the case of non-commitment is the lower equation in (3.45). After some simple, but onerous calculations it is seen that, *ceteris paribus*, debt issued in the debtor country is smaller if commitment is available compared to the case when it is not. Rather than going through these calculations we shall outline the economic reason behind this seemingly paradoxical result.

We know from condition (8.13) that the marginal investment cannot be fully debt-financed in a constrained equilibrium. Instead, marginal investment must be partially financed by additional savings. These additional savings cause, *ceteris paribus*, a reduction in debt raised. That, *ceteris paribus*, savings are larger in a constrained equilibrium when commitment is feasible, can be seen from the lower equation in (3.41) and from equation (8.17) upon noting that $\zeta^2(k_1^*, r_1^{i*}) < 1$ in a constrained equilibrium, where $r_1^{i*} < r_1^*$.

Replacing $-b/(1+n)$ and $b^*/(1+n)$ in the world credit market clearing condition (3.47) by the steady-state values of conditions (3.46) and (8.18) and noting that under debt-financing $r^i = r$ entails

$$H^6(\cdot)\equiv\left[\frac{\dfrac{\Omega}{1+n}\cdot w-k-\dfrac{1}{1+r}\cdot v^d}{\dfrac{r^s-n}{r-n}}\right]+\left[\frac{\dfrac{1}{\Omega^*+(1-\Omega^*)\cdot\zeta^1(k^*,r^{i*})\cdot(1+r^*)}\cdot\dfrac{\Omega^*}{1+n}\cdot w^*-k^*}{1+\zeta^2(k^*,r^{i*})\cdot(1-\Omega^*)\cdot\left[\dfrac{1+r^{i*}}{1+r^*}-1\right]}\right]=0 \tag{8.19}$$

The world credit market-clearing condition (8.19) corresponds to condition (3.48) in the case when commitment is feasible and capital transfers are debt-financed. Condition (8.19) represents therefore the role of commitment for all forms of debt-financing.[5] The $H^6(\cdot)=0$ schedule is depicted in Figure 8.1.

As in a constrained equilibrium debt issued by the borrowing country is, *ceteris paribus*, smaller, the first term in square brackets in equation (8.19) must be smaller too. For $k \geqslant \tilde{k}$ this requires from Figure 4.1(c) and $\partial r/\partial k < 0$ that k must increase, given k^*. Under commitment, the credit

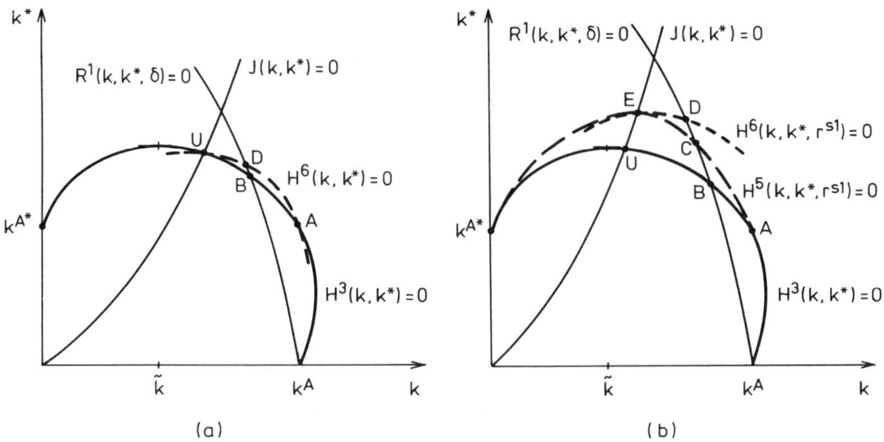

Figure 8.1 *Steady states and the role of commitment.*

market-clearing condition therefore shifts to the right in $k - k^*$ space whenever the steady state is constrained by debtor sovereignty. For $r^{i*} = r^*$ the steady state is unconstrained. As from the definition in (8.14) $\varsigma^1(k^*, r^{i*}) = 1/(1 + r^*)$ and from the definition of $\varsigma^2(k^*, r^{i*})$ in (8.16) $\varsigma^2(k^*, r^{i*}) = 1$ if $r^{i*} = r^*$, it follows that $H^6(\cdot) = H(\cdot)$ if $r^{i*} = r^*$ under debt-financing. In $k - k^*$ space, the world credit market-clearing conditions under commitment and non-commitment intersect on the $J(k, k^*) = 0$ curve.

Figure 8.1(a) depicts the case of bond-financing. From equation (5.4), under non-commitment the relevant credit market-clearing function is $H^3(k, k^*) = 0$.[6] Under commitment the steady state is at D. Compared to the non-commitment steady state B, commitment involves a smaller steady-state capital stock in the creditor country and a larger one in the debtor country. The domestic component of disposable income therefore declines in the creditor country, and it increases in the debtor country. As from the derivative (5.10) the foreign component of disposable incomes is larger in the creditor country and smaller in the debtor country, the welfare effects of commitment are ambiguous.

As the capital stock in the creditor country is smaller at D than at B it follows furthermore that debt outstanding in the steady state is larger under commitment compared to non-commitment. Hence, contrary to the *ceteris paribus* result obtained earlier, the general equilibrium analysis reconciles theory with intuition. The ability to commit improves world financial integration.

The case of bank credit-financing is depicted in Figure 8.1(b). Under non-commitment the relevant credit market-clearing condition is $H^5(k, k^*, r^{s1}) = 0$ (from equation (6.6)). Under commitment, the credit market-clearing condition is given by equation (8.19), with $r^{i*} = r^s$. Given $r^s = r^{s1}$, the commitment steady state is at D, whereas without commitment the steady state is at C. Welfare effects of commitment, given r^s, are again ambiguous.

It should be noted that commitment also influences the solvency restriction $H(k, k^*, \underline{r}^s) = 0$. The solvency condition under commitment is derived if we replace the second term in square brackets on the LHS of equation (6.17) by the RHS of equation (8.18). As under commitment, *ceteris paribus*, debt issued in the debtor country is smaller, it follows from Figure 4.1(b) that k must increase (decrease) for $k > \tilde{\tilde{k}}$ ($k < \tilde{\tilde{k}}$). This is depicted in Figure 8.2.

Under commitment, the steady state where banks make a zero profit from all their activities is given by C. Under non-commitment the zero-profit steady state is at B. The minimal capital stock in the creditor country is therefore smaller if the debtor country can commit herself to an investment plan. The maximal capital stock in the debtor country is increased, as is the maximal net transfer, z.

The steady-state analysis confirms the earlier result that the ability to commit has real effects only when sovereignty is a binding constraint. For large enough δ the $R^1(k, k^*, \delta) = 0$ function in Figure 8.1 intersects the $H^3(k, k^*) = 0$ function to the left of U. In this case sovereignty is not binding and the steady state is given by U under both the presence and the absence of an ability to commit.

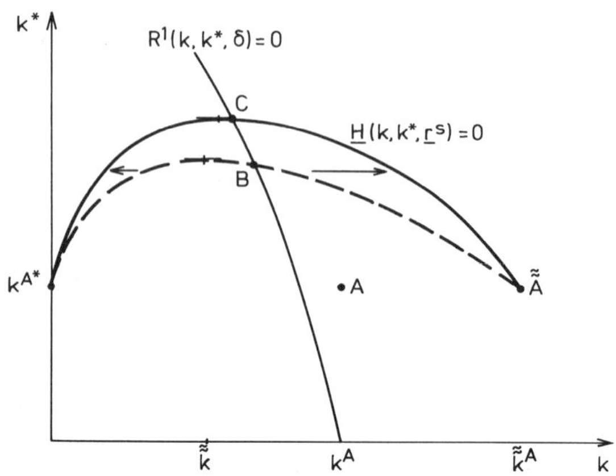

Figure 8.2 *Commitment and bank solvency.*

V. Repudiation Risk, Commitment and Credit Demand

In Section III and Section IV we have obtained a number of unambiguous results. These results, however, are not robust. In particular they are obscured by repudiation risk. To analyse risk we revoke Assumption 3.1 and presume that Assumption 7.1 holds.

Under risk of repudiation the problem of debt externalities in the borrowing economy arises. Households raise debt when young. When debt is due at old age their utility from consumption depends on the government's repudiation decision. To be precise, when repudiation occurs the old generation's utility depends on whether they have to bear the full costs of repudiation or whether some of these costs are paid by the young. A rational household will take this into account when borrowing abroad. To abstract from this complication, in this section we make

Assumption 8.2: The social costs of repudiation have to be fully borne by those households who raised debt in the first place. In addition to the social costs of repudiation further costs do not accrue to these households.

Assumption 8.2 implies that generation t must compensate generation $t+1$ for the loss of access to international credit markets if in period $t+1$ repudiation occurs. This requires a payment $b_1^* \cdot (1+n)$ by each member of generation t in period $t+1$. Furthermore, an old debtor household has to bear $\delta \cdot f^*(k_1^*) \cdot (1+n)$ upon repudiation from the imposition of economic sanctions. Old-age consumption under repudiation, $\tilde{\bar{c}}^{o*}$, is therefore given by

$$\tilde{\bar{c}}^{o*} = (1+n) \cdot (1+r_1^*) \cdot k_1^* - [(1+n) \cdot b_1^* + \delta \cdot f^*(k_1^*) \cdot (1+n)] \tag{8.20}$$

Hence

$$\partial \tilde{\bar{c}}^{o*} / \partial b^* = 0 \tag{8.21}$$

and

$$\partial \tilde{\bar{c}}^{o*} / \partial k_1^* = (1+n) \cdot [1 + r_1^* - \delta \cdot f^{*\prime}(k_1^*)] \tag{8.22}$$

If $\delta = \bar{\delta}(b^*, k_1^*)$ then the debtor country is indifferent to the alternatives of either honouring or repudiating debt. As the young generation is fully compensated, the old generation must be indifferent too. Therefore

$$U^*(c^{j*}, \tilde{\bar{c}}^{o*}, \bar{\delta}(b^*, k_1^*)) = U^*(c^{j*}, \bar{c}^{o*}, \bar{\delta}(b^*, k_1^*)) \tag{8.23}$$

For equations (8.21)–(8.23) the first-order optimality condition for loan demand, (8.5) simplifies to

$$\frac{\Phi(z_1, k_1^*) \cdot U^*_{\bar{c}^{j*}} + \int_0^{\bar{\delta}(\cdot)} g(\delta) \cdot U^*_{\bar{c}^{j*}} d\delta}{\Phi(z_1, k_1^*) \cdot U^*_{\bar{c}^{o*}} + \xi} = 1 + r_1^{i*}(b^*, k_1^*) + b^* \cdot \frac{\partial r_1^{i*}}{\partial b^*} \tag{8.24}$$

Condition (8.24) can be further simplified if preferences are additively separable in consumption. In this case

$$\int_0^{\bar{\delta}(\cdot)} g(\delta) \cdot U^*_{\bar{c}^{j*}}\, d\delta = [1 - \Phi(z_1, k_1^*)] \cdot U^*_{\bar{c}^{j*}}$$

so that optimal loan demand is given by

$$\frac{U^*_{\bar{c}^{j*}}}{\Phi(z_1, k_1^*) \cdot U^*_{\bar{c}^{o*}} + \xi} = 1 + r_1^{i*}(b^*, k_1^*) + b^* \cdot \frac{\partial r_1^{i*}}{\partial b^*} \tag{8.25}$$

To determine the role of repudiation risk for loan demand, equations (8.24) and (8.25) respectively have to be compared with equation (8.8) which holds under certainty. The impact of risk on loan demand and the consumption plan can be disaggregated into a direct and an indirect effect.

The direct effect results from a positive probability that old-age consumption benefits from the windfall of avoided repayment. Under risk of repudiation $\Phi_1(z_1, k_1^*) < 1$. Hence for a given RHS, the LHS in condition (8.25) is larger than in equation (8.8), implying that in an optimum under risk, consumption must be shifted into the first period of life. Economically, consumption smoothing requires that part of the expected windfall from repudiation is shifted into consumption when young. The direct effect of risk on optimal loan demand (8.25) requires therefore additional loans to finance that consumption.

The direct effect of risk on the intertemporal consumption plan and on credit demand is, however, ambiguous if preferences are not additively separable. If

$$U^*_{\bar{c}^{j*}c^{o*}} \begin{Bmatrix} > \\ < \end{Bmatrix} 0 \Rightarrow \int_0^{\bar{\delta}(\cdot)} g(\delta) \cdot U^*_{\bar{c}^{j*}} d\delta \begin{Bmatrix} > \\ < \end{Bmatrix} [1 - \Phi(z_1, k_1^*)] \cdot U^*_{\bar{c}^{j*}}$$

Hence the numerator on the LHS of equation (8.24) is larger than the numerator on the LHS of equation (8.25) if consumption in the two periods of life is complementary.[7] Consumption when young has therefore to be increased even more. Complementarity therefore reinforces the direct effect of risk on consumption and credit demand. However, if consumption in the two periods of life are substitutes the numerator on the LHS in (8.24) is smaller than in (8.25). The LHS in condition (8.24) can therefore be larger or smaller than the LHS in (8.25). Under substitutability the direct effect of risk on intertemporal consumption and borrowing is ambiguous. Economically, under substitutability, consumption smoothing is less necessary than under additively separable utility because the windfalls from repudiation at old age can at least partially replace additional consumption when young.

The indirect effect of repudiation risk on intertemporal consumption and borrowing is due to the fact that the loan supply schedule is increasing under repudiation risk. In the optimality conditions (8.24) and (8.25) this is represented by the last term on the RHS. It is positive. Given r_1^{i*}, the RHS in condition (8.24) and (8.25) is larger than in (8.8). The LHS must therefore increase too. Consumption must be shifted from the first period of life into the second. Borrowing to finance consumption decreases. We now turn to optimal investment under risk.

For equations (8.21)–(8.23) the condition for optimal investment (8.6) simplifies to

$$\frac{EU^*_{c^{j*}}}{EU^*_{c^{o*}}} \equiv \frac{\Phi(z_1, k_1^*) \cdot U^*_{\tilde{c}^{j*}} + \int_{\underline{\delta}}^{\bar{\delta}(\cdot)} g(\delta) \cdot U^*_{\tilde{\tilde{c}}^{j*}} d\delta}{\Phi(z_1, k_1^*) \cdot U^*_{\tilde{c}^{o*}} + \int_{\underline{\delta}}^{\bar{\delta}(\cdot)} g(\delta) \cdot U^*_{\tilde{\tilde{c}}^{o*}} d\delta}$$

(i) $$= (1 + r_1^*)$$

(ii) $$+ \frac{\xi}{EU^*_{c^{o*}}} \cdot \bar{\delta} \cdot f^{*\prime}(k_1^*)$$

(iii) $$- \frac{\xi}{EU^*_{c^{o*}}} \cdot \frac{b^*}{1+n} \cdot \frac{\partial r_1^{i*}}{\partial k_1^*}$$

(iv) $$- \frac{\Phi(z_1, k_1^*) \cdot U^*_{\tilde{c}^{o*}}}{EU^*_{c^{o*}}} \cdot \frac{b^*}{1+n} \cdot \frac{\partial r^{i*}}{\partial k_1^*}$$

(v) $$- \frac{\int_0^{\bar{\delta}(\cdot)} g(\delta) \cdot U^*_{\tilde{\tilde{c}}^{o*}} \cdot \delta \cdot f^{*\prime}(k_1^*) d\delta}{EU^*_{c^{o*}}} \qquad (8.26)$$

To determine the role of repudiation risk for investment, condition (8.26) has to be compared with condition (8.9) which holds under certainty.

The LHS of condition (8.26) is the expected ratio of marginal utility from consumption in the two periods of life. Under risk it is determined by the terms (i)–(v) on the RHS of condition (8.26).

The term (i) represents the ordinary investment incentive to finance consumption when old. This term corresponds to the first term on the RHS of condition (8.9) and to the RHS of the lower equation in condition (3.27).

The term (ii) corresponds to the second term on the RHS of condition (8.9) for the case of repudiation risk. It represents the incentive to raise the credit limit, $\bar{b}^*$, when sovereignty is a binding constraint and commitment is possible. The investment incentives (i) and (ii) are present also under certainty whereas the terms (iii)–(v) represent the role of risk.

Term (iii), like term (ii), is due to the ability to commit. It represents the investment incentive that commitment not only directly increases the credit limit, $\bar{b}^*$, through an increase in economic sanctions pending, but also through a decrease in the costs of borrowing associated with any given level of debt outstanding. If sovereignty is not a binding constraint, then $\xi = 0$ and the incentive to commit vanishes.

The fourth term also represents the availability of better loan conditions from higher investment. Here, however, it is the investment incentive due to lower repayment obligations when debt is not repudiated. It should be noted that the term (iv) is also due to the ability to commit. This term is always positive, that is, irrespective of whether the sovereignty constraint is binding or not. The reason is simply that investment reduces the repudiation risk for lenders. Competitive credit markets reward this by lowering the interest rate on debt at *all* levels of risky debt outstanding.

As $\partial r_1^{i*}/\partial k_1^* < 0$ and $\xi \geqslant 0$ the terms (i)–(iv) are non-negative. For $\xi > 0$ they are positive and therefore contribute to raising expected marginal utility of consumption when young. The terms (i)–(iv), therefore, shift the consumption profile from consumption in the first period of life towards consumption in the second period of life.

The fifth term on the RHS of condition (8.26), contrary to the first four terms, represents a disincentive to invest. It is negative and due to the possibility that, under risk, repudiation actually can occur. As economic sanctions therefore may have to be incurred there is an incentive to constrain these costs by decreasing investment. Term (v) corresponds to the incentive to constrain economic sanctions discussed in Chapter 7.[8] It is now a simple task to determine the role of commitment in optimal investment in the debtor country.

Commitment possibilities are represented by the terms (ii), (iii), and (iv). The sum of these three terms is always positive. Therefore, the ability to commit raises investment in the domestic capital stock in the debtor country.

The role of risk is a bit more difficult to understand. It is represented by the LHS and the terms (iii), (iv), and (v) on the RHS of condition (8.26). The LHS takes account of the risk-aversion of debtor households.

The impact of risk-aversion is best seen in the case of additively separable utility functions. In this case $EU^*_{c^{o*}} = U^*_{c^{o*}}$. From Assumption 3.3, $U^*_{c^{o*}c^{o*}} < 0$ and households are therefore averse to risk concerning variations in old-age consumption. For $U^*_{c^{o*}c^{o*}} < 0$, $EU^*_{c^{o*}} > U'[E(c^{o*})]$ whereas under risk-neutrality $EU^*_{c^{o*}} = U^{*\prime}[E(c^{o*})]$. Hence under risk-aversion the denominator on the LHS of condition (8.26) is larger compared to risk-neutrality. As the first term on the RHS of condition (8.26) is independent of $EU^*_{c^{o*}}$ the RHS decreases by less due to the impact of risk-aversion. Hence, compared to risk-neutrality the denominator on the LHS must increase. Consumption when young decreases. Risk-aversion creates an incentive for additional investment in the domestic capital stock in the debtor country.

The intuitive explanation transpires once we have noted that 'good' states of nature from the point of view of a debtor household involve $\delta < \tilde{\delta}(z_1, k_1^*)$, in which case windfalls from repudiation occur in the form of extra consumption when old. That is, $\tilde{\tilde{c}}^{o*} > \tilde{c}^{o*}$ if $\delta < \tilde{\delta}(z_1, k_1^*)$. Risk-aversion then creates an incentive to cater for the 'bad' states of nature when repudiation does not occur at the expense of 'good' states. This provision for the 'bad' states of nature is achievable by investment in the domestic capital stock. It increases old-age consumption if debt is to be repaid at the expense of additional economic sanctions which, however, have to be borne only in the 'good' states of nature.

It is now readily seen that the role of repudiation risk for investment is ambiguous. Under non-commitment and risk-neutrality the role of risk is limited to the impact of the fifth term on the RHS of equation (8.26) which causes investment to decline due to the dependence of sanctions on economic activity. Under risk-aversion there is a second effect on the LHS of equation (8.26) which works against the investment disincentive associated with repudiation risk. Hence the impact of risk on investment is ambiguous. Risk, however, is more likely to constitute an overall incentive to invest if commitment is feasible, as in this case the terms (iii) and (iv) create an additional investment incentive.

VI. The Credit-cost Externality

If there exists a risk of repudiation, credit markets react to higher risk with a higher surcharge on the risk-free rate. If individual debt contracts are strategically independent, each debtor faces the entire credit costs associated with raising additional debt. Other debtors, being a party to different debt contracts, do not suffer from credit-cost externalities.

Matters are different, however, if individual debt contracts are strategically interdependent. Under a jumbo loan agreement, for example, individual borrowers in the debtor country ultimately raise debt. The government, however, makes its repudiation decision on the basis of a comparison of aggregate debt obligations with aggregate costs of repudiation rather than separately on the basis of each ultimate loan. Repudiation risk then depends on total indebtedness. Total indebtedness, however, is determined by the sum of individual debts raised. An individual debtor is hence confronted with a higher risk premium if other debtors raise more debt. Yet each borrower takes into account only the impact of total indebtedness on his individual credit costs. Let B^* be the country's total indebtedness and let b^{*j} be total indebtedness of borrower j in the country. Then household j's additional interest cost associated with raising marginally more debt is given by

$$b^{*j} \cdot \frac{\partial r_1^{i*}}{\partial B^*} \cdot \frac{\partial B^*}{\partial b^{*j}},$$

where $B^* \equiv \sum_{h=1}^{n} b^{*h}$.

Total credit costs associated with an increase in b^{*j}, however, are given by

$$B^* \cdot \frac{\partial r_1^{i*}}{\partial B^*} \cdot \frac{\partial B^*}{\partial b^{*j}}$$

The marginal increase in individual indebtedness therefore creates credit-cost externalities. These externalities are not taken into account when individual loan demand is determined.

To see the implications of credit-cost externalities for aggregate borrowing and investment return to equations (8.24) and (8.26). We can represent these externalities by taking $\partial r_1^{i*}/\partial b^* = \partial r_1^{i*}/\partial k_1^* = 0$. In this case individual decisions with respect to investment and borrowing are made as if they had no effect on aggregate credit costs.

From the optimality condition with respect to loan demand, equation (8.24), it follows that borrowing is excessive if individual borrowers set $\partial r_1^{i*}/\partial b^* = 0$. From the optimality condition with respect to investment, equation (8.26), it follows that the terms (iii) and (iv) on the RHS disappear if individual decision-makers set $\partial r_1^{i*}/\partial k_1^* = 0$. As in the aggregate these terms are positive it follows that individual investment is socially too small.

Credit-cost externalities motivate economic policy interventions. To reduce the socially excessive private borrowing in the debtor country the government can raise borrowing taxes.[9] Subsidizing private investment can raise aggregate investment to the socially optimal level.

VII. The Repudiation Externality

The costs of servicing debt are usually borne by the party who borrowed in the first place. The costs of repudiation usually fall on others too.

Neither credit embargoes nor economic sanctions seem to be tailored to hurt only those within the debtor economy who raise debt abroad. Sovereignty exerted by governments even creates an incentive for lenders to punish the country at large. Even if the group of borrowers in the debtor country exclusively is the direct target of a credit embargo and economic sanctions, costs may be transmitted onto other groups in the debtor economy.

To analyse the implications of this repudiation externality we revoke Assumption 8.2. In this case equations (8.21)–(8.23) do not hold. Then from equation (8.5), the optimality condition for loan demand is given by

$$\frac{EU^*_{c^{j*}}}{\Phi(z_1, k_1^*)\cdot U^*_{\tilde{c}^{o*}} + \xi}$$

$$\text{(i)} \qquad = 1 + r_1^{i*}(b^*, k_1^*) + b^* \cdot \partial r_1^{i*}/\partial b^*$$

$$\text{(ii)} \qquad + \frac{g[\tilde{\delta}(\cdot)]\cdot[\partial\tilde{\delta}(\cdot)/\partial b^*]\cdot\{U^*(c^{j*}, \tilde{c}^{o*}, \tilde{\delta}(\cdot)) - U^*(c^{j*}, \tilde{\tilde{c}}^{o*}, \tilde{\delta}(\cdot))\}}{\Phi(z_1, k_1^*)\cdot U^*_{\tilde{c}^{o*}} + \xi}$$

$$\text{(iii)} \qquad - \frac{\int_{\underline{\delta}}^{\tilde{\delta}(\cdot)} g(\delta)\cdot U^*_{\tilde{\tilde{c}}^{o*}}\cdot[\partial\tilde{\tilde{c}}^{o*}/\partial b^*]\, d\delta}{\Phi(z_1, k_1^*)\cdot U^*_{\tilde{c}^{o*}} + \xi} \qquad (8.27)$$

Compared to the case when repudiation costs are internalized (see equation (8.24)) repudiation externalities are responsible for two additional terms. If the young in period $t+1$ have to bear part of the costs from repudiation in period $t+1$, then

$$U^*(c^{j*}, \tilde{c}^{o*}, \tilde{\delta}(\cdot)) - U^*(c^{j*}, \tilde{\tilde{c}}^{o*}, \tilde{\delta}(\cdot)) < 0 \qquad (8.28)$$

As $\partial\tilde{\delta}(\cdot)/\partial b^* > 0$, term (ii) on the RHS of equation (8.27) is negative. Compared to the case when repudiation costs are fully internalized this term represents an additional incentive to borrow in order to finance consumption in the first period of life. The reason for this incentive is that in the presence of repudiation externalities borrowers strictly prefer repudiation in the state $\delta = \tilde{\delta}(z_1, k_1^*)$ whereas they are indifferent to this state when costs are internalized.

If repudiation creates lump-sum costs for borrowers then term (ii) represents the sole effect of repudiation externalities. Repudiation externalities then imply excessive borrowing. However, externalities may be endogenous to the level of borrowing. In this case, old-age consumption of the indebted generation depends on the level of borrowing also when repudiation occurs. Under endogeneity, repudiation externalities have a second effect on the optimal level of individual borrowing. This is represented in equation (8.27) by term (iii) on the RHS.

The natural presumption is $\partial \tilde{\bar{c}}^{o*}/\partial b^* < 0$, that is, the costs of repudiation accruing to borrowers increase with the amount of debt raised. This can be justified on a number of grounds. If borrowing is an indicator of the level of economic activity then debtors have to bear a large share of economic sanctions imposed on the country. Another justification is in the spirit of political economy. If the level of debt raised by a group is low, political pressure on that group to take over an extra share in the national burden exerted on the country by economic sanctions may be weak. The pressure perhaps increases if debt raised by the group is large. Other groups may convincingly argue that debtors should not get a free lunch, and that the burden imposed on them should be made proportional to the repayment obligation they would have faced if repudiation had not occurred.

If $\partial \tilde{\bar{c}}^{o*}/\partial b^* < 0$ the third term on the RHS of equation (8.27) is positive and hence represents an incentive to reduce borrowing at the cost of consumption in the first period of life. In this case the total effect of repudiation externalities on borrowing is ambiguous.

On the other hand, if $\partial \tilde{\bar{c}}^{o*}/\partial b^* > 0$ term (iii) is negative. Then borrowing is even more excessive than in the case when repudiation costs to borrowers are exogenous. This situation may also be justified by arguments borrowed from political economy. A large private foreign debt of an interest group is more likely to be perceived as a national problem than a small one. With large debt outstanding, the debtor group may be therefore able to argue that other groups or the country at large benefitted from the debt raised. The group of borrowers thus may get away with a socialisation of some of their private costs of repudiation.

For these reasons the role of repudiation externalities in determining the optimal private demand for international loans is ambiguous in general. From the point of view of someone concerned about the smooth flow of international capital the prospect of excessive loan demand is troublesome. If debt raised is extremely high then the probability of repudiation is too. Reducing debt to the socially optimal level is therefore in the interest of stabilizing international credit markets.

The condition for optimal loan demand shows how economic policy can attain a socially optimal level of private loan demand. Repudiation taxes proportional to debt, levied on debtors in case of repudiation, decrease $\partial \tilde{\bar{c}}^{o*}/\partial b^*$ and therefore induce borrowers to issue less debt. Such taxes have to be levied only in the case when repudiation actually occurs. The associated reduction in debt outstanding increases the probability that these taxes do not need to be levied.

To analyse how private investment depends on repudiation externalities let D be equal to the RHS of equation (8.26) which is the condition for optimal investment if repudiation costs are fully internalized. Under repudiation externalities the condition for optimal investment (8.6) can be reformulated to entail

$$\frac{EU^*_{c^{j*}}}{EU^*_{c^{o*}}} = D - \frac{g[\tilde{\delta}(\cdot)] \cdot [\partial\tilde{\delta}(\cdot)/\partial k^*_1] \cdot \{U^*(c^{j*}, \tilde{c}^{o*}, \tilde{\delta}(\cdot)) - U^*(c^{j*}, \tilde{\tilde{c}}^{o*}, \tilde{\delta}(\cdot))\}}{(1+n) \cdot EU^*_{c^{o*}}} \tag{8.29}$$

The additional term is negative due to inequality (8.28) and because $\partial\tilde{\delta}(\cdot)/\partial k^*_1 < 1$. The intertemporal consumption plan is therefore biased towards excessive consumption when young. Repudiation externalities therefore create an additional disincentive to invest into the domestic capital stock in the debtor country. As repudiation risk negatively depends on the level of the capital stock, repudiation risk is excessively high.

What must be borne in mind when evaluating the effect of repudiation externalities on investment is that in our model investment and borrowing decisions are made by the same group of decision-makers in the debtor country. Repudiation externalities are therefore defined with respect to the group of borrowers-cum-investors. Although this is perhaps a good approximation to reality it need not necessarily be the case. If borrowers and investors are not the same, then repudiation externalities, in their effect on investment, have to be defined with respect to the group of decision-makers in charge of investment.

VIII. Conclusions

Let us sum up:

(1) The ability to commit to investment implies higher savings and investment in the debtor country if the equilibrium is constrained by debtor sovereignty. This is true under both certainty and repudiation risk.

(2) In general equilibrium the ability to commit allows for a larger world capital stock. The constrained bond-financed steady state under commitment involves a larger capital stock in the debtor country and a smaller capital stock in the creditor country compared to non-commitment. Under bank credit-financing the same holds for the steady state where the banking sector makes zero profits. If the equilibrium is unconstrained commitment opportunities have no effects on the world economy.

(3) Repudiation risk has an ambiguous effect on international loan demand. Credit demand may increase or decrease if repudiation costs are fully internalized by borrowers.

(4) Risk-aversion in the debtor country creates an additional incentive for investment in the domestic capital stock. The overall effect of repudiation risk on investment, however, is ambiguous.

(5) For a number of reasons we must expect that effects of borrowing are not fully borne by debtors. Credit-cost externalities are responsible for socially excessive borrowing due to the increase in the risk premium charged on all loans if individual borrowers raise more debt.

(6) Repudiation externalities of investment arise if investors do not bear the full costs of repudiation imposed on the debtor economy. If repudiation externalities exist, private investment in the debtor country is socially too small.

(7) Repudiation externalities of borrowing arise if borrowers do not bear the full costs of repudiation imposed on the debtor country. If repudiation creates lump-sum costs for borrowers, repudiation externalities cause borrowing to be socially excessive. The same holds for the case where costs from repudiation for borrowers decrease with the level of indebtedness.

CHAPTER 9

Debt Renegotiation

I. Introduction

We have already made considerable headway in exploring the theoretical ramifications of sovereign debt. Throughout the previous chapters we have, however, kept our analysis unrealistically simple. We have restricted the alternatives of parties to a debt contract to only two extreme alternatives. Debtors could either fully honour debt contracts or else repudiate debt and make no payments at all. Creditors had no alternative to imposing the full measure of costs on debtors for even the slightest contract violation. This 'take-it-or-leave-it' alternative does not conform with real world observations.

Debtor countries regularly try to enter negotiations with creditors when falling behind on their payments.[1] In these negotiations the parties try to settle the issue in order to avoid an outright confrontation associated with debt repudiation and declaring the country to be in default. If such negotiations succeed debt contracts are in effect redefined. Renegotiation of existing contracts can end in a variety of agreements. Debtors may insist on the full repayment of principal and interest due, yet help the debtors by infusing fresh money or roll over debt altogether. Alternatively, creditors can agree that principal be paid back at a later date at the going rate of interest. Still other forms involve a partial forgiveness of principal or interest.

Such concessions of lenders aiming at a rescheduling of old debt on terms favourable for the borrower often require similar concessions by debtors. These can involve some payments of interest or principal due. Other concessions by debtors may involve an agreement to pursue a certain economic policy or a commitment to use fresh loans for certain investment projects.

The implications of debt renegotiation and rescheduling are wide. We begin by analysing the incentives for the parties to a debt contract to enter such negotiations. If negotiations are on the table once a loan is in jeopardy rational lenders will anticipate this when making a loan. We can therefore expect that debt rescheduling has a role to play in the determination of loan supply in the first place. We shall therefore investigate the consequences of rescheduling for the loan supply under certainty, risk and adverse selection.

A question of particular interest is, what are the determinants of agreements reached in debt renegotiations. We address this question in detail by viewing negotiations as a dynamic and strategic decision problem of parties to a debt contract. According to this view agreements possess the properties of a perfect equilibrium. We determine such equilibria for a variety of debt situations. Finally, we investigate the implications of such equilibrium agreements for the general equilibrium of sovereign debt. As we cannot take it for granted that the different forms of financing are neutral with respect to a negotiated equilibrium we distinguish in the partial and general equilibrium between bank- and bond-financing.

To inquire into all these aspects of sovereign debt we revoke Assumption 2.2 and make

Assumption 9.1: Parties to a debt contract can avoid the imposition of the costs from contract violations by reaching an agreement in debt renegotiations.

II. The Efficiency of Debt Renegotiation

If parties waive some or all stipulations to an existing debt contract the question arises as to what is the role of such contracts in the first place. Although debt contracts may fail to fix in advance the transactions during a contractual debt relationship they are nevertheless important in defining the object of negotiations.

In fixing debt service obligations, contracts define the maximum which lenders can obtain at the end of renegotiations.[2] Contracts thus define the most debtors can gain in negotiations. Renegotiating debt repayment obligations is a zero-sum game in that achieving some agreement or failing to do so always involves some distribution of a cake of a given size, where the size of the cake is given by the amount due to servicing.

The role of contracts, however, is not limited to defining the size of the cake. A contractual debt relationship is often a precondition which allows those involved to appeal to institutional mechanisms designed to exert economic sanctions. Bondholders, for example, can only prevent debtor countries issuing new bonds, if the latter have violated contracts that these bondholders are a party to. At least to some extent economic sanctions require an involvement of governments in the creditor countries. One can expect governments to be rather reluctant to exert economic sanctions if lenders cannot point to the exact contractual stipulation the debtor country has violated. Debt contracts therefore also define implicitly the nature and size of economic sanctions pending.

Thus debt contracts can be responsible for the fact that a negotiated agreement is a positive-sum game, compared to a failure to come to an agreement. In the context of our model, if the failure to reach an agreement results in the imposition of economic sanctions in period t, an agreement avoids dead-weight losses of size $\delta \cdot f^*(k^*)$.

This creates an incentive to enter into negotiations after the country has fallen behind on payments due. This, however, is only possible if lenders can decide after an initial contract violation whether economic sanctions should be imposed. Lenders may forsake the imposition of economic sanctions if they receive at least some repayment. Negotiations to avoid dead-weight losses can make lenders and borrowers better off compared to repudiation if, following repudiation, the imposition of economic sanctions ensues automatically. The set of Pareto-efficient agreements about the distribution of avoided dead-weight losses is shown in Figure 9.1.

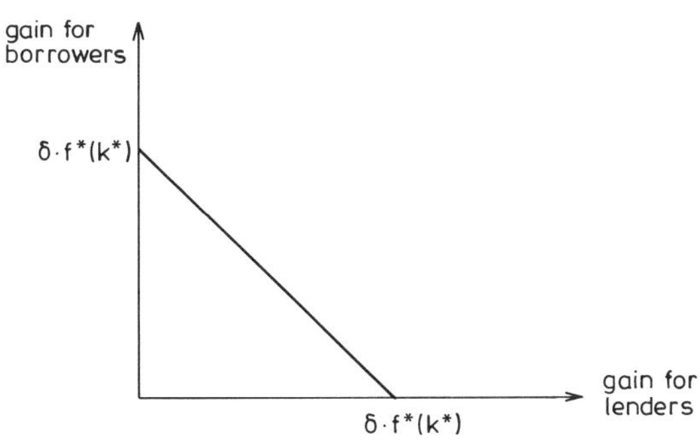

Figure 9.1 *Gains from renegotiation.*

Any agreement under which the debtor country repays an amount not in excess of $\delta \cdot f^*(k^*)$, Pareto-dominates repudiation cum the imposition of economic sanctions of size $\delta \cdot f^*(k^*)$. Debtors and borrowers therefore have an incentive to enter into negotiations to avoid deadweight losses.

An agreement can be characterized by the share $(m, 0 \leqslant m \leqslant 1)$ lenders receive from the total negotiation gains. The debtor country then makes a payment $m \cdot \delta \cdot f^*(k^*)$ in exchange for lenders waiving their right to impose economic sanctions. The debtor country's gain from reaching an agreement is then given by $(1 - m) \cdot \delta \cdot f^*(k^*)$.

It should be noted that in our model economic sanctions constitute dead-weight losses for the world economy, as it is presumed that lenders gain nothing from the imposition of sanctions. It is, however, clear that this assumption is unnecessarily restrictive for making Pareto-superior re-negotiation feasible. It suffices that some of the costs from economic sanctions are dead-weight losses, that is, that some costs do not constitute gains for the lenders. It is also clear that it can never be optimal for a debtor country to repudiate debt if it can enter into such negotiations.

Here we have left it open as to what agreement lenders and debtors will strike, that is, what size of m they agree upon. Before analysing the determinants of a debt agreement we first investigate the implications a future agreement has for the loan supply debtor countries face in the first place.

III. Anticipated Renegotiation and Loan Supply

Renegotiation influences the effective costs of not fully honouring a loan contract. If the debtor country can reach an agreement m in negotiations then the effective costs of not fully honouring a loan contract is given by $m \cdot \delta \cdot f^*(k^*)$. It is then optimal to honour a contract only if $z \leqslant m \cdot \delta \cdot f^*(k^*)$. If this is not fulfilled it pays for the debtor country to violate the contract, enter into negotiations, and settle for $m \cdot \delta \cdot f^*(k^*)$, to be repaid in exchange for the lenders forsaking economic sanctions.

In our general equilibrium model this has the implication that the sovereignty restriction (5.7) has to be replaced by

$$R^3(k, k^*, \delta, m) \equiv (r - n) \cdot \left[\frac{\Omega}{1+n} \cdot w - k - \frac{1}{1+r} \cdot v^d\right] - m \cdot \delta \cdot f^*(k^*) = 0 \tag{9.1}$$

For $m = 1$ lenders obtain all the efficiency gain from avoiding economic sanctions. In this case the sovereignty restriction is identical to the case when negotiations are impossible. If the debtor country can reap some of the efficiency gain, that is, if $m < 1$, then renegotiations influence the

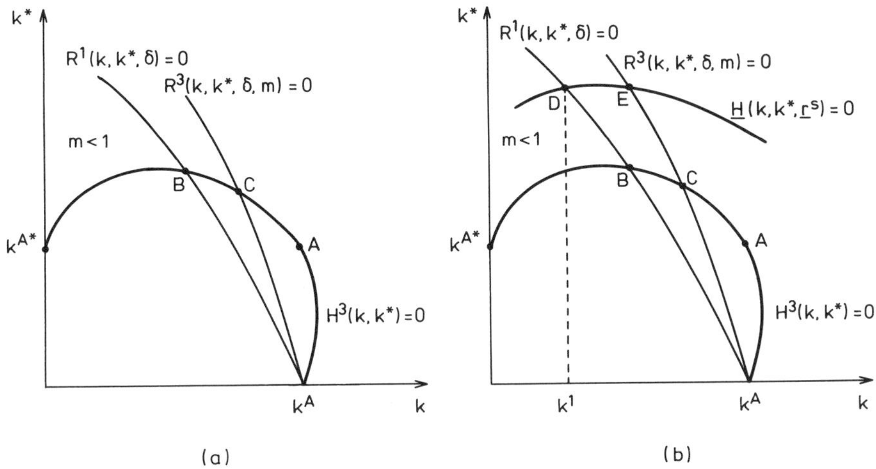

Figure 9.2 *Renegotiation in general equilibrium.*

sovereign-debt steady state. The general equilibrium in the presence of renegotiation is depicted in Figure 9.2.

For $m < 1$ the sovereignty restriction $R^3(k, k^*, \delta, m) = 0$ is situated to the right of $R^1(k, k^*, \delta) = 0$. Renegotiations to avoid dead-weight losses have the property of a decrease in the sovereignty parameter, δ, that is, of an increase in the country's sovereignty unless lenders reap the entire gain from avoiding economic sanctions (compare Figure 5.2). The bond-financed steady state under renegotiations is given by C in Figure 9.2(a). Compared to the steady state when negotiations are impossible, B, it involves a higher capital stock in the creditor country and a lower capital stock in the debtor country. Bank-financed steady states are depicted in Figure 9.2(b). Under renegotiation, steady states are located between C and E on $R^3(k, k^*, \delta, m) = 0$.

From this analysis we conclude that for $m < 1$, negotiations to avoid dead-weight losses, if anticipated by lenders, lead to a reduction in the credit limit. This, however, is not the sole effect of negotiations. To see this we return to the partial equilibrium model of international loan markets under risk.

Without renegotiation, risk implies that repudiation can be an equilibrium phenomenon. By analogy, if renegotiation is possible, risk implies that a negotiated settlement ensuing a contract violation can be an equilibrium phenomenon.

Given Assumptions 7.1, 7.2 and 7.3, the critical value of the state of the world, $\tilde{\delta}$, where the debtor country is indifferent between honouring and repudiating debt, is given by

$$z(b^*, r^{i*}) = m \cdot \tilde{\delta} \cdot f^*(k^*), \tag{9.2}$$

instead of equation (7.2). For $m < 1$ this implies that $\tilde{\delta}$ is larger under potential renegotiation than in the case when renegotiation is impossible. From the definition of the repayment probability in equation (7.4) it then immediately follows that the probability that debt is fully repaid is smaller if negotiations are feasible. *Ceteris paribus*, lenders therefore require a higher risk premium.

In order to determine the credit market equilibrium condition we must note that lenders now obtain some repayment also in bad states of the world, provided $m > 0$. Replacing equation (7.6), the credit market equilibrium condition is now given by

$$\Phi(z, k^*, m) \cdot (1 + r^{i*}) + \frac{m}{b^*} \cdot \int_{\underline{\delta}}^{\tilde{\delta}(\cdot)} \delta \cdot f^*(k^*) d\delta = (1 + r) \tag{9.3}$$

The additional term on the LHS of equation (9.3) is the expected repayment the debtor country makes per dollar lent, due to a negotiated settlement.

It is now apparent that the effect of renegotiation on creditworthiness is ambiguous. The decreased probability that debt is altogether repaid requires the debtor country to pay a higher risk surcharge on the interest rate. However, there is an effect which works against the decrease in $\Phi(z, k^*, m)$. In bad states of the world the country now receives some payments too. This effect reduces the interest rate on sovereign debt. It is therefore not apparent whether renegotiation leads to a decrease or increase of the interest rate for a given loan size.

Given renegotiation, the effect of a change in m is readily obtained. A larger m creates a disincentive for the debtor country to enter negotiations; hence $\Phi(z, k^*, m)$ increases. As the expected repayment to lenders from a negotiated settlement is furthermore increased, the debtor country is charged a lower interest rate for every loan size if m increases.

Let us now turn to the adverse selection problem. It is not difficult to show that negotiations to avoid dead-weight losses have an ambiguous effect on the adverse selection problem. Replacing equation (7.13), the condition for the optimal efficiency level is now given by

$$\Gamma(z, k^*, \Psi, m) \equiv -\partial f^*(k^*, \Psi)/\partial\Psi + m \cdot \int_{\underline{\delta}}^{\tilde{\delta}(\cdot)} g(\delta) \cdot \delta \cdot \partial f^*(k^*, \Psi)/\partial\Psi \, d\delta \leqslant 0 \tag{9.4}$$

Taking the derivative with respect to m we obtain

$$\partial\Gamma(z, k^*, \Psi, m)/\partial m = \int_{\underline{\delta}}^{\tilde{\delta}(\cdot)} g(\delta)\cdot\delta\cdot\partial f^*(k^*, \Psi)/\partial\Psi\, d\delta$$
$$+ m\cdot g[\tilde{\delta}(\cdot)]\cdot\tilde{\delta}(\cdot)\cdot[\partial f^*(\cdot)/\partial\Psi]\cdot\partial\tilde{\delta}(\cdot)/\partial m \quad (9.5)$$

The first term on the RHS of equation (9.5) is positive. A negotiated agreement with $m < 1$ therefore implies a reduction of $\Gamma(z, k^*, \Psi, m)$. Given an interior solution for the optimal choice of Ψ in the case when negotiation is impossible, this implies that Ψ is larger if negotiation is possible. Intuitively, a negotiated settlement with $m < 1$ decreases the effective costs of not fully honouring debt. It therefore creates a disincentive to invest in the containment of these costs.

There is, however, a second effect represented by the second term on the RHS of the derivative (9.5) which works against the first. From the condition for the critical value $\tilde{\delta}$, equation (9.2), we obtain for a given repayment obligation, z,

$$\frac{\partial\tilde{\delta}}{\partial m} = -\frac{z(b^*, r^{i*})}{m^2\cdot f^*(k^*)} < 0$$

The second term in the derivative (9.5) is therefore negative. This term thus represents an additional incentive to invest in the containment of costs from violating a debt contract. This incentive is due to the increased probability that debt will not be fully honoured if $m < 1$.

However, if negotiations entail $m \to 1$, negotiations lessen the adverse selection problem. For $m \to 1$ $\partial\tilde{\delta}/\partial m \to -z(\cdot)/f^*(k^*)$. From equation (9.2) $|z(\cdot)/f^*(k^*)| \leqslant 1$ as $m \to 1$ and as $\delta \leqslant 1$. The second negative term in equation (9.5) is therefore smaller in absolute terms than the first term. If lenders obtain almost the entire gains from avoiding economic sanctions, then the ability to enter negotiations entices the debtor government to choose projects and technologies with a higher efficiency parameter, Ψ. For lower values of m this is not necessarily the case.

The role of negotiations for the adverse selection problem therefore depends on the properties of the agreement reached. We address this issue next.

IV. Bargaining and Equilibrium Agreements

More than one approach exists as to how to determine the outcome of negotiations. In the axiomatic approach the procedure is to define a set of axioms, which the outcomes ought to fulfil, and then apply these axioms to determine the set of solutions from the set of feasible agreements.[3] In this approach the negotiation process preceding an agreement is a black box to which little or no attention is paid.

An alternative procedure, known as the non-cooperative bargaining approach, starts from the observation that the outcome of negotiations depends on a set of factors which may be labelled the relative bargaining power of the parties involved. Bargaining power must be expected to hinge on the precise conditions under which negotiations are to take place. Pursuing this approach, it is therefore necessary to specify precisely the rules under which bargaining takes place. Bargaining is then defined as a dynamic game between opponents, and the solution to the bargaining process is an equilibrium satisfying non-cooperative optimality conditions.[4] In analysing debt renegotiations we follow this approach.

To do that we take up a variant of the simple non-cooperative bargaining model presented in Sutton (1986). Suppose there are two bargaining parties which possess complete information. The structure of the bargaining process is depicted in Figure 9.3.

After a debt contract has been violated the two parties to the contract enter negotiations by taking turns in making proposals concerning the division of a cake. Let m be the proposed share for the lending party and let $1 - m$ be the share for the borrower party. The size of the cake is defined per member of a young generation in either of the two countries. It depends on the object of negotiations.

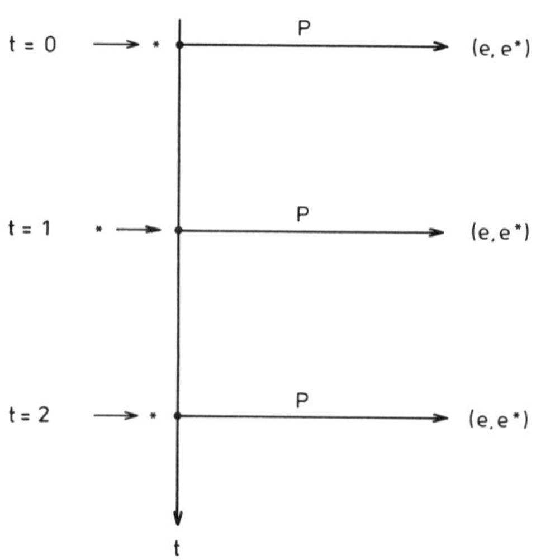

Figure 9.3 *The bargaining rules.*

We arbitrarily presume that the first proposal is made by the creditors. Each proposal by one party induces an immediate reply by the other. It takes the form of either accepting or refusing the proposal. If the debtor refuses the offer obtained in $t = 0$, an i.i.d. random event occurs with probability p. If it occurs, the debtor has available an option to exit negotiations without reaching a bargaining agreement. Taking this option gives the lending party e and the debtor party e^*, where e and e^* are defined in terms of the party's share in the negotiated cake. Contrary to a negotiated agreement, the outside option may entail $e + e^* \gtreqless 1$.

The outside option is unavailable if the random event does not occur. In this case, just as in the case when the debtor party does not take the available option in $t = 0$, negotiations enter a new round in $t = 1$, where it is up to the debtor party to make a proposal to the creditor. If creditors refuse the offer obtained they have the outside option available with probability p.

The same pattern recurs until an agreement is reached or until one party takes its outside option. Let h be the discount factor common to both parties. If the game thus ends in round $t = T$ the parties receive the discounted payoffs $(h^T \cdot m, h^T \cdot (1 - m))$ and $(h^T \cdot e, h^T \cdot e^*)$ respectively. Furthermore, we take it that $h^T < 1 \; \forall \, T$. The bargaining game is stationary. This completes the description of the rules under which negotiations take place.

Although the bargaining rules are admittedly rather special, the model allows investigation into a number of interesting issues. The size of the cake to be divided depends on the object under negotiation. The model can thus accommodate, for example, bargaining over the avoidance of deadweight losses, gross repayment or the infusion of fresh loans.

The options may be the ability to end the debt relationship by declaring the debtor in outright default. Bankruptcy of banks may also be represented as an outside option in the bargaining process. Furthermore, the outside option can represent the existence of a third party of higher authority to which parties can appeal to.

Some of these outside options are naturally available with probability 1. Others may not always be available. For example, we analyse the role of a lender-of-last-resort by making the bankruptcy option available with a probability of less than 1. Furthermore, the bargaining model also accommodates the possibility of outside intervention. It thus allows for an analysis of a forced settlement of the issue under negotiation.

As in general the outside option is not available with certainty, the parties' attitude towards risk ought to be taken into account. We abstract, however, from this complication and make

Assumption 9.2: Parties to debt renegotiations are risk-neutral.

This assumption is innocuous in most of our applications as the outside option will be available with probability 1.

The rules of the game depicted in Figure 9.3 determine the bargaining power of the parties involved. Impatience, which is represented by the discount factor, gives an incentive to come to an early agreement. A high probability of having an outside option of sufficient value available can act as a threat to leave the bargaining table. It thus improves a party's bargaining power.

Threats to exit negotiations without a settlement influence a bargaining process between rational parties only if they are credible. Strategies of the parties involved, that is, sequences of proposals, reactions to proposals and reactions to the availability of options must therefore have the property of subgame-perfection introduced in Chapter 2. As, according to its rules, the game automatically ends if one party takes its option, subgame-perfection is also a sufficient condition for the credibility of threats in this bargaining game. A solution of the bargaining process then is a subgame-perfect equilibrium to the game depicted in Figure 9.3.

In determining the subgame-perfect equilibrium we follow Sutton (1986). Let m be the supremum of the share of the cake the creditor party receives in a perfect equilibrium. The relationship between three successive offers is depicted in Table 9.1.

The subgame-perfect equilibrium partition of the cake is determined recursively. If creditors obtain the supremum m if negotiations end in period $t = 2$, creditors will accept an offer in $t = 1$ only if they obtain at least η. There is no point in borrowers then offering more in $t = 1$.

The security share in period $t = 1$, η, depends on creditors' decision whether to take their option if available or not. If creditors do not take their outside option (case (i)), η is given by the discounted value of the

Table 9.1 Payoffs from reaching an agreement in consecutive periods

Time	Creditors obtain at most share	Borrowers obtain at least share	Case
$t = 0$	$m = \begin{cases} 1 - h \cdot (1 - \eta) \\ 1 - (1 - p) \cdot h \cdot (1 - \eta) - p \cdot e^* \end{cases}$	$(1 - m) = \begin{cases} h \cdot (1 - \eta) \\ (1 - p) \cdot h \cdot (1 - \eta) + p \cdot e^* \end{cases}$	(i*) (ii*)
$t = 1$	η	$1 - \eta$	
$t = 2$	m	$1 - m$	
where	$\eta = \begin{cases} h \cdot m \\ (1 - p) \cdot h \cdot m + p \cdot e \end{cases}$	in case	(i) (ii)

supremum m. If creditors do take their option (case (ii)), η is given by the expected discounted value of not accepting an offer in $t = 1$.

As borrowers can make an offer η in period $t = 1$, which they can expect that lenders will accept, this offer will determine the minimum offer in period $t = 0$ which borrowers are prepared to accept. Again, lenders have no incentive to offer more. This minimum offer will depend on borrowers' decision whether to take their outside option if available. If they do not (case (i*)), lenders need to offer no more than the discounted value of $1 - \eta$. If borrowers do take their outside option if available (case (ii*)), lenders need to offer in $t = 0$ the discounted expected value for borrowers of not accepting an offer in this round of negotiations.

The bargaining equilibrium is now easily determined from the element in the first row and first column in Table 9.1. As both bargaining parties may take two decisions with respect to the availability of the outside option four cases exist. Solving the first row and column element in Table 9.1, entails for the bargaining equilibrium m

$$\left.\begin{aligned}
m &= \frac{1-h}{1-h^2} && \text{in case (i, i}^*\text{)}\\
m &= \frac{1-h+p\cdot h\cdot e}{1-h^2\cdot(1-p)} && \text{in case (ii, i}^*\text{)}\\
m &= \frac{1-(1-p)\cdot h-p\cdot e^*}{1-h^2\cdot(1-p)} && \text{in case (i, ii}^*\text{)}\\
m &= \frac{1-p\cdot e^*-(1-p)\cdot h\cdot(1-p\cdot e)}{1-h^2\cdot(1-p)^2} && \text{in case (ii, ii}^*\text{)}
\end{aligned}\right\} \tag{9.6}$$

For a full description of the bargaining equilibrium it only remains to make precise under which conditions which of the four alternative cases will hold. The parties' decisions with respect to the outside option must fulfil the criterion of subgame-perfection. To determine the conditions under which case (i, i*) holds, note that subgame-perfection requires creditors to abstain from taking the option if continuing negotiations entails a larger gain. As lenders can take their option at the earliest in $t = 1$ this requires $e \leqslant h \cdot m$, or from the bargaining equilibrium

$$e \leqslant h \cdot \frac{1-h}{1-h^2} \tag{9.7}$$

In case (i), $\eta = h \cdot m$ and borrowers abstain from taking their option in $t = 0$ only if $e^* \leqslant h \cdot (1 - h \cdot m)$. From this we obtain

$$e^* \leqslant h \cdot \frac{1-h}{1-h^2} \tag{9.8}$$

upon using the equilibrium partition for the case (i, i*) in (9.6). The equilibrium for the case (i, i*) is therefore only relevant if conditions (9.7) and (9.8) hold.

Applying the same procedure to the case (ii, i*) we obtain as conditions for its relevance

$$e > h \cdot \frac{1-h}{1-h^2} \tag{9.9}$$

and

$$e^* \leqslant h \cdot \frac{1 - p \cdot e - (1-p) \cdot h}{1 - h^2 \cdot (1-p)} \tag{9.10}$$

Applying the same procedure for case (i, ii*) it is readily shown that this case holds if and only if

$$e \leqslant h \cdot \frac{1 - h(1-p) - p \cdot e^*}{1 - h^2 \cdot (1-p)} \tag{9.11}$$

and

$$e^* > h \cdot \frac{1-h}{1-h^2} \tag{9.12}$$

The case (ii, ii*) holds if conditions for none of the other cases are fulfilled.

The critical value of options where parties are indifferent to the two alternatives available, the RHSs of conditions (9.7)–(9.12), are given by the discounted value of arriving at an agreement in the next round of negotiations. Options which would not be taken if available have no impact on the bargaining equilibrium. The bargaining equilibrium has therefore the property that only credible threats matter.

As the problem is stationary, the parties face the same problem in each round of negotiations. As for $h < 1$ there exist time-costs of bargaining, parties have an incentive to come to an agreement earlier rather than later. Having complete information available rational parties will therefore agree immediately.[5]

From case (i, i*) in the bargaining solution (9.6) it follows that $m > 1 - m$. Although both parties have no credible outside option available, the lenders are in a better bargaining position due to a first mover advantage. This allows them to take advantage of the borrower's impatience by offering them

$$1 - m = h \cdot \frac{1-h}{1-h^2}$$

This bargaining advantage for lenders is arbitrary as the choice is arbitrary as to which party is to make the first offer in the game. This arbitrariness can be eliminated if negotiations take place continuously. Then borrowers can make an immediate counter-offer if they neither accept a bid nor take their outside option, if it is available.

To that end let the time interval between successive offers be Δ. Replace the single round discount factor h by h^{Δ} and let $p = 1 - e^{-\varkappa \cdot \Delta}$. Note that $p \to 0$ for $\Delta \to 0$ and $p \to 1$ for $\Delta \to \infty$. Let $\Delta \to 0$. Then the bargaining equilibrium given by equations (9.6)–(9.12) simplifies to

$$\left.\begin{array}{lll} m = 1/2 & \text{if } e, e^* \leqslant 1/2 & \text{(case (i, i}^*\text{))} \\ m = (1 - L') \cdot 1/2 + L' \cdot e & \text{if } e > 1/2,\ e^* \leqslant 1/2 & \text{(case (ii, i}^*\text{))} \\ m = (1 - L') \cdot 1/2 + L' \cdot (1 - e^*) & \text{if } e \leqslant 1/2,\ e^* > 1/2 & \text{(case (i, ii}^*\text{))} \\ m = (1 - L) \cdot 1/2 + L \cdot [e + 1/2 \cdot (1 - e - e^*)] & \text{otherwise} & \text{(case (ii, ii}^*\text{))} \end{array}\right\} \tag{9.13}$$

where the auxiliary variables L and L' are given by

$$L \equiv \frac{1}{1 - \dfrac{\ln h}{\varkappa \cdot \ln \varkappa}} \tag{9.14}$$

and

$$L' \equiv \frac{1}{1 - \dfrac{2 \cdot \ln h}{\varkappa \cdot \ln \varkappa}} \tag{9.15}$$

Note that $0 \leqslant L,\ L' \leqslant 1$. The factors L and L' evaluate the probability that the option will be available.

If the option is available with certainty, $p = 1 - e^{-\varkappa \cdot \Delta} = 1$ which requires $\varkappa \to \infty$. For $\varkappa \to \infty$, from the definitions in (9.14) and (9.15) it follows that

$$L = L' = 1 \tag{9.16}$$

We now turn to applying the Sutton model of bargaining to different debt rescheduling situations. These situations differ, first in the size of the cake to be divided, second in terms of the outside options available, and last in the probability with which these options are available.

V. Bargaining to Avoid the Imposition of Economic Sanctions

Once an international debt contract is violated economic sanctions are on the table. The implications of anticipated negotiations to avoid deadweight losses have been examined in Section III for any given agreement,

m. As it was presumed that dead-weight losses are equal to the costs of economic sanctions, it only remains to determine the equilibrium agreement, m, in order to analyse the bargaining over the avoidance of economic sanctions.

As dead-weight losses are supposed to be equal to the costs of economic sanctions the size of the cake is given by $\delta \cdot f^*(k^*)$. In accordance with Assumption 9.1 sanctions are imposed if negotiations fail. Hence borrowers have no outside option available. In the bargaining model of Section IV this can be represented by setting $e^* = 0$. The value of an outside option to lenders, e, is positive if economic sanctions exerted on the debtor country can be repatriated as gains in the creditor country. The value of taking their option, that is of declaring the debtor country in default then is given by $e \cdot \delta \cdot f^*(k^*)$, where $0 \leqslant e \leqslant 1$. The natural presumption for the availability of these outside options is $p = 1$.

The availability of an outside option for creditors has two implications. First, if after a breakdown of negotiations economic sanctions are triggered only by specific actions to be undertaken by creditors, the debtors must consider this threat credible if $e > 0$. Second, if $e > 0$ debtors cannot negotiate forever in order to postpone indefinitely the execution of economic sanctions or a negotiated partial repayment of debt. In this case it would be optimal for lenders to take their outside option as soon as possible.

The bargaining equilibrium is now easy to determine. As $e^* = 0$ it never pays for debtors to leave the bargaining table. Therefore from the equilibrium partition (9.13) either case (i, i*) or case (ii, i*) holds. If $e \leqslant 1/2$ case (i, i*) holds and the bargaining solution is given by $m = 1/2$. If $e > 1/2$ case (ii, i*) holds. From equation (9.16) $L' = 1$ if $p = 1$ and therefore $m = e$. The non-cooperative bargaining equilibrium is therefore given by

$$m = \max[1/2, e] \tag{9.17}$$

Presumably, the case which is relevant in reality is $e < 1/2$ as economic sanctions are to a large extent dead-weight losses. If $e < 1/2$ the size of the gains lenders can obtain from the imposition of economic sanction or a marginal change in this size has no effect whatsoever on the outcome of negotiations. The gains lenders obtain from imposing economic sanctions are simply too low to make sanctions a credible threat.

In terms of the general equilibrium model, the sovereign debt steady state for $e \leqslant 1/2$ is given by point C, in Figure 9.2, respectively points on the sovereignty restriction between C and E, if we let $R^3(k, k^*, \delta, m) = R^3(k, k^*, \delta, 1/2)$. The outside option for lenders determines the sovereign debt steady state only if $e > 1/2$. In this case $R^3(k, k^*, \delta, m) = R^3(k, k^*, \delta, e)$. An increase in e, $1/2 < e < 1$, causes a counterclockwise turn of the sovereignty restriction in Figure 9.2. A larger gain for lenders from letting negotiations break down implies therefore that the sovereign debt steady state is associated with a larger capital stock in the debtor country and a smaller capital stock in the creditor country. The intuition behind this result is simply that a more valuable outside option for lenders increases the effective costs of violating a debt contract and hence works like a decrease in the debtor's sovereignty, i.e. like an increase in δ.

The reader should bear in mind that an increase in e, given $e^* = 0$, implies a reduction of inefficiencies associated with the imposition of economic sanctions. We can then conclude that bargaining to avoid economic sanctions has no real effect on the world economy if sanctions do not cause dead-weight losses. This conclusion is motivated by noting that in this case $e = 1$. Hence the steady state is given by B, respectively points on $R^1(k, k^*, \delta) = 0$ between B and D in Figure 9.2.

VI. Renegotiating Gross and Net Repayment Obligations

So far, the object of renegotiations has been the avoidance of economic sanctions. Under risk of repudiation, violations of debt contracts do actually occur. Therefore negotiations to avoid economic sanctions are actually undertaken. If the world is riskless, however, lenders impose a credit limit such that contract violations are always avoided. Consequently renegotiations never occur.

It would be premature, however, to conclude that renegotiation can only be an equilibrium phenomenon under risk. The reason for this is that a sovereign has, almost by definition, the freedom to initiate renegotiation not only if the repudiation restriction is violated. Rather, a sovereign debtor has the freedom to initiate renegotiation at will.

That such renegotiation actually does take place depends, however, on three conditions. First, lenders must be able to be a party to renegotiations. Given the ability to renegotiate, the second precondition is that debtors can make gains from initiating them. Although the precise outcome will depend on the bargaining power of the parties involved, non-trivial negotiations take place only if lenders also gain from engaging in negotiation. This precondition is fulfilled, for example, if debtors fall behind on their payment obligation and bargain over a partial repayment of the loan in arrears. It is obviously in the interest of debtors to first fall behind in payments before entering negotiations with lenders. For simplicity, we take it therefore that the sovereign stops servicing debt entirely before entering debt renegotiations.[6]

Renegotiating parts of a debt relationship other than those involving the avoidance of economic sanctions leaves a degree of freedom as to what is the object under negotiation. There are two important alternatives, renegotiating gross repayment and renegotiating net repayment of the debtor. In what follows we call bargaining over gross repayment bargaining situation I and bargaining over net repayment bargaining situation II. We first turn to bargaining over gross repayment obligations.

In bargaining situation I the amount of fresh loans is not an object under negotiation. With new loans being exogenous, the size of the cake is $(1 + r^{i*}) \cdot b^*/(1 + n)$.

The parties have available as their outside options an outright repudiation of debt and the declaration of default which is associated with economic sanctions. Throughout we take it that the outside option for lenders, e, is too small to constitute a credible threat. In other words, we restrict our analysis to the case where lenders reap only a minor gain from imposing economic sanctions.

The value of the outside option for the debtor country, e^*, is given by the costs saved under repudiation. Hence in a steady state

$$e^* \cdot \frac{b^*}{1+n} \cdot (1 + r^{i*}) = \frac{b^*}{1+n} \cdot (1 + r^{i*}) - [\delta \cdot f^*(k^*) + b^*]$$

from which we obtain the steady-state value of the debtor country's outside option

$$e^* = 1 - \frac{\delta \cdot f^*(k^*) + b^*}{(1 + r^{i*}) \cdot b^*/(1 + n)} \equiv e_{\mathrm{I}}^* \tag{9.18}$$

To close the bargaining model we set $p = 1$ to represent the presumption that repudiation and the imposition of economic sanctions are always available as an alternative to bargaining.

If e does not constitute a credible threat, the bargaining equilibrium is given either by case (i, i*) or (i, ii*) in (9.13). As for $p = 1$, $L' = 1$, it follows from equation (9.18) that in a bargaining equilibrium

$$m = \begin{Bmatrix} 1/2 \\ \dfrac{\delta \cdot f^*(k^*) + b^*}{(1 + r^{i*}) \cdot b^*/(1 + n)} \end{Bmatrix} \equiv m_{\mathrm{I}} \qquad \text{if} \qquad e_{\mathrm{I}}^* \begin{Bmatrix} \leq \\ > \end{Bmatrix} 1/2 \tag{9.19}$$

Two properties of the equilibrium partition (9.19) are noteworthy. First, if the debtor country's option is credible, it follows from case (i, ii*) in (9.13) that $m < 1/2$.

Second, from equation (9.18) $e^* < 1$ even if $\delta = 0$. In this case $e^* > 1/2$ if $r^{i*} > n$. As under bank-financing $r^{i*} = r^s$ and inequality (6.2) holds, it follows that $e^* > 1/2$ in a reputational equilibrium. Bargaining over gross repayment implies therefore that the debtor country's threats of repudiating debt altogether is credible if economic sanctions are impossible. The equilibrium partition in the case $\delta = 0$ therefore gives lenders less than an equal share of the gross repayment obligations of the debtor country.

We now turn to bargaining over net repayment obligations. In the bargaining situation II fresh loans are part of the negotiation package. The size of the steady-state cake is given by $(r^{i*} - n) \cdot b^*/(1 + n)$. To make the problem meaningful we take it that this size is positive. Hence, from the analysis in Chapter 5 and Chapter 6 we exclude the possibility that the steady state under bond-financing is inefficient.

Outside options are the same as under bargaining over gross repayment. As before, we take it that e is too small to constitute a credible threat. The outside option of the debtor country is again given by the costs saved under repudiation. However, under bargaining over the net repayment this requires

$$e^* \cdot \frac{b^*}{1+n} \cdot (r^{i*} - n) = \frac{b^*}{1+n} \cdot (r^{i*} - n) - \delta \cdot f^*(k^*)$$

or

$$e^* = 1 - \frac{\delta \cdot f^*(k^*)}{(r^{i*} - n) \cdot b^*/(1+n)} \equiv e^*_{\text{II}} \tag{9.20}$$

Furthermore, $p = 1$. Again, cases (i, i*) and (i, ii*) in the equilibrium partition (9.13) are relevant. As $L' = 1$ we obtain from (9.13) and (9.20)

$$m = \begin{Bmatrix} 1/2 \\ \dfrac{\delta \cdot f^*(k^*)}{(r^{i*} - n) \cdot b^*/(1+n)} \end{Bmatrix} \equiv m_{\text{II}} \quad \text{if} \quad e^* \begin{Bmatrix} \leqslant \\ > \end{Bmatrix} 1/2 \tag{9.21}$$

As in the case where fresh loans are not part of negotiations, $m < 1/2$ if the debtor country's outside option is a credible threat. However, contrary to that case, if $\delta = 0$, $e^* = 1$ and $m = 0$. This result is not surprising in the light of the analysis in Chapters 5 and 6. If economic sanctions are impossible, a steady state involves a pure roll-over or else it involves net transfers out of the creditor country. In other words, the size of the cake is zero if $\delta = 0$.

Let us next compare the two equilibrium partitions in (9.19) and (9.21). What is of particular interest is which negotiation party prefers which object under renegotiations. The first idea, perhaps, is that lenders would like to include the provision of new loans in the package under negotiation as this supposedly improves the bargaining power of lenders compared to the case when new loans are off the table. However, we must be careful with this conclusion as bargaining power also depends on the credibility of the debtor's outside option, which in turn depends on the size of the cake. As this size is not independent of the negotiation package we cannot be sure about this conclusion beforehand.

To analyse this problem formally let index I(II) denote variables associated with negotiations over gross (net) repayment. Then upon using equations (9.18) and (9.20) it follows that

$$e_{\mathrm{I}}^{*}\begin{Bmatrix}\geqslant\\ \leqslant\end{Bmatrix}e_{\mathrm{II}}^{*}$$

if

$$(r^{i*}-n)\cdot b^{*}/(1+n)\begin{Bmatrix}\leqslant\\ \geqslant\end{Bmatrix}\delta\cdot f^{*}(k^{*}) \tag{9.22}$$

Hence the value of the debtor country's outside option in case I is larger (smaller) if under 'take-it-or-leave-it' the debtor country would honour (repudiate) debt. Alternatively, from (9.20) and (9.22)

$$e_{\mathrm{I}}^{*}\begin{Bmatrix}\geqslant\\ \leqslant\end{Bmatrix}e_{\mathrm{II}}^{*}\Leftrightarrow e_{\mathrm{II}}^{*}\begin{Bmatrix}\leqslant\\ \geqslant\end{Bmatrix}0 \tag{9.23}$$

Bargaining over gross repayment provides the debtor country with a larger value of the outside option if the value of the outside option under net repayment negotiations is negative.

From the equilibrium partitions (9.19) and (9.21) e^{*} influences the bargaining outcome only if $e^{*}>1/2$. From (9.23) three cases are therefore possible:

$$\left.\begin{array}{lll}\text{Case a: } e_{\mathrm{I}}^{*}, e_{\mathrm{II}}^{*}\leqslant 1/2 & \Leftrightarrow & m_{\mathrm{I}}=m_{\mathrm{II}}=1/2\\ \text{Case b: } e_{\mathrm{I}}^{*}\leqslant 1/2<e_{\mathrm{II}}^{*} & \Leftrightarrow & m_{\mathrm{I}}=1/2>m_{\mathrm{II}}\\ \text{Case c: } 1/2<e_{\mathrm{I}}^{*}, e_{\mathrm{II}}^{*} & \Leftrightarrow & 1/2>m_{\mathrm{I}}, m_{\mathrm{II}}\end{array}\right\} \tag{9.24}$$

Although (9.24) already provides an insight into relative bargaining power under the negotiation alternatives in terms of equilibrium shares, what really matters to the parties is the effective net transfer, z, agreed upon in negotiations. The effective net transfer under both negotiation alternatives is given by

$$z_{\mathrm{I}}=m\cdot(1+r^{i*})\cdot b^{*}/(1+n)-b^{*} \tag{9.25}$$

and

$$z_{\mathrm{II}}=m\cdot(r^{i*}-n)\cdot b^{*}/(1+n) \tag{9.26}$$

Inserting the equilibrium partition (9.19), respectively into (9.21), (9.25), and (9.26) we obtain for the cases in (9.24)

$$\left.\begin{array}{l} \text{Case a: } z_{\mathrm{I}} < z_{\mathrm{II}} \\[2ex] \text{Case b: } z_{\mathrm{I}} \left\{\begin{array}{c} \geqslant \\ \leqslant \end{array}\right\} z_{\mathrm{II}} \\[2ex] \text{Case c: } z_{\mathrm{I}} > z_{\mathrm{II}}. \end{array}\right\} \tag{9.27}$$

The relative bargaining power in the two bargaining situations is therefore indeterminate.

To interpret the results in (9.27) note that in bargaining situation I any agreement involves a fresh loan of that same size as if the debtor country had fully honoured its debt obligations in the first place. On the contrary, under net payment renegotiations the sovereign cannot avoid when trying to bargain over a reduction in repayment obligations that the creditors also bargain over a reduction in fresh loans. This increases the bargaining power of lenders which in turn implies $z_{\mathrm{I}} < z_{\mathrm{II}}$ if the debtor country's outside option is an incredible threat (Case a).

A conceded reduction in fresh loans, however, makes an agreement for the debtor country less attractive in bargaining situation II, compared to situation I. Consequently, for some parameter constellations (Case b) the sovereign's outside option is credible in bargaining situation II whereas it is incredible in bargaining situation I. This worsens the bargaining power of lenders. Therefore, in Case b two bargaining power effects work against one another. Net transfers in situation I can therefore be larger or smaller than in situation II.

The result in Case c is due to the fact that in this case, in both bargaining situations, the sovereign's outside option is credible and consequently lenders must offer at least e^*. As from (9.23) $e_{\mathrm{I}}^* < e_{\mathrm{II}}^*$ if the outside option is credible, lenders receive a larger net transfer if gross payments are the object under negotiation.

In conclusion we can say that in general neither lenders not the debtor country can be expected always to prefer one or other negotiation situation. Rather, preferences with respect to the object under negotiation will depend on the precise situation at hand. However, a result which holds throughout, except if incidentally $z_{\mathrm{I}} = z_{\mathrm{II}}$ in Case b, is that the parties are neither indifferent with respect to the object under negotiation nor do they unanimously prefer the same object. Rather, in general the parties will disagree as to what *should* be under negotiation. This poses the question as to what the object under negotiation *is*, a question which we take up next.

VII. Renegotiation and the Bond- Bank-credit Dichotomy

The ability to initiate debt renegotiations and the relative bargaining power therein must be expected to be sensitive to the form of financing.

The ability to bargain must be expected to depend, amongst other things, on the costs individual lenders have in joining negotiations relative to the stake they have in the case at hand. As a debtor country is likely to be unable to bargain with individual lenders, in particular, if there is a large number of them, these costs of individual lenders in effect relate to joining groups which represent their interests.

With the necessity of acting collectively, however, another obstacle arises for lenders who enter negotiations jointly. Lenders must be jointly able to prohibit individual free-riding. Free-riding in debt renegotiations occurs if an individual lender participates in gains from an agreement without bearing part of the associated costs. To give an example, if individual debt contracts are strategically connected, an agreement may have to involve all loans being treated equally. An individual lender may then be able to reap some repayment without participating in the collective provision of new loans necessary to reach the agreement.

Free-riding can be expected to pose a problem if the group of lenders is large, non-homogeneous and difficult to monitor. On the contrary, mechanisms of collective enforcement and arm-twisting can perhaps prevent free-riding if the group of lenders is small and easy to monitor.

Under bond-financing the supply side of international loans consists of a large number of individual lenders. Compared to bond-financing, bank credit-financing is characterized by a larger concentration on the supply side of international debt. Furthermore, banks engaged in international lending have a stake in international debt relations which is larger than a representative bondholder's stake.

For these reasons banks must be expected to be much better able than bondholders to participate in debt renegotiations. In the extreme, under bond-financing the costs of bargaining to lenders are prohibitive or free-riding is so excessive that debt renegotiations are impossible. It is therefore of particular interest to investigate the special case where renegotiation is feasible under bank-credit financing whereas under bond-financing it is not.

If bond-financing prevents renegotiation, bond holders will restrict loans so that the sovereignty restriction (3.11) is fulfilled. Hence from condition (9.22) the interesting case is $e_{\mathrm{I}}^* \geqslant e_{\mathrm{II}}^*$ which from (9.23) requires $e_{\mathrm{I}}^*, e_{\mathrm{II}}^* \leqslant 0$. Therefore from the equilibrium partition in (9.24) $m_{\mathrm{I}} = m_{\mathrm{II}} = 1/2$. From this we immediately derive interesting results.

Given any situation under which bond-financed debt is sustainable without repudiation, under a complete substitution of bond-financing by bank-credit financing, banks prefer the inclusion of fresh loans in the package under negotiation. In turn, the debtor country wants to exclude fresh loans from debt renegotiations and only wants to bargain over repayment obligations.

What perhaps is of even more interest is that we have identified situations in which, *ceteris paribus*, the sovereign wants to fully honour debt if it is bond-financed whereas it is in the interest of the debtor country to violate contracts under bank credit-financing.[7] This makes it obvious as clearly as possible that it need not be in the interest of lenders to be able to enter into negotiations with a sovereign. The point is that the ability to negotiate has a non-negative value to lenders only in cases in which it is an option for them. However, if lenders *are* able to negotiate they are *not* able to avoid entering into debt renegotiations with a sovereign. Hence renegotiation is not an option banks can credibly promise to forsake.

The presumption that bondholders are unable to renegotiate debt is at best an approximation to real world observations. The empirical evidence rather suggests that the preconditions for contract violations and the initiation of renegotiation are different under bond- and bank-credit-financing.[8] It is therefore worthwhile to investigate the consequences of different forms of debt-financing if bondholders cannot avoid becoming a party to debt renegotiation. To distinguish as much as possible the analysis here from the analysis above, let us suppose now that banks and bondholders are identical in terms of their ability to enter negotiations.

Nevertheless an important distinction between the forms of financing remains. From the analysis in Chapter 5 we know that in the long run bond holders regularly leave the market for international loans and are replaced by new lenders. Banks, by contrast, stay in the market for much longer. In the long run it is therefore reasonable to suppose that on average a bondholder, already having a stake in a sovereign debt relationship, will find it much more difficult to make the provision of new loans be part of the package under negotiation. The two-period-lived household in the overlapping generations model illustrates this vividly. On the contrary, banks are into a debt relationship now and in the future and are therefore also able to bargain over the provision of new loans. Furthermore, if banks have no interest in renegotiating new loans, the debtor country has. Given the banks's ability to renegotiate new loans, the sovereign can force banks into such negotiations.

We bring this difference between bank-credit and bond-financing to the fore by supposing now that under bond-financing the exclusive object of debt renegotiations is the gross repayment obligation (bargaining situation

I) whereas under financial intermediation it is the net repayment obligation (bargaining situation II). In the last two sections of this chapter we address the implications of these presumptions for general equilibrium.

VIII. Renegotiation and Bond-financing in General Equilibrium

In Section III we discussed the consequences of bargaining over the avoidance of economic sanctions for the general equilibrium steady state. In Section VI we concluded that renegotiations can in fact be an equilibrium phenomenon if the object of bargaining is gross or net repayment obligations. In this section and the following we therefore introduce such repayment renegotiations into the general equilibrium steady-state analysis.

In doing this we go beyond the view that debt renegotiations *can* be an equilibrium phenomenon. As we investigate the implications of bargaining for the steady state we entertain the view that debt renegotiations *are* a long-run phenomenon. Hence, incidences in international debt relations which, perhaps, are second to none in buttressing the popular view that international debt relations are in a 'crisis' are seen here instead as phenomena which are permanent.[9]

An implication of debt renegotiations under bond-financing is that households in the creditor country must rationally anticipate concessions, made in the endeavour to entice the sovereign to service debt. This implies that the portfolio equilibrium condition (5.3) does not hold any longer. Instead, if $m \leqslant 1$, bondholders will require a surcharge $r^i \geqslant r$ on the interest rate on the international component in their portfolios. Precisely, portfolio equilibrium requires

$$(1 + r) = m_{\mathrm{I}} \cdot (1 + r^i) \qquad (9.28)$$

Following the dichotomy developed in Section VII we take it that under bond-financing, parties bargain over the debtor country's gross repayment obligation. Hence $m = m_{\mathrm{I}}$.

The portfolio equilibrium condition (9.28) requires that bonds must bear a nominal interest rate

$$r^i = \frac{1}{m_{\mathrm{I}}} - 1 + \frac{r}{m_{\mathrm{I}}} \qquad (9.29)$$

so that bondholders can obtain an effective interest rate on bonds equal to r.

It is not necessary to elaborate further on the fact that the world credit market clearing condition must be based on the effective interest rate on international debt, r. Therefore debt renegotiations have no impact on the credit market clearing conditions $H^3(k, k^*) = 0$ in equation (5.4).[10]

Let us next turn to the sovereignty restriction under debt renegotiation. It is necessary to distinguish between the two regimes in the equilibrium partition (9.19).

If the sovereign's outside option to repudiate debt is an incredible threat, $m_{\mathrm{I}} = 1/2$. From (9.29) the nominal interest rate on bonds is then given by

$$r^i = 2 \cdot (1 + r) - 1 \ \forall \, b^* \tag{9.30}$$

Put differently, the credit market equilibrium condition is independent of the size of the loan, b^* as long as $e_{\mathrm{I}}^* \leqslant 1/2$. The loan is therefore increased until credit demand vanishes or else until repudiation becomes a credible threat in negotiations, that is $e_{\mathrm{I}}^* > 1/2$.

For $e_{\mathrm{I}}^* > 1/2$ it follows from the equilibrium partition (9.19), the credit market equilibrium condition (9.28), and $r^i \equiv r^{i*}$ that

$$(1 + r) = \frac{\delta \cdot f^*(k^*) + b^*}{(1 + r^{i*}) \cdot b^*/(1 + n)} \cdot (1 + r^{i*})$$

from which one obtains, after collecting terms,

$$\frac{b^*}{1 + n} = \frac{\delta \cdot f^*(k^*)}{r - n} \tag{9.31}$$

The portfolio equilibrium condition is now independent of the nominal interest rate $r^i = r^{i*}$. Whereas credit markets react to anticipated debt renegotiation solely by setting an appropriate spread over the domestic interest rate if the sovereign cannot credibly threaten to leave the bargaining table, matters are different if the threat is credible. If it is, credit markets sustain an equilibrium solely by setting an appropriate credit limit.

Under bond-financing $b^*/(1 + n) = [\Omega \cdot w/(1 + n)] - k - [v^d/(1 + r)]$ (see, for example, equation (5.4)). Bearing this in mind it immediately follows that the portfolio equilibrium condition (9.31) is nothing but the sovereignty restriction $R^1(k, k^*, \delta) = 0$ in (5.7). The incentive for bondholders to prevent outright repudiation if debt renegotiation is impossible and the incentive to obtain at least a return on foreign assets equal to domestic assets if bargaining over repayment obligations takes place lead therefore to the same restriction on international capital flows.

As debt renegotiation impacts neither on the world credit market clearing condition $H^3(k, k^*) = 0$ nor on the sovereignty restriction $R^1(k, k^*, \delta) = 0$, it follows that the steady state under renegotiation is the same as the steady state without renegotiation. In Figure 9.2(a) the bargaining steady state is therefore at B.[11] Hence the steady state under the 'take-it-or-leave-it' alternative can also be interpreted as a permanent bargaining equilibrium. There are a number of remarks due with respect to this neutrality result.

Whereas the irrelevance of anticipated concessions for the world credit market clearing condition is apparent, neutrality with respect to the sovereignty restriction is more of a surprise. Under anticipated bargaining over gross repayment marginal creditworthiness depends on the lenders' ability to reap a larger repayment for a larger loan size. This ability, however, depends on the bargaining power of lenders. It ends as soon as the sovereign's outside option becomes a credible threat. *When* the outside option becomes a credible threat in turn depends also on the sovereign's bargaining power. In the model at hand, repudiation becomes a credible threat in repayment negotiation under exactly the same conditions under which repudiation becomes a credible threat under the 'take-it-or-leave-it' alternative.

To see this, note that from the equilibrium partition (9.19) the critical value is $e_{\mathrm{I}}^* = 1/2$. Inserting the portfolio equilibrium condition for $e_{\mathrm{I}}^* > 1/2$, equation (9.31), into definition (9.18) we obtain after collecting terms

$$e_{\mathrm{I}}^* = 1 - \frac{1+r}{1+r^{i*}} \tag{9.32}$$

For the critical value $e_{\mathrm{I}}^* = 1/2$, equation (9.30), that is the portfolio equilibrium condition under an incredible outside option, immediately follows from equation (9.32). Hence, if the loan size is increased under a simultaneous equilibrium adjustment of the nominal interest rate, the credit limit is reached exactly when the value of the outside option, e_{I}^* attains its critical value 1/2.

As at the credit limit $e_{\mathrm{I}}^* = 1/2$, it follows from the equilibrium partition (9.19) that $m = 1/2$ along the sovereignty restriction $R^1(k, k^*, \delta) = 0$. Hence, bargaining over the gross repayment obligation between a debtor country and foreign bondholders results in an equal split of the nominal gross repayment obligation.

IX. Renegotiation and Financial Intermediation in General Equilibrium

Following the dichotomy developed in Section VII of this chapter we take it that under bank credit financing the object of debt renegotiation is the net payment obligation of the debtor country. As we know from the analysis in Chapter 6, due to the idiosyncratic nature of a sovereign debt relationship under financial intermediation, banks are prepared to accept a negative spread on financial intermediation only in a constrained equilibrium. The equilibrium condition (9.28) holds therefore under bank credit-financing whenever repudiation is not a credible threat. In an unconstrained situation, there is therefore no difference between bargaining under bond-financing and bargaining under financial intermediation. Therefore financing matters with respect to debt renegotiations only in situations when the sovereignty restriction is a binding constraint. Hence, we presume that bargaining takes place in a constrained steady state such as on $R^1(k, k^*, \delta) = 0$ in points between B and D in Figure 9.2(b).

In a constrained steady state the net repayment obligation is equal to the costs from the imposition of economic sanctions. Therefore the size of the cake under negotiation is $\delta \cdot f^*(k^*)$. As the size of the cake is $\delta \cdot f^*(k^*)$, it follows from the definition of e_{II}^* in (9.20) that $e_{\mathrm{II}}^* = 0$. From the equilibrium partition (9.21) it follows therefore that repudiation is not a credible threat.[12]

If the outside option of banks were also incredible it would follow from the equilibrium partition (9.21) that $m = 1/2$. It is, however, easily verified that permanent negotiations over the reduction of the net repayment obligation cannot be part of a steady state when an agreement involves the repayment of half the payments due.

A steady state depends on the value of banks, v, and hence on the effective net repayment of the sovereign. Effective net repayments, however, depend on the size of the cake, that is on nominal net repayment obligations as specified when the loan was made. Hence, a steady state is simultaneously determined by both nominal and effective net repayment obligations. This is consistent with a single steady-state value of k only if nominal and effective repayment obligations are the same. That is, in a steady state with negotiations over net repayment obligations $m_{\mathrm{II}} = 1$, or else k cannot be a fix-point.

As $e_{\mathrm{II}}^* = 0$, from the equilibrium partition (9.13), $m_{\mathrm{II}} = 1$ is only possible in case (ii, i*). As $p = 1$ and hence from (9.16) $L' = 1$, $m_{\mathrm{II}} = e_{\mathrm{II}}$ in case (ii, i*). Hence, bargaining equilibrium under financial intermediation requires

$$m_{\mathrm{II}} = e_{\mathrm{II}} = 1 \qquad (9.33)^{13}$$

We are left to tackle the question what is the outside option of banks when bargaining over net repayment obligations takes place.

If the gains of lenders from inflicting trade sanctions on the debtor country are as negligible as we continue to presume, the sole potentially credible outside option for banks is bankruptcy.[14] The solvency restriction depends on the effective net repayment obligation z.

The minimal effective net repayment obligation, $\underline{z}$, is given by

$$\underline{z} = (\underline{r}^s - n) \cdot b^* / (1 + n) \qquad (9.34)$$

where $\underline{r}^s$ is to be interpreted as an effective interest rate net of concessions made in renegotiation, given by equation (6.13). Furthermore, $b^*/(1+n)$ is given by the RHS of equation (6.16). Substituting equation (6.13) and the RHS of equation (6.16) into equation (9.34) we obtain, upon taking account of equation (3.13),

$$\underline{z} = (r-n) \cdot \left[\frac{\Omega}{1+n} \cdot w - k - \frac{1}{1+r} \cdot v^d \right] \tag{9.35}$$

The minimal net transfer (9.35) and the size of the cake $\delta \cdot f^*(k^*)$ determine the value of a bank's outside option

$$e_{\text{II}} = \frac{(r-n)\left[\dfrac{\Omega}{1+n} \cdot w - k - \dfrac{1}{1+r} \cdot v^d \right]}{\delta \cdot f^*(k^*)} \tag{9.36}$$

Using (9.33) we obtain from (9.36) the sovereignty restriction (5.7), that is $R^1(k, k^*, \delta) = 0$. A steady state with bargaining over net repayment obligations between a sovereign and foreign banks is therefore located at the intersection of the solvency restriction, $\underline{H}(k, k^*, \underline{r}^s) = 0$, and the sovereignty restriction under the 'take-it-or-leave-it' alternative, $R^1(k, k^*, \delta) = 0$. In Figure 9.2(b) the bargaining steady state is at D.[15] In the steady state banks charge a nominal interest rate $\underline{r}^s(k^1)$. As a smaller effective interest rate, agreed upon in renegotiations, would push banks into bankruptcy they are able to receive $\underline{r}^s(k^1)$ as the effective return on internation loans.

Bargaining hence resolves the problem of multiple equilibria arising under financial intermediation. In Figure 9.2(b), amongst the steady states under 'take-it-or-leave-it' between B and D on $R^1(k, k^*, \delta) = 0$, the steady state under bargaining is that one which features the smallest capital stock in the creditor country, respectively the largest capital stock in the debtor country.

In the steady state banks reap the entire cake under negotiations. Rather than being due to their general bargaining power, this result is due to the fact that in the steady state banks bargain with their backs to the wall.[16] Although the debtor country must make maximal concessions it extracts from the creditor economy all the profits banks make from providing domestic bank services.[17]

The model suggests therefore that debtor sovereignty can be responsible for an instability of international capital markets which goes beyond the instability of loan contracts alone. In a long-run equilibrium the ability of banks to act as financial intermediaries and to provide services to the domestic economy is imperilled. This is a rather extreme result and depends on the assumption that banks have no credible alternative to bankruptcy in leaving the bargaining table without having reached an agreement. Bank regulation, a 'lender of last resort' and taxes can change the bargaining power of banks and modify this result. We shall address these institutional schemes in Chapter 11.

X. Conclusions

To sum up:

(1) We interpreted international debt renegotiation as a long-run equilibrium phenomenon of sovereign debt.

(2) If punishments in the wake of debt repudiation cause dead-weight losses for the world economy, parties to debt contracts have an incentive to negotiate over a rescheduling of debt. If, as a result of such negotiations, lenders forsake some of their claims, then negotiations further tighten the sovereignty restriction and decrease the credit limit borrowers face.

(3) Under risk of repudiation concessions made by lenders increase the probability that debt will not be fully honoured. However, if the negotiated concessions of lenders are not too large, then debt renegotiations decrease the credit costs debtors face compared to a 'take-it-or-leave-it' situation.

(4) Debt renegotiation has an ambiguous effect on the incentive of the debtor country to invest in the containment of economic sanctions. If the lenders' concessions are small enough, then bargaining alleviates the adverse selection problem.

(5) Whether gross or net repayment is the object under negotiation is important. If outside options do not constitute a credible threat, then the net transfer from the debtor country to the creditor country is larger if net transfers are under negotiation compared to gross repayment negotiations. The reverse holds if both lenders and borrowers have a credible outside option available. If only the debtor country has a credible outside option available, then net transfers are indeterminate.

(6) If bondholders cannot be forced into renegotiation, then situations exist in which a debtor country fully services loans under bond-financing, whereas it falls behind on payments due under bank-credit financing. If bondholders are able to be a party to renegotiation, for a number of reasons the object of debt renegotiation is likely to be gross repayment. On the contrary, under bank credit financing net repayment obligations are likely to be the object under negotiation.

(7) Under bond-financing, debt renegotiation has no real effect on the long-term general equilibrium of the world economy.

(8) Under bank credit-financing, debt renegotiation has a real effect on the general equilibrium steady state. In the steady state the debtor country is able to extract from the creditor country the entire value of domestic bank services and banks are on the brink of bankruptcy.

CHAPTER 10

Rescheduling Instruments and Crisis Management

I. Introduction

In the previous chapter we have inquired, in a rather general and abstract form, into efforts to contain the consequences of debt in arrears. With the heavy increase of unserviced debt in the early 1980s such crisis management has gained preeminence in international debt relations. The experience participants in international debt markets made thereby has filled the tool-chest of crisis management with an array of special debt management instruments. In this chapter we shall therefore broaden our analysis of the previous chapter and investigate some import rescheduling instruments.

We begin with a general equilibrium analysis of equity-based forms of financing international capital transfers which have been proposed as an alternative to debt-financed capital transfers. Then we continue with an investigation of indexed debt contracts and of the consequences of indexation for the adverse selection problem. We proceed with an analysis of non-market and market-based rescheduling instruments. Amongst them are involuntary lending and debt forgiveness, debt-equity swaps, securitization and buybacks. The concepts of a debt overhang and the 'debt-relief Laffer curve' are introduced. Debt instruments are compared with one another and crisis management at large is evaluated in light of the view we entertain in this book that sovereign debt is a long-term problem.

II. Direct Investment

A debt management instrument which has drawn considerable publicity is debt-equity swaps. Although a debt-equity swap usually involves a number of transactions in the debtor and creditor country, the central transaction is a substitution of debt by equity.[1] Creditors sell claims from past loans in exchange for shares in the domestic capital stock in the debtor country. Hence a debt-equity swap is a substitution of debt-financing by direct investment financing of international capital. Although the application of debt-equity swaps has been limited, a theoretically interesting question is what the consequences are if such swaps are carried to the limit such that all international capital is financed by direct investment. In this section we shall inquire into this issue in the context of the general equilibrium model. To that end we revoke Assumption 5.2 and Assumption 6.1 respectively and make instead

Assumption 10.1: All foreign capital is equity financed.

Apart from this we maintain all assumptions underlying the general equilibrium model. However, we leave it open whether Assumption 3.2 or Assumption 8.1 holds. It will turn out that under Assumption 10.1 the existence of commitment possibilities is irrelevant for the long-run equilibrium.

The central difference between raising debt abroad and attracting direct investment is that under the latter the interest rate on the foreign component in the portfolio of households in the creditor country is linked to the real interest rate in the debtor country. As we know from the analysis in Chapter 5 and Chapter 6 it is linked to the real interest rate in the creditor country under any form of debt-financing. Formally, under direct investment, equation (5.3) has to be replaced by

$$r^* = r^i \tag{10.1}$$

If households hold shares in the foreign capital stock the return on these shares must be equal to r^*. This in turn implies

$$r^{i*} = r^* \tag{10.2}$$

that is, the cost of attracting foreign capital in the debtor country is equal to the domestic rate of return on real capital. Furthermore, under direct investment

$$r \equiv r^d \equiv r^s \Rightarrow \theta = v^i = 0 \tag{10.3}$$

Under direct investment banks do not operate as financial intermediaries. Hence a comparison between direct investment and debt financing requires that bond-financing is the frame of reference. Therefore, it does not matter whether a real store of wealth in the creditor country exists. Therefore we can assume without loss of generality that banks provide only domestic services. We are now ready to point to some important differences between debt- and equity-financing.[2]

For simplicity we maintain the convention of calling one country the debtor economy and the other country the creditor economy. Furthermore, under direct investment, b^* has to be interpreted as equity held by the creditor country in the debtor country. Accordingly, $-b$ is the direct investment undertaken by a representative household in the creditor country.

Upon using equations (10.1) and (10.2) we obtain from equation (3.42) for the steady state

$$\left.\begin{aligned} i &= \Omega \cdot w - \frac{1+n}{1+r} \cdot v + b \cdot \left[(1-\Omega) \cdot \frac{1+r^*}{1+r} + \Omega\right] \\ i^* &= \Omega^* \cdot w^* + b^* \end{aligned}\right\} \tag{10.4}$$

Comparing equations (10.4) with equations (5.13) it follows that the structure of the investment functions in the two countries is reversed if debt-financing is substituted by equity-financing. The reason for this is that under debt-financing households in the debtor country face different interest rates on different assets in their portfolios, whereas under direct investment it is the households in the creditor country which earn different returns on different assets.

In a constrained steady state $r^* > r$ and therefore investment in the *domestic* capital stock in the creditor country is, *ceteris paribus*, smaller under direct investment than under debt-financing. This is due to the bonus, $r^* - r$, households receive from investing in the foreign capital stock. The associated increase in old-age consumption is in part shifted into consumption when young, financed by a smaller investment in the domestic capital stock.

From the upper investment function in (10.4) it also follows that domestic investment in the creditor country decreases by more than foreign investment, b, if $r^* > r$. Each dollar invested abroad therefore reduces the world capital stock.

Comparing investment in the debtor country in the two cases of financing (the lower equations in (5.13) and (10.4)) it follows that under direct investment an incentive problem with respect to capital supplied from abroad does not exist. Whereas in a constrained debt steady state households in the debtor country use some of the foreign capital for consumption, under direct investment foreign capital is not used for consumption.

Upon using (10.1)–(10.3) in the world capital market clearing condition (3.48) we obtain

$$H^7(k, k^*) \equiv \left[\frac{\frac{\Omega}{1+n} \cdot w - k - \frac{1}{1+r} \cdot v^d}{(1-\Omega) \cdot \left[\frac{1+r^*}{1+r} - 1 \right]} \right] + \left[\frac{\Omega^*}{1+n} \cdot w^* - k^* \right] = 0 \qquad (10.5)$$

To determine the properties of the capital market clearing condition (10.5) in $k = k^*$ space we need to compare it with the corresponding condition (5.4), that is with $H^3(k, k^*) = 0$ in Figure 5.1 or in Figure 5.3.

Given (k, k^*), under direct investment the use of foreign capital in the debtor country is smaller than under bond-financing if $r^* > r$. Economically, the reason for this is that under bond-financing households in the debtor country enjoy a discount, $r^* - r$, on the cost of borrowing, which they have to forsake under direct investment.[3] Likewise, given (k, k^*), the supply of foreign capital in the creditor country is also smaller under direct investment than under debt-financing if $r^* > r$. Although the return on foreign capital is larger under direct investment the supply decreases because savings decrease due to induced extra consumption during old age, associated with a larger return on foreign capital.

It therefore follows that for a given (k, k^*), both the first term in square brackets and the second term in square brackets in equation (10.5) are smaller than the respective terms in equation (5.4). We cannot therefore say *a priori* whether $H^7(k, k^*) = 0$ lies above or below the $H^3(k, k^*) = 0$ locus in $k - k^*$ space.

It should by now be an easy task for the reader to verify that $H^7(k, k^*) = 0$ and $H^3(k, k^*) = 0$ intersect at A and U in Figure 5.3. It is furthermore straightforward that between A and U the two functions cannot intersect, as below the $J(k, k^*) = 0$ function $r^* > r$. Hence between A and U the $H^7(k, k^*) = 0$ function is located either entirely above or entirely below the $H^3(k, k^*)$ locus. These two cases are depicted in Figure 10.1.

To determine the conditions under which either Figure 10.1(a) or 10.1(b) holds it should be noted that a sufficient condition for either case is the relative slope of $H^3(k, k^*) = 0$ and $H^7(k, k^*) = 0$ at U. To be precise, if at U the slope of $H^7(k, k^*) = 0$ is smaller (larger) than the slope of

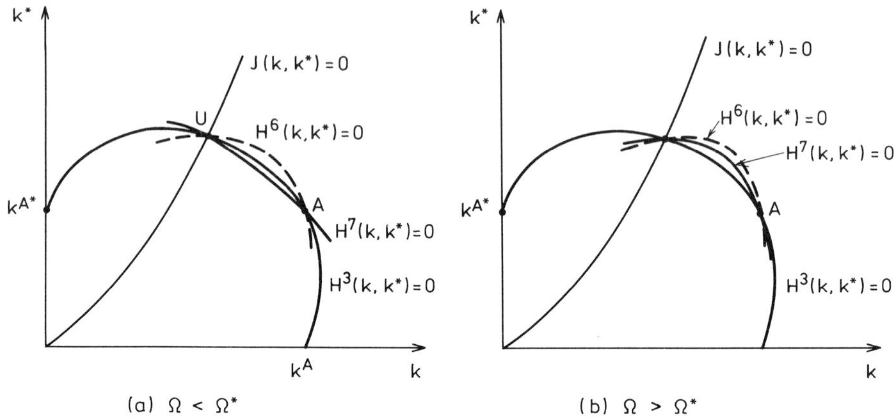

Figure 10.1 *World capital market clearing under direct investment.*

$H^3(k, k^*) = 0$ then $H^7(k, k^*) = 0$ is located below (above) $H^3(k, k^*) = 0$ in between U and A. Let

$$\gamma(k) \equiv \frac{\Omega}{1+n} \cdot w - k - \frac{1}{1+r} \cdot v^d \gtrless 0$$

and

$$\gamma^*(k^*) \equiv \frac{\Omega^*}{1+n} \cdot w^* - k^* \lessgtr 0$$

From the implicit functions (5.4) and (10.5) the slopes are then given by

$$\frac{dk^*}{dk}_{|H^3(\cdot)=0} = -\frac{\gamma'(k) - \gamma^*(k^*) \cdot \dfrac{1-\Omega^*}{1+r^*} \cdot r'(k)}{\gamma^{*\prime}(k^*) + \gamma^*(k^*) \cdot \dfrac{1-\Omega^*}{1+r^*} \cdot r^{*\prime}(k^*)} \tag{10.6}$$

and

$$\frac{dk^*}{dk}_{|H^7(\cdot)=0} = -\frac{\gamma'(k) + \gamma(k) \cdot \dfrac{1-\Omega}{1+r} \cdot r'(k)}{\gamma^{*\prime}(k^*) - \gamma(k) \cdot \dfrac{1-\Omega}{1+r} \cdot r^{*\prime}(k^*)} \tag{10.7}$$

respectively. Upon noting that at U $r = r^*$ and $\gamma(k) = -\gamma^*(k^*)$, and from our general assumption that the slope of $H^3(k, k^*) = 0$ is negative in U it follows from equation (10.6) and (10.7), after some simple but onerous calculations, that

$$\Omega \begin{Bmatrix} \leqslant \\ > \end{Bmatrix} \Omega^* \Rightarrow \frac{dk^*}{dk}_{|H^7(\cdot)=0} \begin{Bmatrix} \leqslant \\ > \end{Bmatrix} \frac{dk^*}{dk}_{|H^3(\cdot)=0} \tag{10.8}$$

at U. Hence $H^7(k, k^*) = 0$ is located below (above) $H^3(k, k^*) = 0$ if the creditor country has a higher (lower) time preference than the debtor country. An economic interpretation of this result is readily given.

If the creditor country has a lower time preference (is more patient) than the debtor country then the improved return on direct investment (compared to holding foreign bonds) in the creditor country and the higher costs of attracting foreign capital in the debtor country will reduce the supply of international capital by less than its demand. Given k, the world capital market clearing condition then requires from Figure 4.1(a) a larger capital stock in the debtor country, k^*, under equity-financing compared to debt-financing. By a similar argument a given capital stock, k, sustains only a smaller capital stock, k^*, if households in the creditor country are more impatient than households in the debtor country.

In the model we entertain, countries can differ in tastes and technology. It is therefore possible that the creditor country is more or less impatient than the debtor country. However, if economies operate under the same technology then necessarily $\Omega > \Omega^*$. The sustainable world capital stock, $k + k^*$, is then larger under equity-financing than under debt-financing.

It is also easily verified that the ability to commit is irrelevant if foreign capital is equity-financed. To see this, return to the world capital market clearing condition under commitment (8.19) and non-commitment (6.6). It follows that the ability to commit does not influence the supply component of the world capital market clearing condition under debt-financing. It is intuitive that the same holds under equity-financing. Furthermore the ability to commit is represented in the demand component in (8.19) by the terms which involve $\zeta^1(k^*, r^{i*})$ and $\zeta^2(k^*, r^{i*})$. From the definition in (8.14), from (8.18) and (6.5) it follows that the demand component in the world capital clearing condition (8.19) is identical to the demand component in (6.6) if $r^* = r^{i*}$. That $H^6(k, k^*, r^s) = 0$ intersects $H^5(k, k^*, r^s) = 0$ on $J(k, k^*) = 0$ at E in Figure 8.1(b) is due to this.

However, under equity financing $r^* = r^{i*}$ holds not only on $J(k, k^*) = 0$. Instead, equation (10.2) also holds below $J(k, k^*) = 0$. Hence the demand component of the world capital market clearing condition under equity-financing must be the same irrespective of the debtor country's ability or inability to commit. The capital market clearing condition $H^7(k, k^*) = 0$ therefore holds for both commitment and non-commitment.

The intuition behind this, once again, is straightforward. As under direct investment $r^* = r^{i*}$, households in the debtor country are always unconstrained on the international capital market (see for example condition (3.34)). That is, decision-makers in the debtor country could attract more capital if they wanted to. The limit on direct investment, $\bar{b}^*$, therefore, is not a binding constraint and therefore decision-makers in the debtor country have no incentive to commit. The ability or inability to commit therefore has no effect on the world economy.

Although the (in)ability to commit has no impact on the world capital market clearing condition under equity-financing, this does not imply that it is unimportant for a comparison of debt- with equity-financing. The (in)ability to commit has an impact on the world capital market clearing condition under debt-financing (see Chapter 8). In particular, from Figure 8.1 we know that this condition shifts northwards in $k - k^*$ space if commitment is feasible. Hence the relative location of the clearing conditions in Figure 10.1 has to be modified if commitment is feasible. The relative location is maintained if $\Omega < \Omega^*$. However, for $\Omega > \Omega^*$ it is possible that $H^7(k, k^*) = 0$ is located above the bond-financing capital market clearing condition under non-commitment, $H^3(k, k^*) = 0$, whereas it lies below the bond market clearing condition under commitment, $H^6(k, k^*) = 0$. This case is depicted in Figure 10.1(b).

As households in the debtor country are always unconstrained under equity-financing the clearing of international capital markets solely by the interest rate $r^* = r$ is prevented only if households in the creditor economy are constrained. We therefore need to address the question of which of the constraints is operative under equity-financing.

Almost by definition, sovereignty is not limited to a debt relationship. Rather, if a country can exercise its sovereignty with respect to one obligation it can in general do so with respect to other obligations as well. Hence what in a debt relationship is the risk of repudiation is in an equity relationship the risk of expropriation.[4] If a host country expropriates foreign investment then it repudiates the title of foreign investors to their investment and to the proceeds from it.

For given sovereignty in principle, both under debt- and equity-financing there are, however, a number of reasons to expect that the degree of sovereignty, δ, varies with the form of financing. With an investor's direct control over the technology employed, he may choose a technology in the host country so that output crucially depends on foreign experts. Similarly, plants can be deliberately designed so that inputs essential for output must be supplied from the mother company abroad. Such precautions increase the costs to the host country from the imposition of economic sanctions. Furthermore the imposition of economic sanctions via the withdrawal of company experts or a cutoff from essential parts is under the direct control of the mother company. The imposition of economic sanctions, therefore, is presumably easier to achieve than under debt-financing where the political process in the creditor countries is likely to play a decisive role in triggering economic sanctions.

On the other hand, under direct investment an embargo of future investment is presumably harder to achieve than a credit embargo. The sovereign can, under direct investment, single out individual investors for expropriation whereas under debt-financing this is prevented by cross-default clauses. Furthermore, a varying ability to choose expropriation-proof technologies across investors need not prevent future investment if some investment were to be expropriated today. Under direct investment the sovereign, therefore, is likely to be able to exploit individual differences between investors, which she perhaps may find it much harder to do under debt-financing.

It is therefore not apparent whether sovereignty poses a greater problem under debt- or under equity-financing. Apart from these institutional and technological differences what perhaps is more interesting for the theorist is whether the form of financing as such influences the sovereignty restriction international capital markets have to observe. To pursue this question let us therefore presume that the sovereignty restriction (3.11) holds identically for both debt- and equity-financing.[5]

Noting that $-b^*/(1+n)$ is given by the first term in square brackets on the LHS of the world capital market clearing condition (10.5) and making use of equation (10.2) we obtain from the sovereignty restriction (3.11)

$$R^4(k, k^*, \delta) \equiv \frac{r^* - n}{1 + (1 - \Omega) \cdot \left[\dfrac{1 + r^*}{1 + r} - 1 \right]} \cdot \left[\frac{\Omega}{1 + n} \cdot w - k - \frac{1}{1 + r} \cdot v^d \right] - \delta \cdot f^*(k^*) = 0 \quad (10.9)$$

The sovereignty restriction under equity-financing (10.9) has to be compared with restriction (5.7) which holds under debt-financing. Given k^* and $k < k^A$ the LHS of equation (10.9) is larger than the LHS of equation (5.7) if

$$r - n < \frac{r^* - n}{1 + (1 - \Omega) \cdot \left[\dfrac{1 + r^*}{1 + r} - 1 \right]}$$

from which we obtain after collecting terms

$$\frac{1 - \Omega}{1 + r} < \frac{1}{r - n} \quad (10.10)$$

if $r^* - r > 0$. As $\Omega > 0$, $n \geqslant 0$, and $r - n > 0$, inequality (10.10) indeed holds. Hence, given k^*, from Figure 4.1(c), for $k^A > k \geqslant \tilde{k}$, k must be smaller in $R^1(k, k^*, \delta) = 0$ than in $R^4(k, k^*, \delta) = 0$. The sovereignty restriction under equity-financing is therefore located to the right of the sovereignty restriction under debt-financing for $r^* > r$. For $k = k^A$ capital supply vanishes and $R^1(k, k^*, \delta) = R^4(k, k^*, \delta)$. Furthermore, $R^1(k, k^*, \delta) = R^4(k, k^*, \delta)$ if $r^* = r$. The sovereignty restriction under debt- and equity-financing therefore intersect on the k-axis and on $J(k, k^*) = 0$. The sovereignty restrictions are depicted in Figure 10.2.

Equity-financing worsens the sovereignty problem in the sense that the sovereign expropriates foreign investors under conditions under which she would not repudiate debt owed to foreign lenders. The reason is that, compared to debt-financing, the costs of attracting foreign investment are higher, as the domestic interest rate, r^*, has to be paid instead of the foreign rate, r, respectively r^s, $r^s \leqslant r$.

For $\delta = 0$, $R^4(k, k^*, \delta) = 0$ requires $k = k^A \; \forall \, k^*$. Hence the sovereignty restriction is vertical as is $R^1(k, k^*, \delta) = 0$ for $\delta = 0$. If economic sanctions are infeasible all forms of financing, bond-, bank credit-, and equity-financing imply the same sovereignty restriction.

The steady state under equity-financing can be determined by bringing together Figure 10.1 and Figure 10.2. The steady state is depicted in Figure 10.3.

The steady state under equity-financing is at C in Figure 10.3. Compared to the steady state under bond-financing, B, under equity-financing the capital stock in the creditor country is larger.[6] However, the capital stock in the debtor country could be smaller or larger. If $\Omega < \Omega^*$ equity-financing lets the steady-state capital stock, k^*, be smaller than under bond-

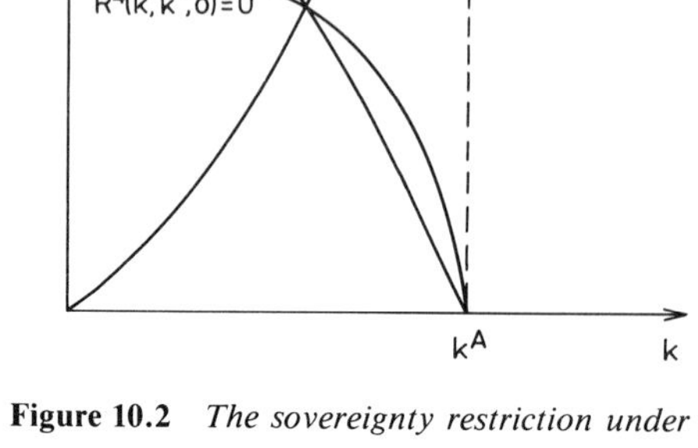

Figure 10.2 *The sovereignty restriction under direct investment.*

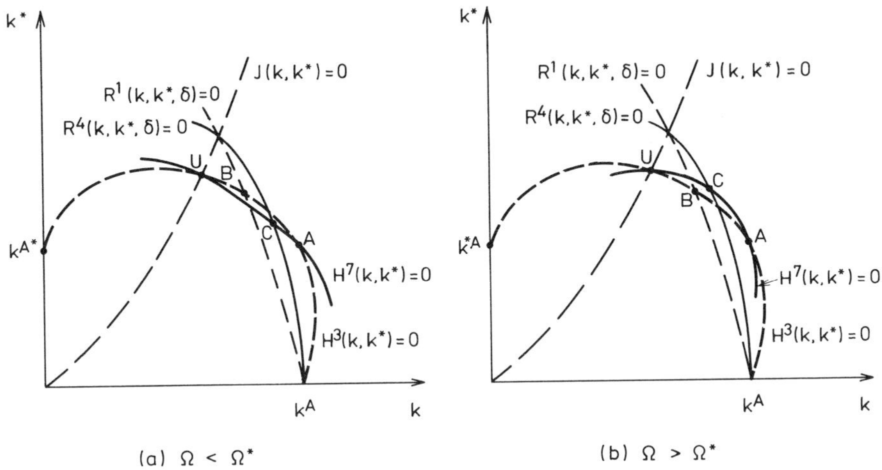

Figure 10.3 *Steady states under direct investment.*

financing.[7] As depicted in Figure 10.3(b), the capital stock in the debtor country can be larger under equity-financing than under bond-financing if $\Omega > \Omega^*$.

Two special cases are not explicitly taken into account in Figure 10.3. If $\delta = 0$ the sovereignty restriction is a vertical line through A. Hence as under bond-financing if $\delta = 0$ the steady state is at A. If economic sanctions cannot be imposed direct foreign investment does not occur in an equilibrium.

The second case not explicitly depicted in Figure 10.3 is when the steady state is unconstrained. As under debt financing, if δ is large enough $R^4(k, k^*, \delta) = 0$ intersects the world capital market clearing condition to the left of U. Then the unconstrained steady state is at U. As U is located on $J(k, k^*) = 0$ it follows from Figure 10.2 that the steady state under equity-financing is unconstrained whenever the debt-financed steady state is unconstrained. Again, if sovereignty is not a binding constraint the particular form of financing is irrelevant for the real economy.

Collecting the results obtained in this section, we can conclude that a substitution of debt- by equity-financing has some advantages as well as disadvantages. Under equity-financing the debtor country has no incentive to divert resources obtained from abroad from investment to consumption. Furthermore, one need not regret the unavailability of institutions enabling the debtor country to commit to a certain behaviour in the future.

On the cost side one has to accept a tighter sovereignty restriction under equity-financing. In the presence of risk this also implies an increased incentive for the debtor country to invest in the containment of economic sanctions. If the debtor country maintains the ability to influence the project and technology choice one must therefore expect adverse selection to pose a greater problem under equity-financing.[8] What perhaps is most worrisome, however, is that although foreign capital is fully invested, direct investment does not guarantee that capital in the debtor country is in the long run at least as large as under debt-financing. In particular, cases can be identified in which a substitution of debt by equity-financing necessarily diminishes the long-run capital stock in the debtor country. An increased reliance on equity-financing in efforts to 'resolve' a debt 'crisis' therefore has to be treated with care.

III. Debt Contract Indexation

Under risk, international loan markets are confronted with contract violations and the need to enter into rescheduling agreements whenever the state of the world allows it to be to the disadvantage of a country to honour debt. In the previous analysis contract violations could occur precisely because the costs of contract violations depended on the state of nature whereas the costs of honouring debt did not. The costs of being faithful to her creditors were independent of the state of nature because we took it that the sovereign was offered an ordinary fixed-rate contract. It is therefore tempting to ask whether the introduction of flexible, or indexed, interest rates could be a contribution to the stability of international debt markets.

Indexing debt contracts allows for a flexibility which is missing under an ordinary fixed-rate contract. From the point of view of lenders a variable interest rate, properly indexed, provides enough leeway when times are bad and allows a feeding of the hogs when they are good. A fixed-rate contract does neither. It is too stringent when times are bad and too lax when they are good.

To formally investigate the merits of flexible loan contracts let us maintain the assumptions underlying the analysis in Chapter 7. In particular we continue to presume that risk has the properties introduced by Assumption 7.1. To extend the scope of our analysis we do, however, take account of the adverse selection problem discussed in Chapter 8. To allow for flexible loan contracts we revoke Assumption 7.3 and make instead

Assumption 10.2: In a loan contract the debt servicing obligation is indexed to the state of nature δ.

There are different forms of indexing to choose from. Perhaps the most natural indexation is to let the interest rate depend on the state of the world, that is $r^{i*} = r^{i*}(\delta)$. Alternatively, or in addition, the amortization or the principal may be indexed. Although in practice the distinction between the two is important, in our one-period loan contracts amortization is identical to the principal due, so that both imply $b^* = b^*(\delta)$.[9] Furthermore, in our model the sovereign is concerned about her net repayment obligation and hence it does not matter whether contracts are indexed to the interest rate or to principal. We therefore let $z = z(\delta)$.[10]

What then is the optimal indexation? The optimization problem of one individual lender is

$$\max_{z(\delta)} \int_{\underline{\delta}}^{\bar{\delta}} g(\delta)\cdot z(\delta)\cdot d^* d\delta$$

$$\text{s.t.} \tag{10.11}$$

$$d^* = \begin{Bmatrix}1\\0\end{Bmatrix} \forall\, z(\delta)\begin{Bmatrix}\leqslant\\>\end{Bmatrix}\delta\cdot f^*(k^*, \Psi)$$

Given an exogenous inflow of new loans into the debtor country a risk-neutral lender chooses that loan contract which maximizes the expected net payment obligation of the debtor subject to the sovereignty restriction. Note that the costs of violating contracts also depends on the technology parameter, Ψ, under the control of the sovereign. We therefore let the lender be aware of the adverse selection problem when choosing an optimal indexation. The optimal contract, $\tilde{\tilde{z}}(\delta)$, has the property

$$\tilde{\tilde{z}}(\delta) = \delta\cdot f^*(k^*, \bar{\Psi}) \tag{10.12}$$

An optimal flexible contract requires lenders to fully exploit the sovereign's willingness to pay in each state of nature. A second aspect of the optimal contract is that lenders calculate the sovereign's willingness to pay on the basis of efficient projects and technologies, $\bar{\Psi}$. In other words, lenders take it that the sovereign has no incentive to invest in the containment of economic sanctions if she is offered the optimal contract $\tilde{\tilde{z}}(\delta)$.

To see that $\tilde{\tilde{z}}(\delta)$ is indeed optimal, note that a contract $z(\delta)$ which implies $d^* = 0$ in at least some states of the world δ, $\delta > 0$, cannot be optimal. Because for a sufficient reduction of the repayment obligation in these states, the sovereign would set $d^* = 1$ and the lender would receive at least some payment.

Hence an optimal contract requires $d^* = 1\ \forall\,\delta$. Consequently, $\Phi(z(\delta)) = 1$, that is the sovereign honours debt in all states of nature.

If an optimal contract is always honoured, then economic sanctions need never be incurred. Hence the critical state of nature, $\tilde{\delta}(z, k^*, \Psi)$, is given by $\underline{\delta}$. For $\tilde{\delta}(z, k^*, \Psi) = \underline{\delta}$, the second term on the LHS in the condition for the sovereign's optimal choice of Ψ in (7.13) vanishes, and condition (7.13) holds as an inequality. It is therefore indeed optimal for the sovereign to set $\Psi = \bar{\Psi}$.

If for some δ, $z(\delta) < \delta \cdot f^*(k^*, \bar{\Psi})$, the lender could increase the expected payment received from the sovereign and therefore the optimal loan contract, $\bar{\bar{z}}(\delta)$, indeed satisfies condition (10.12).

Credit market equilibrium requires that the contract $\bar{\bar{z}}(\delta)$ provides an expected return to a lender equal to the return on a risk-free loan. Therefore the original loan size agreed upon in the contract $\bar{\bar{z}}(\delta)$ is given by

$$b^* = \frac{1}{1+r} \cdot \int_{\underline{\delta}}^{\bar{\delta}} g(\delta) \cdot \delta \cdot f^*(k^*, \bar{\Psi})\, d\delta \qquad (10.13)$$

For a smaller loan size the optimal contract $\bar{\bar{z}}(\delta)$ implies an expected return in excess of the risk-free rate r. Hence competition amongst lenders increases the loan size until (10.13) is fulfilled. For a larger loan size the risk-free rate cannot be obtained from the contract $\bar{\bar{z}}(\delta)$. There are several interesting aspects to the flexible loan contract, characterized by equations (10.12) and (10.13).

Indexing is in the interest of lenders. It allows lenders to skim off the cream in good states of the world. Furthermore it allows risk-averse lenders to completely protect themselves against the risk of repudiation.

Optimal indexation can solve the problem of adverse selection. A contract flexible enough to avoid contract violations in each state of nature poses no incentive for a sovereign to choose an inefficient project or technology.

It is noteworthy that a *fixed* contract which is so lax as to imply $\tilde{\delta} \leqslant \underline{\delta}$ also prevents the occurrence of an adverse selection problem. The most stringent, yet sufficiently flexible, contract therefore solves the adverse selection problem as well as the least stringent, fixed contract.

The optimal indexed contract maximizes the loan supply sustainable in a credit market equilibrium because $\bar{\bar{z}}(\delta)$ maximizes the expected repayment for any loan size. Indexation therefore helps to mitigate the sovereignty problem in improving the creditworthiness of the debtor country.

We have obtained a number of results advocating an increased reliance on flexible loan contracts. In particular the optimal contract has been a particularly simple one. One should, however, be careful when generalizing this. We have presumed single-period loan contracts; allowing for multiple-period contracts, in particular if the stochastic process is not i.i.d., substantially complicates the properties of an optimal contract.

There is another problem associated with indexation which remains to be addressed. In our model we indexed loan contracts to δ, that is to an exogenous variable. This, however, need not necessarily be the case. Contracts could as well be indexed to variables endogenous to the debtor country.

Exogenous variables to which contracts could be indexed to are, for example, the prices of raw materials the debtor country obtains for the export of natural resources on a competitive world market. Endogenous variables could for example be GNP, the export volume or its value. The question arises whether loan contracts should be indexed to variables which are exogenous or endogenous to the debtor country.

It is perhaps tempting to argue that the advantage of indexing contracts to endogenous variables is that this takes better account of the country's ability to service debt. Linking repayment obligations to changes in the debtor country's foreign currency account may be viewed as a point in case. The ability to pay, however, is irrelevant if sovereignty is the binding constraint.

More importantly, indexing contracts to endogenous variables can cause a moral hazard problem. For example, the debtor country can reduce debt service payments by discouraging exports if repayment obligations are indexed to the export earnings of the country.

It has been therefore advocated that loan contracts should be indexed by lenders to exogenous variables (Krugman, 1988). The validity of this recommendation, however, can be sustained in general only if information is symmetric. If information is asymmetric indexing contracts to endogenous variables can be in the interest of lenders (Froot *et al.*, 1989). The reason is that the debtor's actions to manipulate an endogenous variable in order to limit repayment obligations can reveal information to lenders which is valuable to them.

Whether contracts should be indexed to endogenous or exogenous variables therefore remains an open question, one which at best is to be answered case by case.

IV. Non-market-based Rescheduling Instruments

Some rescheduling instruments can be applied on an individual basis in a one-to-one market-based transaction between a debtor and a lender. In this section we shall be concerned, however, with rescheduling instruments which require some coordination within the group of lenders. As markets fail to implement those transactions which require collective actions we call them non-market-based rescheduling instruments to distinguish them from market-based instruments. Non-market-based rescheduling instruments are involuntary lending or financing and collective debt forgiveness. We shall address them in turn.

If rescheduling is on the table one method of granting a debtor country some leeway is to infuse additional loans into the country. With these loans repayment due can be (partially) financed. Formally, in our model, if the sovereignty restriction (2.3) is violated repudiation can be avoided if lenders sufficiently increase the supply of new loans, b^*. Such financing is usually involuntary.

In Chapter 6 we have enquired into the rationale of involuntary lending. In order to protect the value of claims due, banks were willing to finance debt servicing with fresh loans at terms below the costs of refinancing, or so the argument went. Obviously, such transactions below the market rate of interest successfully kept new lenders off the stage. Rescheduling by way of financing was involuntary in the model we entertained. Yet there was no need for collective action.

We carried through with the analysis in Chapter 6, however, under the restrictive and, perhaps, unrealistic Assumption 6.2. Loosening the assumption that debt contracts are strategically independent reveals why financing requires collective actions by banks. Realistically, what matters to a debtor country is its obligations with respect to all lenders. In addition, cross-default clauses link individual loan contracts to one another. All debt is therefore repudiated or all debt is honoured.

This provides an individual bank with an incentive to free-ride on the effort of other banks to reschedule debt by way of financing. Precisely, in order to protect their own claims other banks could be willing to fill the gap an individual bank leaves behind when refusing to participate in the provision of new loans. If this is the case an individual bank can fade out of an unprofitable debt relationship without having to forsake payments it has a title to. Involuntary lending, or financing, can therefore be in the collective interest of banks, yet free-riding is in the interest of an individual bank. Debt rescheduling by way of providing additional loans therefore requires collective action.

An alternative to financing a country's repayment obligation is debt forgiveness. Forgiveness, like financing, reduces the net repayment obligation of a sovereign. In terms of our model, forgiveness would require that the gross repayment obligation, for example in condition (2.3), would be based on a loan size below b^*_{-1} or on an interest rate below r^{i*}. Again, sufficient forgiveness could restore the inequality in the sovereignty restriction (2.3) if it were violated. Like financing, forgiveness requires collective actions by lenders. By the same reasoning as above, individual lenders have an incentive to free-ride on other lenders' readiness to forgive debt.

We have identified some similarities between financing and forgiveness. We next turn to some important differences between the two.

Table 10.1 Gains and costs from financing and forgiveness

	Financing	Forgiveness
Costs in t	$b^* = (1 + r^{i*}) \cdot b^*_{-1} - \delta' f^*(k^*, \Psi)$	$(1 + r^{i*}) \cdot b^*_{-1} - \delta' \cdot f^*(k^*, \Psi)$
Gains in t	$(1 + r^{i*}) \cdot b^*_{-1} - b^* = \delta' \cdot f^*(k^*, \Psi)$	$\delta' \cdot f^*(k^*, \Psi)$
Option Value in t	$\Pi > 0$	$\Pi = 0$

For lenders, financing has the advantage over forgiveness that claims lenders have a title to are never forsaken for good. Rather, under financing, claims are only temporarily given up when times are bad in the hope that at some future time they can be reclaimed. Financing therefore can have a positive option value, whereas forgiveness never has. To investigate this more deeply, let us return to our model under risk introduced by Assumption 7.1.[11]

Suppose in period t a realization of the state of nature $\delta = \delta'$ requires rescheduling because $(1 + r^{i*}) \cdot b^*_{-1} > \delta' \cdot f^*(k^*)$. In Table 10.1 the effects of financing and forgiveness are compared.

Under the application of both rescheduling instruments it is required that the sovereign's net repayment obligation in period t is reduced so as to make her indifferent between honouring and repudiating debt. The immediate costs for lenders in period t therefore are the same whether $(1 + r^{i*}) \cdot b^*_{-1} - \delta' \cdot f^*(k^*, \Psi)$ is forgiven or financed by a new loan, b^*. As the application of both instruments triggers a repayment $\delta' \cdot f^*(k^*, \Psi)$ the immediate gains to lenders are also the same. However, the option value of the repayment obligations forgiven is zero by the definition of forgiveness, whereas under financing it is given by

$$\Pi = \frac{1}{1 + r_1} \cdot \left\{ (1 + r_1^{i*}) \cdot b^* \cdot \Phi(z_1, k_1^*, \Psi_1) + \int_{\underline{\delta}}^{\bar{\delta}(\cdot)} [\delta \cdot f^*(k_1^*, \Psi_1) + \Pi_1(\delta_1')] \cdot g(\delta) d\delta \right\} \quad (10.14)$$

The first term in the bracket on the RHS of equation (10.14) is the expected repayment in period $t + 1$ from financing in t, given the probability that further reschedulings will not be necessary in period $t + 1$. The second term is the expected value in period $t + 1$ of financing in period t if 'bad' states of nature require further rescheduling. This value is the sum of expected repayments in period $t + 1$ triggered by the application of further rescheduling instruments and the option value of the instrument applied.

As at least one of the two terms on the RHS of equation (10.14) is positive it follows that the option value under financing is positive. Given identical immediate costs and gains from both rescheduling instruments the analysis suggests that lenders prefer financing over forgiveness.[12]

Whereas there is an advantage for banks in financing rather than in forgiving, debtors prefer forgiveness as under financing debt is piled upon debt with the prospect that the associated additional repayment obligations might have to be met at some time in the future. There is therefore a conflict of interest between the parties to rescheduling negotiations in as far as the choice amongst different instruments is concerned.

This conflict, however, need not necessarily occur. Under certain circumstances lenders also prefer forgiveness over financing.

To see this let $\tilde{\Pi}$ be the market value of a sovereign's debt outstanding. To fix ideas suppose that $\tilde{\Pi}$ is determined on a secondary market for sovereign debt where unenforceable claims are traded. To keep matters simple, suppose that the current value of debt not serviced is zero.[13] The market value in period t of debt due in period $t+1$ then is

$$\tilde{\Pi} = \Phi[z_1(b^*, r_1^{i*}), k_1^*(b^*), \Psi(z_1(b^*, r_1^{i*}))] \cdot z_1(b^*, r_1^{i*}) \cdot \frac{1}{1+r_1} \qquad (10.15)$$

The market value of sovereign debt as a function of debt outstanding is depicted in Figure 10.4.

To motivate $\tilde{\Pi}(b^*)$ in Figure 10.4, return to Figure 6.3. For low values of debt outstanding, associated with a capital stock k, $k^2 < k < k^A$, the equilibrium is unconstrained, requiring $r_1^{i*} = r_1$. Allowing for risk we know from the credit market equilibrium condition (7.6) that the risk-adjusted interest rate r_1^{i*} provides an expected return equal to r_1. It therefore follows that in an unconstrained equilibrium $\tilde{\Pi} = b^*$ and $\partial\tilde{\Pi}/\partial b^* = 1$, that is the market value is equal to the nominal value of debt. This is represented in Figure 10.4 by the linear section of $\tilde{\Pi}(b^*)$ between the original and A. In our risk-free model A corresponds to B in Figure 6.3.

For debt in excess of b^{*1} lending is involuntary at an interest rate r_1^{i*} below the market rate r_1. A movement from A in the direction of B in

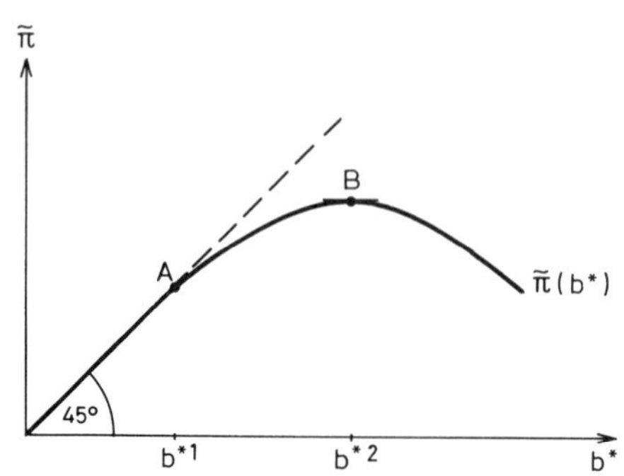

Figure 10.4 *The debt overhang.*

Figure 10.4 corresponds to a movement from B in the direction of D on the $R^1(k, k^*, \delta) = 0$ function in Figure 6.3, as steady states above B involve involuntary lending at increasingly unprofitable terms as debt rises. If risk is present, involuntary lending is characterized by lending at an expected return below the certainty rate r_1. Hence in Figure 10.4 $\tilde{\Pi} < b^*$ for $b^* > b^{*^1}$.

To see that $\Pi(b^*)$ has a negative slope for a large enough debt outstanding take the derivative of $\tilde{\Pi}$ with respect to b^* in equation (10.15). This entails, after collecting terms,

$$\frac{\partial\tilde{\Pi}}{\partial b^*} = \frac{1}{1+r_1} \cdot \left\{ \Phi(\cdot) \cdot \frac{\partial z_1}{\partial b^*} + z_1(\cdot) \cdot \frac{\partial \Phi}{\partial z_1} \cdot \frac{\partial z_1}{\partial b^*} + z_1(\cdot) \cdot \left[\frac{\partial \Phi}{\partial k^*} \cdot \frac{\partial k^*}{\partial b^*} + \frac{\partial \Phi}{\partial \Psi} \cdot \frac{\partial \Psi}{\partial b^*} \right] \right\} \tag{10.16}$$

The first term on the RHS of (10.16) is the volume effect of a larger debt. It is positive. The second term is the risk effect. It is negative, as the probability that debt is honoured decreases if debt is larger.

The third term on the RHS of equation (10.16) is the total incentive effect of varying the debt size. It is itself composed of two effects. The first takes account of the fact that investment in the debtor country varies with the loan size. We know from the lower equation in (3.42) that under certainty and non-commitment investment increases as b^* is increased. Furthermore, from the condition for the optimal investment under risk and commitment possibilities, equation (8.26), a larger debt, *ceteris paribus*, increases the positive terms (iii) and (iv). Hence a larger loan size also increases investment under risk and the ability to commit. The first of the two incentive effects therefore is positive. The second incentive effect takes account of adverse selection. We know from condition (7.18) that for a larger debt the sovereign chooses lower quality projects. The adverse selection effect in equation (10.16) is therefore negative. Hence the total incentive effect can be positive or negative.

We conclude that $\partial\tilde{\Pi}/\partial b^*$ can in general be positive, zero, or negative. For a small z_1 and hence a small b^*, however, $\partial\tilde{\Pi}/\partial b^* > 0$. On the other hand for a very large z_1 and hence a large b^* and k_1^*, marginal productivity of capital is very small. Hence for large enough b^*, the investment effect disappears and the total incentive effect becomes negative. Therefore for large enough b^* the negative risk and incentive effects outweigh the positive volume effect. $\tilde{\Pi}(b^*)$ therefore declines for $b^* > b^{*^2}$ in Figure 10.4.

The rationale by which debt forgiveness can be in the interest of lenders is now obvious. If debt is so large that $\tilde{\Pi}(b^*)$ is declining, a marginal forgiveness increases the value of debt for lenders. Economically, lower debt gives an overall positive incentive to invest, efficiency-adjusted, in the debtor country. This raises output of the country and hence the repayment lenders obtain for a given probability of repayment.[14] Furthermore, forgiveness reduces the risk of debt outstanding.

The function $\tilde{\Pi}(b^*)$ has been dubbed the 'debt-relief Laffer curve'. Forgiveness can be in the interest of lenders only if the debtor country is located on the declining, 'wrong' side of the debt-relief Laffer curve. Burdened with a debt overhang, $b^* > b^{*^2}$, the overall situation in the debtor country improves and the value of debt increases if some debt is forgiven.

In determining whether forgiveness is in their interest, lenders compare the advantage of forgiveness with the advantage of financing under which the option value is preserved. Hence only if the option value is small compared to the increase in $\tilde{\Pi}$ due to forgiveness, will lenders agree to forgive debt. If the country is located on the increasing part of the debt-relief Laffer curve it is never optimal for lenders to forgive debt.

As a last remark in this section the reader should be aware that forgiveness faces the same incentive problem as debt contract indexation, discussed in Section III. Forgiveness requires lenders to discriminate between countries which have a debt overhang and those which do not. Hence a country has an incentive to *be* on the wrong side of the debt-relief Laffer curve. Furthermore countries which did not give in to the temptations causing adverse selection are punished *ex post* as they do not qualify for forgiveness. To insulate debtor countries against the incentive effects forgiveness creates, forgiveness ought to be made contingent on variables which are exogenous to the country.[15]

V. Market-based Rescheduling Instruments

Market-based debt relief instruments take advantage of secondary markets for sovereign debt.[16] The purpose of market-based instruments is to reduce debt outstanding by exploiting the discount on sovereign debt on secondary markets. Contrary to forgiveness, market-based instruments do not require collective actions of lenders. Amongst the most important market-based debt rescheduling instruments are buybacks, securitization or exit bonds, and debt-equity swaps.

A buyback is a cash repurchase of existing old debt on the secondary market by a debtor country. It is financed either by the country's own foreign currency reserves or by foreign aid. It transpires that financing is the crux of buybacks. It depends on the creditor country's generosity or the debtor country's ability or readiness to give up foreign currency. Securitization (exit bonds) and debt-equity swaps are buybacks where financing of buybacks is an essential part of the program.

Under securitization buybacks are financed by the emission of new debt (exit bonds).[17] The financing of buybacks under a debt-equity swap scheme is a bit more complicated. An investor buys debt owed by a country at a discount on the secondary market. The investor exchanges these foreign currency obligations of the debtor country against the country's domestic currency to finance foreign direct investment. It should be noted that debt-equity swaps neither permit additional direct investment nor do they provide additional opportunities for the country to retire debt outstanding. Debtor countries, if anything, restrict the outflow of foreign currencies. Foreign investors therefore are always able to obtain the local currencies needed for direct investment. Furthermore, the country can retire the same amount of debt with a given amount of foreign currency obtained from foreign direct investment whether the foreign investor participates in a debt-equity swap or not.

The similarities between market-based schemes and collective forgiveness are, however, not restricted to the common reduction in debt outstanding. Just as with collective forgiveness, all market-based debt reduction schemes require that the debtor country is on the wrong side of the debt-relief Laffer curve. To see this return to equation (10.15) and Figure 10.4.

For $b^* > b^{*^1}$ the market value of debt is below the nominal value. More precisely the discount on total sovereign debt outstanding is $b^* - \tilde{\Pi}(b^*) > 0$. Hence for $b^* > b^{*^1}$, $\tilde{\Pi}(b^*)/b^* < 1$, that is, the market price of purchasing 1 dollar of sovereign debt is less than a dollar. A debtor country therefore can take advantage of secondary markets and retire debt at a discount.

There are, however, important caveats with buybacks (and hence with other forms of market based rescheduling schemes). First, there is an incentive problem as the 'worst' debtor enjoys the largest discount on retiring debt. Second, and perhaps more importantly, the value per dollar of the remaining debt outstanding may decrease as the buyback runs down the resources of the country and hence can negatively affect the probability that the remaining debt will be honoured.[18] If this is the case it immediately follows that buybacks can only be in the collective interest of lenders if the debtor country has a debt overhang. It is easily seen that other market-based debt relief instruments require the same.

Under securitization the debtor country issues exit bonds at the market price $\bar{\Pi}$ per dollar issued. Apparently securitization can help to retire debt only if $\bar{\Pi} > \tilde{\Pi}(b^*)/b^*$. The market price of new debt can, however, only exceed the price of existing debt if new debt is made senior to existing debt.[19] If exit bonds are made senior, once again the value problem is pending as existing debt may decrease in value. Again, a necessary condition for securitization being in the collective interest of lenders is that the debtor country is on the wrong side of the debt-relief Laffer curve.

Let ω be the price of the debtor country's equity. Then, again, in a debt-equity swap the country can retire debt only if $\omega > \tilde{\Pi}(b^*)/b^*$. That is, if a debt-equity swap is to be of any help in retiring debt, equity must be made senior to debt.[20] With this seniority requirement, the value problem for the remaining debt makes it necessary that the country has a debt overhang.

We can therefore conclude that the preconditions for market-based debt relief instruments to function are the same as for collective debt forgiveness. One is therefore bound to deny that market-based instruments possess important advantages over simple forgiveness.

VI. Crisis Management and Long-term Debt

In this chapter we have browsed in the tool-chest of debt managers. In doing so, perhaps with the exception of Sections II and III, we took a vacation from the idea we entertain in the rest of this book.

In this book we view sovereign debt from a long-term perspective. Problems associated with debtor sovereignty accordingly are seen as long-term problems. Contrary to this view, debt crisis management, almost by definition, takes up a different, short-term view of the issue. With repudiation pending today, debt managers are called upon to produce a quick solution to save the day. The problems of tomorrow are the problems of the next day. 'Muddling through' has become the name for such activities.

Apart from the obvious caveats of a 'muddling through' approach there is, however, one aspect to it which perhaps warrants further investigation. Explicitly or implicitly, debt crisis management takes up the view that the status quo, a 'crisis', is a disequilibrium situation on an unstable path. This justifies some intervention to put it on a stable path, leading to an equilibrium which in some sense is 'nicer' than the crisis.

It is not intended to criticize this view by claiming that international debt is actually in long-run equilibrium. Rather the analysis in the previous chapters suggests that the long-run debt equilibrium has some properties which are in no way any 'nicer' than the 'crises' which debt managers try to overcome. In the debt steady state, debtor countries are constrained on the international credit markets. Debtor countries are unable to maintain a net inflow of resources, they may even have to accept a permanent outflow of resources. The banking system faces losses from its international debt engagement and, in addition, banks make further concessions in perpetual debt renegotiations that cost them dear. Furthermore, the world economy is battered by an entire array of incentive problems accruing in the debtor country.

The gist of the analysis in these other chapters therefore is that the international debt problem needs to be tackled by improving upon the long-run equilibrium rather than manging 'crisis' after 'crisis'.

VII. Conclusions

Let us sum up:

(1) Equity-financing of international capital transfers can increase or decrease the world capital stock sustainable in a steady state, compared to debt-financing. If the creditor country has a higher (lower) time preference than the debtor country then the sustainable world capital stock is smaller (larger) under equity-financing than under debt-financing if commitment is impossible.

(2) Equity-financing resolves a number of incentive problems. The debtor country has no incentive to divert foreign capital from investment to consumption. Furthermore the inability to commit poses no problem.

(3) Equity-financing worsens the sovereignty problem compared to debt-financing in the sense of further constraining admissible capital stocks in the debtor and creditor economies.

(4) Under equity-financing the steady-state capital stock in the creditor country is larger than under debt-financing. It can be larger or smaller in the debtor country.

(5) An appropriate indexation of debt contracts can resolve the adverse selection problem and maximize the loan size the debtor country can obtain. Indexation, however, can also create an incentive problem.

(6) Financing and forgiveness require collective action by lenders. From the point of view of lenders, financing has the advantage over forgiveness that the option value of debt is preserved. Lenders agree to forgiveness only if the debtor country is on the wrong side of the debt-relief Laffer curve.

(7) Market-based debt relief schemes, just like forgiveness, involve a reduction of debt outstanding. Like forgiveness, they require that the debtor country is on the wrong side of the debt-relief Laffer curve.

CHAPTER **11**

Institutions and the Regulation of Sovereign Debt

I. Introduction

In the previous analysis the role of institutions in international debt relations has been rather limited. The debtor country government was the sole body to intervene on international debt markets. In this chapter we shall therefore extend the analysis by incorporating into the model of sovereign debt a number of institutions and regulatory interventions in the market for sovereign debt.

If the banking system exhibits opportunism, bank regulation may be attributed an increased importance. We therefore investigate the implications of bank regulation and the existence of a lender of last resort for debt renegotiation and the long-term debt equilibrium.

Besides bank regulation, authorities in the creditor countries can intervene on debt markets with a number of fiscal policy instruments. We therefore introduce taxes and subsidies into the model. This is to analyse the effects of taxing financial intermediation, the socialization of losses from foreign lending and tax-financed debt-relief schemes.

The role in sovereign debt markets is, however, not limited to domestic authorities acting domestically. Neither is it limited to authoritative actions. Nor need such institutions have to act at all in order to exert an impact on the economy. Institutions can have an intricate impact on the world economy when debtor countries and lenders enter into debt re-negotiation. We therefore analyse the role of a variety of institutions in the debt bargaining process.

II. Bank Regulation and Fiscal Policy in General Equilibrium

In this section we set the formal preconditions for the analysis of bank regulation, taxes on financial intermediation, the socialization of losses and tax-financed debt-relief schemes.

Bank regulation is an intervention on international debt markets by an institution with authoritative power over banks. Regulatory authorities can act in several ways. Banks can be forbidden to engage in certain activities, or activities permissible in principle may be limited in volume. Although regulation of this kind is to be observed in reality, what is more important for our problem at hand is the regulation of the accounting practices of banks.

We have seen in Chapter 6 that rational banks in an unregulated market have an incentive to lend below the costs of refinancing in order to protect the value of existing claims. Long-term losses are thus incurred for the sake of short-term profits. The rationale for banks behind this strategy is that for as long as the costs of postponing necessary write-downs are moderate, banks can exploit the market discounting of the future while protecting current claims at face value.

For a regulatory authority concerned about opportunism it is therefore tempting to intervene in the market by forcing banks into an instantaneous write-down of non-performing loans. We shall therefore investigate the consequences of regulatory write-down requirements.[1] To that end we make

Assumption 11.1: Bank regulation requires banks to write down immediately non-performing loans outstanding, in proportion to the (positive) difference between the face value and the market value of the loans.

Of course, when analysing bank regulation we take it that Assumption 6.1 holds. Let σ be the constant proportionality factor. Under bank-financing $r^{i*} = r^s$. Under certainty the steady-state market value of bank loans that mature in the following period is given by

$$\tilde{\Pi} = \frac{b^*}{1+n} \cdot \frac{1+r^s}{1+r} \tag{11.1}$$

If banks exhibit opportunism $r^s < r$ so that $\tilde{\Pi} < b^*/(1+n)$. Given a face value of the loan, $b^*/(1+n)$, the proportional write-down requirement then implies additional profits to a bank per period, $\tilde{\theta}$, equal to

$$\tilde{\theta} = \sigma \cdot \frac{b^*}{1+n} \cdot \left[1 - \frac{1+r^s}{1+r}\right]$$

Upon using $-b = b^*$ and the steady-state value of the period profit from financial intermediation (3.14), this implies

$$\tilde{\theta} = \frac{\sigma}{1+r} \cdot \theta \tag{11.2}$$

As from definition (3.14) $\theta < 0$ under involuntary lending, the proportional write-down requirement causes costs for banks in each period proportional to the losses per period from involuntary lending. Let us now turn to fiscal policy.

In a general equilibrium model taxes and subsidies are paid and simultaneously received by different groups in the economy. As in the overlapping generations model there are only two groups of individuals in a country, fiscal policy is a redistribution between generations. In our model, banks are owned by the old generation. The old finance consumption by the liquidation of their possessions in the banking sector. In as far as taxes reduce and subsidies increase the value of banks, taxes are a redistribution from old to young and subsidies are a redistribution from young to old in the creditor economy. We therefore make

Assumption 11.2: Fiscal policy induces a transfer between banks and the young generation in the creditor country.

Formally, let τ be the transfer per member of the young generation in the creditor country to the banking system induced by fiscal policy. Then consumption when young is given by

$$c^j = w - \tau + \lambda \cdot f(k) + \theta + \tilde{\theta} + b - (1+n) \cdot k_1 - v \tag{11.3}$$

and consumption when old is now

$$c^o = (1+n) \cdot [(1+r_1) \cdot k_1 + (v_1 + \tau_1)] + (1+r_1^i) \cdot (-b) \tag{11.4}$$

Furthermore, instantaneous capital market equilibrium requires

$$v - \lambda \cdot f(k) - \theta - \tilde{\theta} = \frac{1+n}{1+r_1} \cdot (v_1 + \tau_1) \tag{11.5}$$

The role of bank regulation and fiscal policy can be seen from equations (11.3)–(11.5). A fiscal policy-induced transfer to banks increases the value of a bank when sold (equation (11.5)) and hence old-age consumption of bank owners. If banks benefit from fiscal policy, youth consumption declines for two reasons. First, from the financing requirement of fiscal policy, τ, and second, as the young generation has to pay a higher price for banks, v.

If bank regulation reduces the value of banks, then old-age consumption decreases. The effect of bank regulation on youth consumption is ambiguous in equation (11.3) because write-down requirements not only reduce the purchasing price of banks but also the dividend the new owners of banks receive.

Noting that each bank receives a steady-state transfer per period from fiscal policy, $(1 + n) \cdot \tau$, and taking account of the write-down requirement (11.2) the fundamental of a representative bank is given by

$$v = \frac{1+r}{r-n} \cdot \left[\lambda \cdot f(k) + \left(1 + \frac{\sigma}{1+r}\right) \cdot \theta\right] + \frac{1+n}{r-n} \cdot \tau \tag{11.6}$$

Comparing equation (11.6) with the fundamental (3.18) it follows that bank regulation decreases the value of banks and subsidies increase the value of banks.

Following the procedure of Section IV in Chapter 3 it is easily verified that for equations (11.2)–(11.6) in a household optimum under bank credit-financing

$$c^j = (1 - \Omega) \cdot (w - \tau) \tag{11.7}$$

$$s = \Omega \cdot (w - \tau) + \lambda \cdot f(k) + \left(1 + \frac{\sigma}{1+r}\right) \cdot \theta \tag{11.8}$$

and

$$\frac{-b}{1+n} = \frac{\dfrac{\Omega}{1+n} \cdot w - k - \dfrac{1}{1+r} \cdot v^d - \left(\dfrac{\Omega}{1+n} + \dfrac{1}{r-n}\right) \cdot \tau}{\dfrac{r^s - n}{r-n} - \dfrac{\sigma}{1+r} \cdot \dfrac{r - r^s}{r-n}} \tag{11.9}$$

We are now ready to analyse various aspects of bank regulation and fiscal policy. We begin with an analysis of write-down requirements.

III. Write-down Requirements

In this section we let $\tau = 0$. As write-down requirements may be seen as an instrument to tackle the problem of involuntary lending it is interesting to see how this affects banks' opportunism. Under write-down requirements a bank is prepared to accept losses from international lending if

$$\frac{-b}{1+n}\cdot(1+r^s)+\frac{1+n}{1+r}\cdot v^i+\tilde{\theta}\geqslant 0 \tag{11.10}$$

where from the fundamentals (11.6) and (3.13)

$$v^i=\frac{1+r}{r-n}\cdot\left(1+\frac{\sigma}{1+r}\cdot\theta\right) \tag{11.11}$$

From condition (11.10) and the value of international operations (11.11) it follows from a comparison with the corresponding condition (6.1) that bank regulation affects the condition for opportunism as it increases the future losses from a continuation of the debt relationship by $\sigma\cdot\theta/(r-n)$ and decreases the dividend payment to current owners by $\tilde{\theta}=\sigma\cdot\theta/(1+r)$ (see equation (11.2)). Making use of equations (11.2), (11.11), and the steady-state value of definition (3.14) we obtain from the condition for opportunism (11.10)

$$r^s\geqslant\frac{(1+r)^2\cdot n+\sigma\cdot r\cdot(1+n)}{(1+r)^2+\sigma\cdot(1+n)}\equiv \underline{\underline{r}}^s(\sigma) \tag{11.12}$$

The properties of $\underline{\underline{r}}^s(\sigma)$ are depicted in Figure 11.1.

For $\sigma=0$ condition (11.12) is identical to the condition for opportunism (6.2) under unregulated banking. From the definition of $\underline{\underline{r}}(\sigma)$ it is easily verified that $\underline{\underline{r}}^s(\sigma)$ is increasing in σ. As $r^d=r$, the maximal negative spread in absolute terms, $r-\underline{\underline{r}}^s(\sigma)$, which banks are prepared to accept therefore decreases if σ is increased. In this sense write-down requirements therefore lessen the opportunism of banks.

It is noteworthy, however, that the enforcement of a complete write-

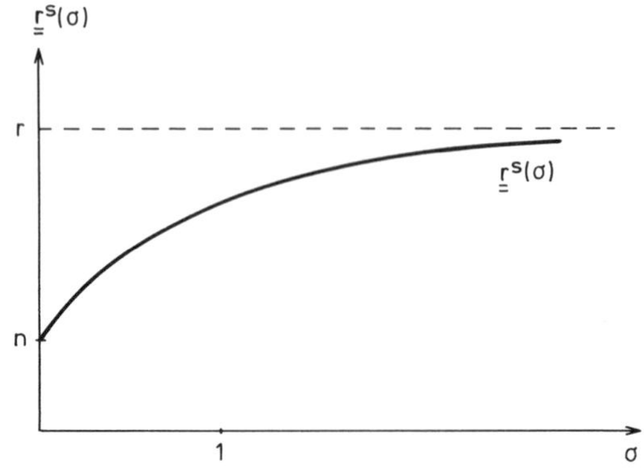

Figure 11.1 *Rational opportunism and the role of write-down requirements.*

down of the face value of non-performing loans to their market value does not suffice to prevent opportunism. A write-down to the market value would require $\sigma = 1$. For $\sigma = 1$

$$\underline{\underline{r}}^s(\sigma) = \frac{(1+r)^2 \cdot n + r \cdot (1+n)}{(1+r)^2 + (1+n)} < r$$

as $n < r$ in an economy with a real store of wealth. Write-down requirements can only prevent opportunism if $\sigma \to \infty$, as from the definition of $\underline{\underline{r}}^s(\sigma)$ in (11.12)

$$\lim_{\sigma \to \infty} \underline{\underline{r}}^s(\sigma) = r$$

For $\sigma > 1$ bank regulation enforces a write-down below the market value of loans outstanding. $\sigma > 1$ therefore can be interpreted as punishment of banks for exhibiting opportunism. The model suggests that bank regulation can prevent opportunism of banks by write-down requirement only if these inflict infinite, prohibitive costs on banks.

If, except for an infinite punishment, write-down requirements lessen but do not prevent opportunism it is interesting in particular to enquire into the long-term effects of bank regulation when banks have reached the limit of their opportunistic behaviour. We know from Chapter 6, however, that under unregulated banking, solvency is the bottleneck restriction. This needs to be verified in the case of write-down requirements.

The zero-profit condition requires a zero dividend per period, that is from equation (11.6) $\lambda \cdot f(k) + (1 + \sigma/(1+r)) \cdot \theta = 0$. For $\tau = 0$ equation (11.8) therefore simplifies to $s = \Omega \cdot w$. Returning to the upper equation in (3.41) and noting that $r_1^i = r_1^d = r_1$, and that $\lambda \cdot f(k) + \theta = 0$ if $v = 0$ under unregulated banking, it follows that savings are unaffected by bank regulation if $v = 0$. As for $v = 0$, wealth, $s/(1+n)$, is either held in the form of domestic capital or international loans we conclude that for given k, international credit supply is unaffected by bank regulation if $v = 0$. It will therefore be clear from a moment's reflection that the zero-profit function $\underline{H}(k, k^*, \underline{r}^s) = 0$ in (6.17) also holds under bank regulation. It would, however, be erroneous to conclude that write-down requirements have no effect on the solvency restriction in $k - k^*$ space. To see this let us determine $\underline{r}^s$.

For $v = 0$, the first term in brackets on the RHS of (6.17) must be equal to the RHS of (11.9), where $\tau = 0$. Setting $r^s = \underline{r}^s$ it follows from this and equation (3.13) that

$$\underline{r}^s(\sigma) = r - \frac{1+r}{1+r+\sigma} \cdot \frac{\lambda \cdot f(k)}{\frac{\Omega}{1+n} \cdot w - k} \tag{11.13}$$

Following the procedure leading to condition (6.15), and taking account of the fact that under bank regulation the willingness to continue an unprofitable debt relationship is given by condition (11.12), it can be verified that

$$\underline{r}^s(\sigma) \geqslant \underline{\underline{r}}^s(\sigma)\ \forall k \leqslant k^A \tag{11.14}$$

given $\sigma \geqslant 0$. Hence solvency indeed remains the bottleneck restriction under bank regulation.

From equation (11.13) $\partial \underline{r}^s(\sigma)/\partial\sigma > 0$ and $\underline{r}^s(\sigma) \to r$ as $\sigma \to \infty$. The minimal interest rate which ensures solvency of banks therefore increases if σ increases. For $\sigma = 0$ equation (11.13) is identical to equation (6.13). Because $\underline{r}^s(\sigma)$ increases if σ increases, the denominator in the second term in brackets in the solvency restriction (6.17) also increases if σ is increased. Given k^*, the second term decreases. Hence the first term must decrease if k^* is held constant. From Figure 4.1(b) it follows that k must increase (decrease) if k is larger (smaller) than $\tilde{\tilde{k}}$.

The solvency restriction therefore shifts upwards in $k - k^*$ space if σ is increased. As $\underline{r}^s(\sigma) \to r$ as $\sigma \to \infty$ it follows from equations (6.17) and (5.5) that $\underline{H}(k, k^*, \underline{r}^s(\sigma)) = 0$ converges to $H^4(k, k^*) = 0$ if $\sigma \to \infty$. The properties of $\underline{H}(k, k^*, \underline{r}^s(\sigma)) = 0$ are depicted in Figure 11.2.

Write-down requirements for non-performing loans increase the world capital stock sustainable with a solvent banking system. The intuition behind this is that bank regulation reduces the maximal discount on the

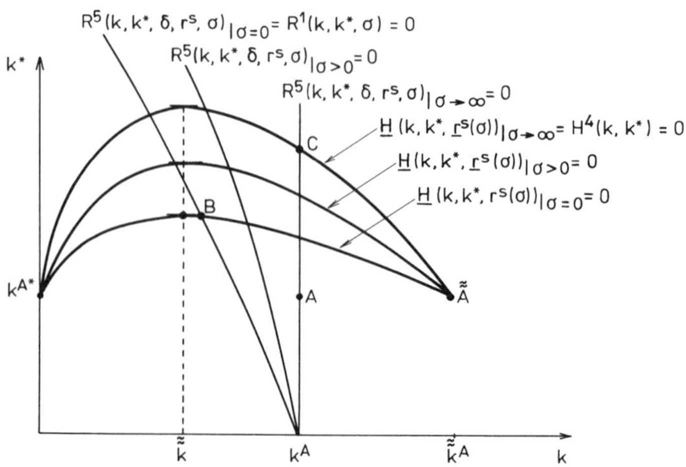

Figure 11.2 *The solvency and sovereignty restrictions and bank regulation.*

costs of borrowing which the debtor country can obtain. Hence the inefficient use of foreign loans for consumption declines.

In order to determine the steady state under bank regulation we need to derive the sovereignty restriction for $\sigma > 0$. Noting that $r^{i*} = r^s$ and $b^* = -b$ it follows from the sovereignty restriction (5.6) and from the credit supply (11.9) that for $\tau = 0$

$$R^5(k, k^*, \delta, r^s, \sigma) \equiv (r - n) \cdot \frac{\frac{\Omega}{1+n} \cdot w - k - \frac{1}{1+r} \cdot v^d}{1 - \frac{\sigma}{1+r} \cdot \frac{r - r^s}{r^s - n}} - \delta \cdot f^*(k^*) = 0 \tag{11.15}$$

It is easy to verify that $R^5(k, k^*, \delta, r^s, \sigma) = 0$ has the properties depicted in Figure 11.2. In particular, an increase in σ implies, *ceteris paribus*, a clockwise turn of $R^5(k, k^*, \delta, r^s, \sigma) = 0$. Furthermore, as $\sigma \to \infty$ the sovereignty restriction converges on the vertical line through A.

The economics behind this is easy to understand if we return to equations (11.6) and (11.9). An increase in σ, *ceteris paribus*, reduces the value of the banking system (equation (11.6)) and hence frees savings for foreign lending (equation (11.9)). The associated increase in debt outstanding raises the net transfer obligations, z, of the debtor country. Hence more severe economic sanctions are required. Bank regulation in the creditor country therefore acts like an increase in the debtor country's sovereignty, that is like a decrease in the gunboat-technology parameter, δ. To sustain the same set of permissible $k - k^*$ combinations the introduction of write-down requirements must therefore be combined with an improvement in the sanctions technology.

Bank steady states are not unique if debt renegotiation does not take place. However, we know from Chapter 9 that under constant debt renegotiations the steady state is given by the unique non-bargaining steady state in which $v = 0$. In terms of Figure 11.2 it is given by the intersection of $R^1(k, k^*, \delta) = 0$ and $\underline{H}(k, k^*, r^s(0)) = 0$ at B under unregulated banking. Apart from uniqueness the bargaining steady state is important in particular as it involves banks being permanently on the brink of bankruptcy, a situation about which bank regulators in particular will be wary. Therefore we investigate here the effect of bank regulation for the bargaining steady state.

Changing σ involves a complication. The sovereignty restriction (11.15) must be based on the steady-state value of $r^s = \underline{r}^s(\sigma)$. In equation (11.5) r^s therefore also varies if σ is changed. The reader will easily verify that for $\partial \underline{r}^s(\sigma)/\partial\sigma > 0$ the isolated effect of an increase in r^s will imply a counterclockwise turn of $R^5(k, k^*, \delta, r^s, \sigma) = 0$ in Figure 11.2. Together with the

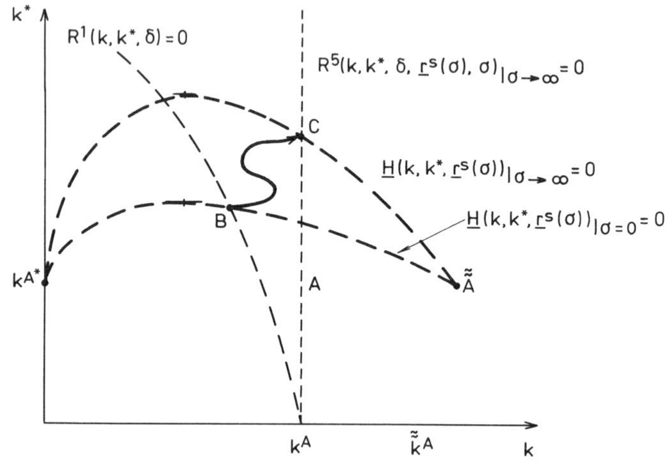

Figure 11.3 *Debt renegotiation and bank regulation in general equilibrium.*

direct effect of an increase in σ, depicted in Figure 11.2, the total effect of an increase in the write-down requirements is ambiguous. It is, however, easy to verify that $R^5(k, k^*, \delta, \underline{r}^s(\sigma), \sigma) = 0$ shifts clockwise for an increase in σ if σ is close to zero or close to infinity. A possible locus of bargaining steady-states for $\sigma \in [0, \infty]$ is depicted in Figure 11.3.

Interestingly, a marginal increase in σ, except for very large σ, need not improve welfare in the creditor country. Although, starting at B, the introduction of write-down requirements improves the domestic component of welfare, x^d, in the creditor country (see equations (4.18) and (4.19)), the international component, z, may initially decrease. For larger σ the domestic component may again decrease. Similarly, the welfare effects in the debtor country of a marginal tightening of bank regulation is ambiguous as the domestic and the international components of welfare work against each other.

IV. Taxing Financial Intermediation

We have seen that write-down requirements neither prevent rational opportunism nor do they prevent banks from going to the limit of their ability in making concessions. An alternative to bank regulation is taxes on banking. Write-down requirements act *like* a transfer from the old generation to the young generation only because the latter obtain a discount on the purchase of bank shares. In the general equilibrium model taxes on banking *are* transfers from old to young.

In order to analyse the effect of taxes on banking let $\sigma = 0$ and set

$$\tau \equiv \zeta \cdot (r^s - r) \cdot \frac{-b}{1+n} \tag{11.16}$$

with $\zeta > 0$, constant. The tax on banking is therefore proportional to the period losses incurred from financial intermediation. From equation (11.6) these taxes are levied before banks change hands and thus constitute a transfer from old to young.

The tax scheme (11.16) should be distinguished from corporate profit taxes. Whereas under corporate profit taxes losses reduce the tax obligation, under the scheme (11.16) it is the losses from financial intermediation which are taxed. The scheme is therefore a tax on rational opportunism.

Following the by now well known procedure we obtain from the tax variant of our model

$$\underline{\underline{H}}(k, k^*, \underline{r}^s(\tau)) \equiv \left[\frac{\frac{\Omega}{1+n} \cdot w - k}{1 - \zeta \cdot (r - \underline{r}^s)(\tau) \cdot \left[\frac{\Omega}{1+n} + \frac{1}{1+r} \right]} \right] + \left[\frac{\frac{\Omega^*}{1+n} \cdot w^* - k^*}{1 + (1 - \Omega^*) \cdot \left[\frac{1 + \underline{r}^s(\tau)}{1 + r^*} \right] - 1} \right] = 0 \tag{11.17}$$

as the solvency restriction. Furthermore, we have

$$R^6(k, k^*, \delta, r^s, \tau) \equiv (r - n) \cdot \frac{\frac{\Omega}{1+n} \cdot w - k - \frac{1}{1+r} \cdot v^d}{1 - \zeta \cdot \frac{r - r^s}{r^s - n} - \zeta \cdot (r - r^s) \cdot \frac{\Omega}{1+n} \cdot \frac{r-n}{r^s - n}} - \delta \cdot f^*(k^*) = 0 \tag{11.18}$$

as the sovereignty restriction.

Necessarily, the zero-profit interest rate $\underline{r}^s(\tau)$ must be larger than $\underline{r}^s$, which is given by equation (6.13), if $\zeta > 0$. Taking this into account it is readily seen that the solvency restriction shifts upwards and the sovereignty restriction turns clockwise in $k - k^*$ space for $\zeta > 0$. This is depicted in Figure 11.4.

Taxing financial intermediation, just like bank regulation, increases the set of $k - k^*$ combinations sustainable under a solvent banking system. Again, the underlying reason is that taxes, like write-down requirements, raise the minimal sustainable interest rate $\underline{r}^s(\tau)$. Furthermore, like bank regulation, taxes on financial intermediation reduce the value of banks and hence free savings for foreign loans. To sustain the same set of $k - k^*$ combinations without repudiation the introduction of taxes on financial intermediation needs to be accompanied by an improvement of the gunboat-technology, that is δ must increase.

V. The Socialization of Losses

Taxes on unprofitable financial intermediation are not observed in reality. On the contrary, unprofitable financial intermediation is subsidized by corporate tax schemes. Because profit taxes are levied on the balance of profits and losses from all activities of firms, the representative taxpayer subsidizes unprofitable financial intermediation as it reduces the effective tax rate on profitable activities.

The investigation into the effects of a socialization of losses from rational opportunism is further motivated by recourse to ideas from political economy. If the international debt situation is seen as a 'crisis' rather than seen to be permanent, pressure on the government to 'temporarily' recruit the taxpayer for a resolution of the 'crisis' may be substantial.

The tax variant of the general equilibrium model accommodates the socialization of losses from financial intermediation if we set $\zeta < 0$ in the tax scheme (11.16). Then $\tau > 0$ under involuntary lending. Banks are now

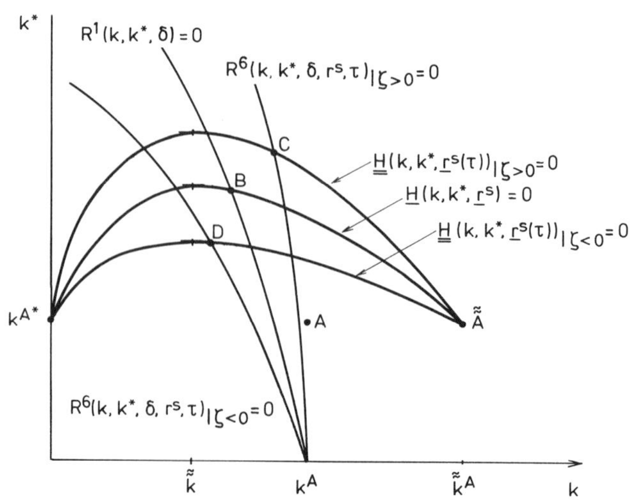

Figure 11.4 *Taxing unprofitable financial intermediation in general equilibrium.*

subsidized by transfers financed by taxes, levied on the income of the young generation.

The implications of socialization are depicted in Figure 11.4. From (11.17) and (11.18) the solvency restriction shifts downwards for $\zeta < 0$, and the sovereignty restriction turns counter-clockwise. Economically, socialization reduces the disposable income of the young in the creditor country. It furthermore raises the value of banks. Both effects diminish the supply of international loans and the world capital stock sustainable under a solvent banking system. As debt outstanding decreases for a given k, the debtor country is now less inclined to repudiate debt. Hence the socialization of losses from financial intermediation loosens the sovereignty restriction.

VI. Tax-financed Debt Relief

In Chapter 10 a number of debt-relief instruments were discussed. All these instruments require concessions to be made by banks. As we have seen, these instruments require their application to be in the collective interest of lenders. Apparently, if debt-relief schemes are tax-financed, preconditions on these schemes are less demanding. Their application does not need to be in the collective interest of lenders. A natural extension of the analysis in Chapter 10 and of the previous section is therefore to enquire into tax-financed debt-relief schemes.

Tax-financed debt relief can be accommodated if we both set $\zeta < 0$ and $\sigma > 0$. The period losses (11.2) now are to be interpreted as the costs or write-downs banks have to bear from the implementation of a debt-relief programme.

Apparently the simultaneous application of write-down requirements and subsidies has an ambiguous effect on the solvency and the sovereignty restriction as both policy instruments individually have opposite effects on each restriction. However, a tax-financed debt-relief scheme requires that the value of banks is unaffected by the programme. This requires from equation (11.6), that

$$\frac{\sigma}{1+r} \cdot \theta + \frac{1+n}{1+r} \cdot \tau = 0 \tag{11.19}$$

so that the value of a bank is given by equation (3.18). Nevertheless, the scheme shows real effects on the creditor economy.

Under condition (11.19) the debt-relief scheme works like a pure subsidy insofar as it reduces the disposable income of the young and hence the supply of international debt. Consequently, the use of international debt in the other country must decrease too. This requires a decline in k^*. Hence the solvency restriction shifts downward as it would under pure subsidization of financial intermediation.[2] As debt outstanding declines for any given k, z declines and consequently the debtor country is less inclined to repudiate debt. The repudiation restriction turns therefore counterclockwise. The qualitative properties of the tax-financed debt-relief scheme are therefore the same as those of pure subsidization of involuntary lending. Insofar as there is nothing sacrosanct about the socialization of debt relief compared to the socialization of plain opportunism.

VII. The Lender of Last Resort

Financial intermediation features a potential instability absent in most other markets. Banks are entwined in a complicated structure of debt contracts, both as creditors and as debtors. Banks are not only a link between the ultimate lenders and the ultimate borrowers, they are also linked to one another via interbank borrowing and lending.

The particular instability arises if, upon the bankruptcy of a bank, depositors and lenders only obtain a fraction of their claims, whereas before the breakdown claims are fully honoured on a first come-first served basis. Whenever news about a bank's solvency or liquidity problem breaks, assets of the bank can therefore be viewed as an exhaustible common property, inducing a run on the bank.[3] Runs not only precipitate the breakdown; they can also make it possible for a bank which would have remained liquid had the run not occurred, to collapse during a run. Expectations of breakdowns thus can be self-fulfilling.[4] Furthermore, runs can snowball through financial markets if banks under a liquidity squeeze try to enforce claims held against other banks.

Several measures can be applied to reduce this instability. Besides deposit insurance the lender of last resort is perhaps the most important. A lender of last resort is an ultimate lender, ready to step in, in order to prevent self-fulfilling runs.[5] The function of a lender of last resort is the following. If depositors expect that the lender of last resort is prepared to provide the liquidity which a bank needs to remain liquid, there is not need to participate in the run. Hence the run does not occur. The mere existence of a lender of last resort can ensure that the phenomenon upon which it is ready to act does not occur.

In this section we investigate the consequences of the existence of a lender of last resort for international debt renegotiations. Such an institution may be seen as particularly important on the international stage if depositors are aware of the unenforceability of the banks' own international claims.[6]

There are several problems arising from the existence of a lender of last resort.[7] Prominent amongst them is moral hazard. If banks believe the lender of last resort will bail them out they will be less cautious in their activities. To contain moral hazard the lender of last resort must randomize its services so that a bank is uncertain whether a lender of last resort will step in to aid it.

We analyse the role of a lender of last resort in the context of the model underlying Section IX in Chapter 9. That is, we take it that banks and the debtor country bargain over the net repayment obligation, z. The size of the cake under negotiation is $\delta \cdot f^*(k^*)$. Furthermore, $e_{\text{II}}^* = 0$ that is, the debtor country has no credible outside option available.

In Section IX of Chapter 9 the sole outside option of a bank which could constitute a credible threat for the debtor country was bankruptcy. This implied that banks received at least the net repayment, $\underline{z}$, given in equation (9.35), and the associated value of the outside option was e_{II}, given in equation (9.36). In fact, we implicitly took it that a lender of last resort bailing out banks did not exist.

If a lender of last resort is known to bail out banks, then bankruptcy clearly cannot constitute a credible threat in debt renegotiations. However, for reasons given above, a lender of last resort is well advised to randomize its strategy. In our model of bargaining this can be represented by setting $p < 1$.[8]

The interpretation of debt renegotiations now is the following. The probability with which the outside option for banks is available, p, is now the probability that the lender of last resort does *not* offer its services. Put differently, $1 - p > 0$ is the probability that due to lender of last resort services, banks do not have available bankruptcy as an outside option in debt renegotiations.[9]

We know from the analysis of Section IX in Chapter 9 that in a bargaining steady state $m = 1$. From the equilibrium partition (9.13), and given $e_{\text{II}}^* = 0$, this implies that case (ii, i*) is relevant. Hence

$$m = (1 - L') \cdot 1/2 + L' \cdot e_{\text{II}} = 1 \tag{11.20}$$

Note that from $p = 1 - e^{-\varkappa \cdot \Delta}$, $p < 1$ requires $\varkappa < \infty$. From the definition of L' in (9.15) $L' < 1$. Hence from (11.20), the existence of a lender of last resort randomizing its activities implies that the value of the banks' bankruptcy option does not exclusively determine the equilibrium partition. To be precise,

$$1 = m < e_{\text{II}} \tag{11.21}$$

This derives from the bargaining equilibrium (9.13) which shows that (11.20) is only relevant if $e_{II} > 1/2$. It follows that banks receive less than their outside option. Intuitively, if the outside option is not available for certain, banks are ready to accept an offer which is worth somewhat less than what the option would entail.

The consequences of (11.21) can be seen from (9.35) and (9.36). Banks receive $z = m \cdot \delta \cdot f^*(k^*) = \delta \cdot f^*(k^*)$. Solvency requires a net transfer $z \geqslant \underline{z}$. As from (11.21) $e_{II} > 1$ it, follows, however, from equation (9.36) that $z < \underline{z}$. Banks cannot maintain solvency. In the absence of a lender of last resort banks would have received $\underline{z}$.

The existence of a lender of last resort providing assistance with some positive probability alone diminishes the bargaining power of banks in debt renegotiations. In our bargaining model the existence of such an institution alone suffices that it will have to get involved. The randomization of lender of last resort strategies therefore does not suffice to prevent the moral hazard of banks in making 'unreasonable' concessions in debt renegotiations. This kind of moral hazard can only be prevented if $p \to 1$, that is if the lender of last resort almost certainly will not get involved.

The strong results obtained depend on the fact that in the absence of a lender of last resort banks are already on the brink of bankruptcy. Under more general conditions concessions leading to bankruptcy need not necessarily emerge. The gist of the result, however, will certainly survive some generalization. Even a remote possibility that institutions, concerned with the stability of the banking system, will be ready to assist banks, changes bargaining power in favour of the debtors. From the lenders' point of view the institution of a lender of last resort should therefore be accompanied by economic policy instruments geared towards an improvement of the bargaining position of banks.

VIII. Institutions of Appeal

The reality of debt renegotiations, undoubtedly more complex than the theoretical bargaining situation we entertain, frequently features actors other than debtor governments and bankers, actors such as the World Bank and the International Monetary Fund. They are drawn by one party or another into debt negotiations and regularly become a party to debt-rescheduling agreements.

Such agreements with third party involvement may involve simply additional loans made by the Fund or the Bank, or an IMF-diet of an economic-policy-change-for-loan deal, or Bank-financed development programmes. All these measures have one thing in common, that is that debtor countries and private banks alone are unable, by themselves, to strike such a deal.

In the context of our bargaining model such an outside involvement can be accommodated by the introduction of an institution of appeal. Formally, outside options, e_{II} and e_{II}^*, now are not determined by the costs of economic sanctions. Rather $(e_{\text{II}}, e_{\text{II}}^*)$ is determined by the specific solution 'imposed' upon the bargaining parties after the Fund or the Bank has become involved. The bargaining rules underlying Figure 9.3 have now to be interpreted so that a party, having declined an offer, can appeal to an outside institution with probability p. If a party appeals to the outside institution bargaining ends as the institution of appeal forces the solution $(e_{\text{II}}, e_{\text{II}}^*)$ upon the parties involved. Without going into the details of the solution, $(e_{\text{II}}, e_{\text{II}}^*)$, which various institutions of appeal have to offer, we are able to derive an important conclusion from the bargaining model.

Intuitively, one is perhaps inclined to expect that the influence of the Bank and the Fund diminishes if they have less resources available to invest in a solution. However, the presence of such institutions of appeal can influence the world economy only if the solutions they offer imply $e_{\text{II}} > 1/2$ or $e_{\text{II}}^* > 1/2$, or both (see the equilibrium partition (9.13)). Hence the influence of the Bank and the Fund is nil rather than small if their resources are below a certain level. A weak Bank is therefore no better than no Bank, and no Fund is no worse than a weak Fund.

We have so far explored some stylized aspects of institutions of appeal in general. In the remainder of this section let us inquire in some greater detail into a hypothetical institution of appeal available to banks.

Suppose banks obtain, upon the termination of an unprofitable debt relationship, a bonus payment, e_{II}, from an institution of appeal. To fix ideas, the institution may be the home government financing the bonus by the tax scheme discussed in Section V. If the bonus is large enough $(e_{\text{II}} > 1/2)$ then the institution has an effect on the bargaining equilibrium. Furthermore, for a large enough bonus payment the incentive of banks to continue an unprofitable debt relationship ends well before their ability. If this is the case, then

$$e_{\text{II}} \cdot \delta \cdot f^*(k^*) > \underline{z} \qquad (11.22)$$

Given $e_{\text{II}}^* \leqslant 1/2$ and $p = 1$, it then follows from the equilibrium partition (9.13) that $m = e_{\text{II}}$. Hence, from (11.22) $z > \underline{z}$, that is, under this institution of appeal, banks do not make concessions that bring them to the brink of bankruptcy. In Figure 6.3 such an institution of appeal would imply that the bargaining steady state would be at F, say, instead of at D.

An institution of appeal which makes the termination of the debt relationship become a credible threat can therefore contribute to a stabilization of financial markets. The attractiveness of such a policy instrument is further raised by the fact that in the steady state such a bonus payment never has to be implemented. Sovereign debtors and banks constantly renegotiate old contracts so that the taxpayer in the creditor country is never called upon. Lastly, the bonus scheme creates no moral hazard problem. This too makes the bonus scheme a more attractive instrument with which to stabilize international financial markets than the lender of last resort.

IX. Outside Intervention

Historically, prolonged debt renegotiations were occasionally brought to an end by outside intervention. Intrusions by military intervention are the classical example.[10] Such gunboat diplomacy has, perhaps fortunately, been the rare exception. To supplement the analysis we shall briefly discuss some implications of gunboat diplomacy for debt renegotiations.

Suppose p represents the probability that an outside institution intervenes in debt negotiations. The bargaining rules underlying Figure 9.3 now have to be interpreted so that after a party has refused an offer, negotiations end with probability p by outside intervention. Contrary to all other bargaining situations in this book, by the very nature of the intervention a party has lost control over the realization of the payoff (e, e^*) once it has turned down an offer. Formally, this corresponds to the case where (e, e^*) is an option for parties with a payoff $e > 1/2$ and $e^* > 1/2$. Intuitively, the occurrence of an outside intervention with probability p and payoff (e, e^*) must have the same implications for the bargaining power of parties as the availability of an outside option (e, e^*) with probability p that will be taken by each party when available.

Hence under outside intervention the bargaining equilibrium is given by case (ii, ii*) in the equilibrium partition (9.13). That is

$$m = (1 - L)\cdot 1/2 + L\cdot [e + 1/2\cdot(1 - e - e^*)] \qquad (11.23)$$

The bargaining equilibrium (11.23) gives some insights into the implications of potential outside intervention.

From the definition of L in (9.14), $L = 1$, if $p = 1$, as $p = 1 - e^{-\varkappa\cdot\Delta} = 1$ for $\varkappa \to \infty$. Hence if outside intervention is certain once the parties do not come to a quick agreement it follows that

$$m = e + 1/2\cdot(1 - e - e^*) \qquad (11.24)$$

The debtor and lenders split the difference between the cake under negotiation and the sum of the values of outside intervention. If outside intervention becomes increasingly unlikely, then the case (i, i*)-partition $m = 1/2$ becomes increasingly important. In the limit $m \to 1/2$ as $p \to 0$.

Under potential outside intervention it is possible that one party reaps a gain from a negotiated agreement which is larger than the size of the cake under negotiation. To see this, suppose $e \simeq 1$, $e^* < 0$, and $p \simeq 1$. This parametric specification may be interpreted as a stylized 19th century gunboat crisis. A debtor country and lenders bargain on the eve of a foreign military intervention in the debtor country. From the proceeds of confiscations in the wake of intervention lenders obtain approximately what they have a title to. Military intervention, however, inflicts dead-weight losses on the debtor country ($e^* < 0$), to be interpreted as the costs from destruction or the loss of national sovereignty. From (11.24) the equilibrium partition of these parametrical values is given by

$$m \simeq 1 - 1/2 \cdot e^* > 1$$

as $e^* < 0$.

Impending gunboat intervention in the debtor country can therefore imply that lenders obtain from debt renegotiations more than they are legitimately entitled to. Intuitively, to avoid the dead-weight losses from military intervention, the debtor country is prepared to 'bribe' lenders to agree to a cooperative settlement of the case. In turn, lenders can blackmail the debtor country.

Bargaining under the threat of military intervention can be viewed as an end point of a string of possible debtor-lender relationships. The other end points are purely reputational situations analyzed in Chapter 5 and Chapter 6. All debtor-lender relationships will, in some sense, be situated between these limits.

X. Conclusions

Let us sum up:

(1) Write-down requirements on non-performing loans imposed by bank regulation do not suffice to prevent rational opportunism of banks, nor do they stabilize financial markets. In particular, bank regulation requiring a complete and instantaneous write-down of loans to the market value achieves neither.

(2) Write-down requirements increase the world capital stock, $k + k^*$, sustainable with a solvent banking system. In that, bank regulation loosens the restrictions international debt is subject to. However, write-down requirements tighten the sovereignty restriction. The effect of bank regulation on the set of sustainable international debt is therefore ambiguous. Taxes on unprofitable financial intermediation have the same effect on the set of sustainable international debt.

(3) Corporate profit taxes are, in effect, subsidies on involuntary lending. Subsidizing unprofitable financial intermediation reduces the world capital stock, sustainable with a solvent banking sector, and loosens the sovereignty restriction.

(4) Tax-financed debt-relief schemes have the same qualitative effect on the set of sustainable international debt as pure subsidies on financial intermediation or corporate profit taxes. The quantitative effects are, however, smaller if tax-financed debt-relief schemes do not affect the value of banks.

(5) The existence of a lender of last resort improves the bargaining power of sovereign debtors. In as far as concessions made by banks in debt renegotiations can destabilize the banking system, lenders of last resort are counterproductive in efforts to stabilize financial markets. A lender of last resort should therefore be accompanied by an institutional improvement of the bargaining power of banks.

(6) Tax-financed bonus payments to banks for the termination of an unprofitable debt relationship can improve the bargaining power of banks and thus stabilize international financial markets.

(7) The World Bank and the International Monetary Fund as institutions of appeal are effective only if they are equipped with sufficient resources to offer in a Bank- or Fund-led settlement. A weak Bank or Fund has no influence at all.

(8) Gunboat diplomacy can worsen the bargaining situation of a debtor country so that it can be blackmailed by lenders. Lenders then obtain in a negotiated settlement more than they have a legal title to.

(9) Bargaining under the threat of military intervention and purely reputational situations can be viewed as natural end points of the string of all possible debtor-lender relationships. It is hoped that the reader, having laboured through this book, has found it a helpful guide to understanding sovereign international debt.

Notes to Chapters

Chapter 2

1. For incentive problems which affect the solvency conditions see e.g. Bulow and Shoven (1978), Jaffee and Russell (1976), and Stiglitz and Weiss (1981).

2. In the prisoners' dilemma game both players can cheat, and the optimal strategy is to do so irrespective of what the other player does.

3. Deterrence equilibria were originally introduced by Friedman (1971). See also, for example, Rubinstein (1979).

4. We shall not use the term 'cooperative' and 'non-cooperative' to distinguish the principles which govern the behaviour of decision-makers in a game. Decision-makers are assumed always to behave egoistically. Rather the terms distinguish the set of opportunities which are open to players to enforce cooperation.

5. A further distinction between implicit contracts relates to the time when the losses, which are to deter cheating, are incurred. In our analysis these losses have to be borne in the long run. Alternatively, an implicit contract could inflict losses in the short run and thus deter the debtor.

6. For an excellent analysis of the rationale behind the Nash equilibrium concept see Johansen (1982).

7. For this rationality axiom see Harsanyi (1977), p. 275, or Luce and Raiffa (1965), p. 107.

8. Empirical observations of this kind of behaviour are vexing to many. Referring to the United Nations, Professor Dasgupta, for example, made the sarcastic comment that '[t]here *is* something unseemly about the sight of mature nations..., taking actions that vitiate the intent of conferences whose inauguration they were a party to in the first place' (Dasgupta, 1982, footnote 21, p. 30). Rather than blaming irrationality one *could* explain such behaviour as emanating from the game at hand.

9. One could also restrict rationality and define a player as a finite automaton (Binmore, 1986). The difference between the finite automaton approach and the 'hazy' proposition criticized at the end of Chapter 1 is that the former makes precise the exact nature of restricted rationality. The formal problems associated with a finite automaton are enormous and its implications are far from being clear.

10. Adler (1987) discusses such a case in the context of long-run consumer-firm relations.

11. Interestingly, legally enforceable contracts can suffer from a caveat related to observability that implicit contracts do not suffer from. A defection from a legally enforceable contract not only needs to be observable, it also must be verifiable before the courts.

12. For a particularly splendid illustration of such endeavours see the satire 'A Tip to our Statesmen' reported in Eichengreen (1988).

13. In Diaz-Alejandro (1984) and Krueger (1987) the observation is made that governments owe the debt while the private sector often owns the resources to meet the obligations entailed by the debt. The government's inability to extract these resources from the private sector is claimed to account for much of the difficulties international debt is plagued with. Far from intending to belittle this problem, it should, however, be noted that it is associated with a country's ability to pay, an issue which is not the subject of our analysis here. Furthermore, viewing it in the spirit of the theory of sovereign debt it is clear that governments, not inclined to service international debt, can create such problems. See also Niehans (1985) for a similar argument relating to a country's balance-of-payments difficulties.

14. For analyses of the history of international debt see, for example, Berg

and Sachs (1988), Eichengreen and Portes (1986), Eichengreen (1988), Jorgensen and Sachs (1988) and Kindleberger (1978).

15. The Guatemalan debt history from 1825 to 1928, reported in Winkler (1933), is a particularly revealing example of the 'short memory' of international credit markets when it comes to implementing credit embargoes. Guatemala, however, is no exception. Sachs (1982a), for example, reports on similar accounts for many other countries.

16. See e.g. Özler (1989) for an econometric analysis of lender monopolization upon repudiation.

17. Having a large stake in a credit relationship does not necessarily twist the arms of bankers in favour of lenience. In Eaton (1986) it is shown that a large stake can entice a bank to engage in a costly punishment of a debtor if a reputation for being a 'hawk' is necessary to preserve the value of the bank.

18. A qualification applies here with respect to the distinction between public and private assets held abroad. The latter may be considerable and there is some empirical evidence of a simultaneity of private foreign investment and public foreign borrowing in a number of indebted countries (Cuddington, 1987). In fact, theoretical considerations suggest a systematic relation between private capital flight and public foreign borrowing (Eaton and Gersovitz, 1989). For the issue at hand, private assets abroad can only be seized if an identity between the owner of assets and the owner of unserviced debt is given and verifiable in the courts of the country where assets are held.

19. Such exceptions are the blockade of Venezuela 1902–3 by naval forces from Great Britain, Germany, and Italy, and occupations of Latin American harbours by the United States. In the case of Mexico defaults on international debt led to the loss of sovereignty in 1861 through the enthronement of Maximilian I by France and Spain. Another example is the British occupation of Egypt from 1881 to 1907.

20. Kaempfer and Lowenberg (1988) also provide an argument why the total costs inflicted on a debtor country need not be large to be an effective deterrent from contract violations. If sanctions are designed to selectively affect certain pressure groups in the target economy they can be an effective threat despite little overall economic impact.

21. Examples of the 'carrot-alone' view are Eaton and Gersovitz (1981), Grossman and Van Huyck (1988), Kletzer (1984), Niehans (1985) and Worrall (1988). The 'stick-also' view is entertained in Cohen and Sachs (1986), Sachs (1982b) and in Sachs and Cohen (1982).

22. Throughout this book, assumptions which are valid for the analysis in all chapters are introduced without accentuation. However, in order to avoid misunderstandings, assumptions which are modified or suspended later on are specially marked.

23. Crawford (1987) has called contracts with immediate punishments 'explicit contracts', alluding to legally enforceable contracts, with respect to which the standard assumption is that legal enforcement is instantaneous.

24. Time is discrete. To simplify notation, the time index, t, of variables is suppressed. Hence, for example, a variable, whose value in period t is x, has the value x_{+j} in period $t + j$. Therefore, r^{i*} denotes the interest rate on international loans which mature in period t.

25. As, under the assumptions made about gunboat-technology, sanctions are restricted to the period in which a contract violation occurs, current costs are identical to the total costs from sanctions. If sanctions also occurred in the future, then the RHS of the sovereignty restriction (2.4) would have to be interpreted as the present value of the additional costs which arise from repudiation today instead of tomorrow.

26. It should be noted that the gunboat-technology is to be interpreted to include the value-function of the sovereign as it is of course necessary for future sanctions to be a deterrent that the sovereign's discount factor for this future period is positive.

27. For a discussion of historical cases of Ponzi-financing see, for example, Kindleberger (1978).

28. Results are stated here and in the conclusions to other chapters without all of the required qualifications and reservations which have appeared in the analysis.

Chapter 3

1. See for example the surveying of Smith (1984) and Frenkel and Mussa (1984).

2. All asterisked variables or parameters refer to the debtor country. All unasterisked variables or parameters refer to the corresponding variables or parameters in the creditor economy.

3. See for example the seminal paper of Barro (1974).

4. See for example Abel (1987), Burbridge (1983), Carmichael (1982), and Sheshinski and Weiss (1981).

5. For arguments leading to this conclusion in a different context see, for example, Sinn (1987).

6. In Berg and Sachs (1988) it is shown that, empirically, outward orientation of a country is a significant predictor of a reduced probability of reschedulings. This suggests that it is the fraction of output which is exported rather than output itself which ought to be the basis for the costs from sanctions in restriction (3.11). However, if exports of a debtor country are proportional to output then this can be accommodated in restriction (3.11).

7. In the present model, for $\delta = 0$, sovereign debt is Ponzi-financed. In particular, although loans from the point of view of single households are fully serviced and hence positively valued, from a macro perspective they are rolled over. Ponzi-financed debt acts therefore in some sense like a 'bubble'. Ponzi-financing and valuing assets at their 'fundamental' may therefore seem to be non-compatible. O'Connell and Zeldes (1988), however, have shown that pricing assets at their 'fundamental' does not exclude the occurrence of Ponzi games in the macro sense.

8. We abstract therefore from domestic financial intermediation. In this model, domestic intermediation could easily be introduced by letting firms finance investment through bank loans instead of, as is assumed, by equity held by private households. In principle, the simultaneity of domestic and international financial intermediation could pose a problem if there is asymmetric information concerning the international exposure of banks. So what we do when abstracting from domestic intermediation is implicitly to have recourse to bank regulation providing complete information to depositors.

9. From footnote 8 it might appear that an alternative formulation to permitting profitable domestic bank services would be to allow for profitable domestic financial intermediation in the creditor country. It will, however, be shown that this is not possible under the assumptions made.

10. Perfect substitutability of all domestic assets also ensures that there could not be a positive spread in domestic financial intermediation (see footnote 9). If this were the case, firms could issue bonds and finance investment under the exclusion of financial intermediaries at the lower refinancing rate of banks.

Chapter 4

1. There is an extensive literature on international aspects of non-sovereign lending. Examples are Fischer and Frenkel (1974), Hamada (1966), Neher (1970), Ruffin (1979) and Siebert (1985), (1989). Non-sovereign debt and international trade in overlapping generations models is discussed, for example, in Dornbusch (1985), and Persson (1985).

2. In Figure 4.2 $J(k, k^*) = 0$ is drawn as a strictly convex function. As a technical point it can be shown that $J(k, k^*) = 0$ is indeed strictly convex if $\alpha < \alpha^*$, linear if $\alpha = \alpha^*$, and strictly concave for $\alpha > \alpha^*$. There is a simple intuition to this. If, for example, $\alpha < \alpha^*$, an increase in k increases output, y, by less than an equal increase in k^* increases y^*. The marginal productivity, r, therefore declines more than r^*. To maintain equality between r and r^*, k^* therefore has to increase by more than k.

3. For a general criterion of efficiency which specializes in condition (3.12) under the assumptions made in the present model, see Abel *et al.* (1989).

4. To derive at the sovereignty restriction (3.11) which involves the same criterion applied to the outflow of goods from a country we needed to make further assumptions as repudiation involves a departure from a steady state.

Chapter 5

1. Bond financing had been the dominant form of international debt financing until up to the world economic crisis in the 1930s (Eichengreen and Portes, 1986). Banks only provided services as issuing houses. Defaults of banks associated with this activity were the rare exception. In Kindleberger (1978), for example, a single case is reported, the default of Barings Bank in 1890 in the wake of the issuance of Argentinian bonds.

2. For $\delta = 1$ the sovereignty restriction is identical to the solvency restric-

tion (2.5). As in the non-sovereignty steady-state, U, solvency is fulfilled, for $\delta \to 1$ the $R^1(k, k^*, \delta) = 0$ function intersects the $H^3(k, k^*) = 0$ function to the left of U.

3. A point which is sometimes raised is that international debt poses a problem *if* loans are not fully invested. The point made here is slightly different and more severe in suggesting that international loans *will* not be fully invested if sovereignty is a binding constraint.

4. The general condition is that the expected discounted value of all future repayments is non-positive.

5. For a dynamic analysis of reputation aquisition see Diamond (1989).

6. In Chapter 10 we shall investigate further reasons why it is in general not in the collective interest of lenders to forgive debt that cannot be expected ever to be paid back. The welfare analysis here is a point in case, for entirely different reasons though. Turning a blind eye to debt that must be perpetually rolled over and returning to financial autarky is not in the collective interest of lenders.

Chapter 6

1. Private bank-financing of international debt became the dominant form of financing LDC debt after World War 2 until net lending came to a halt in the early 1980s. While in the early 1960s the share of private bank credits in total LDC debt outstanding was roughly 3%, it rose to approximately 40% of the 1 trillion US $ of LDC debt outstanding in 1985 (World Bank, 1986). This rise is attributed in part to US bank deregulation in the 1960s and recycling of petro-dollars in the 1970s.

2. In Kyle and Sachs (1984) it is reported that banks have suffered heavy losses from international lending and the banks engaged in this activity sold at a discount.

3. Across creditor countries, US banks suffer an especially high exposure to sovereign debt. Although on average sovereign debt in the portfolios of US banks in the 1980s is moderate, it is highly concentrated on the New York money centre banks, whose Latin America loans alone amounted to over 100% of capital in 1986 (Scott, 1989). Loan-loss reserves and write-offs vary substantially across banks (Hentschel, 1988).

4. See for example Sachs (1986). This threat is aggravated if there exists a risk of bank runs. For a historical account of bank runs see for example again Kindleberger (1978) and, in contrast, Moggridge (1981).

5. For a related point see Hellwig (1977).

6. 'Involuntary lending' here relates to lending which is made solely for the sake of preserving the value of old debt; it does not relate to pathologies of the underlying decision-making process. Coercion by third parties like home governments would fall under such pathological cases of involuntary lending.

7. In fact in our model, as $t \to \infty$, the number of banks and total debt outstanding go to infinity. Debt owed to an individual bank is therefore infinitesimal in the long run compared to total debt and compared to total costs from repudiation.

8. Strategic aspects of inter-bank relations will be taken up in Chapter 10.

9. For an empirical analysis of involuntary lending see for example Nunnenkamp (1989). The implications of opportunism for share prices of banks is consistent with the empirical analysis of Kyle and Sachs (1984) which reports that banks have suffered heavy losses from international lending and that banks engaged in this activity sold at a discount.

10. In Edwards (1984a) it is shown that in 1976–80 many LDCs had to pay interest rates considerably above the London Interbank Offer Rate (LIBOR), suggesting a positive spread in international financial intermediation. However, this surcharge contains risk premia. The underlying risk-free interest rate on sovereign debt therefore could have been below the refinancing rate.

11. Formally, this readily follows from setting $r^s = \underline{r}^s$ in equation (6.6) and then substituting in equations (6.13) and (3.13).

12. The indeterminacy in banking steady states will vanish when we allow for renegotiation between banks and debtor countries in Chapter 9.

13. In Eaton (1986) a bank steady state is derived in which banks make profits on their international activities. If banks fail to punish a debtor upon repudiation they lose their reputation for collecting payments due and hence the value of their international activities disappears. Profits therefore

ensure that threats of economic sanctions are credible, which otherwise would not be. A problem with such reasoning, however, is that a failure to take an action which is optimal, under perfect information does not imply that such optimal action is forsaken in the future.

Chapter 7

1. For a general analysis see Eaton and Gersovitz (1981).

2. Involuntary lending under risk would be characterized by an expected return on sovereign debt below the risk-free rate r. Apparently, this is possible even if $r^{i*} = r^s > r^d = r$ (compare also Footnote 10 in Chapter 6).

3. The analysis follows Kletzer (1984).

4. Here we simply take it that credit demand is decreasing in b^*. In Chapter 8 the role of repudiation risk for the demand for loans is formally analysed.

5. This can be due to the different stakes in international debt, which presumably are low for individual households compared to banks. Together with the presumably better ability of banks to set up creditor clubs which monitor and control debtors this creates a comparative advantage for bank-credit financing.

6. Contrary to what is implied in Footnote 1 in Chapter 6 this suggests that the expansion of bank credit-financing is due at least in part to reasons to be found in the debtor countries.

7. For an early treatment of adverse selection problems in domestic loan markets under bankruptcy risk see Stiglitz and Weiss (1981).

Chapter 8

1. The incentive to commit under debtor sovereignty is analysed for example, in Sachs and Cohen (1982).

2. The commitment-facilitating services of large-scale projects may help explain why heavily indebted countries sometimes seem to have an 'unseemly' predilection for prestigious large projects.

3. The IMF, for example, when getting involved in 'high conditionality' lending requires a debtor country to pursue certain economic policy changes. For private lenders such an IMF involvement may be seen as an indication that the country will stick to a certain type of behaviour in the future. Sachs (1988) has argued, however, that IMF conditionality is barely able to commit debtor countries.

4. That domestic output increases under commitment critically depends on output being a reproduceable good. If a country's output is in exhaustible resources, investment in creditworthiness requires a resource-conserving policy at the expense of current income (Mohr, 1988b). Debtor countries exporting primary goods therefore face a potential conflict between income generation and creditworthiness.

5. Intuitively, under direct investment the dichotomy between commitment and non-commitment is meaningless. In fact, when formally analysing direct investment we will verify that this intuition is indeed correct.

6. The case when a real store of wealth does not exist is isomorphic. It is therefore not discussed here.

7. We take it that under complementarity the second-order optimality conditions are fulfilled.

8. Contrary to Chapter 7, here the decision variable in containing economic sanctions is the level of investment and not the efficiency variable, Ψ, under the control of the government. Nevertheless, lenders face the adverse selection problem discussed in Chapter 7. If both the private sector and the government can invest in the containment of economic sanctions, then under Assumption 8.2 the private sector fully internalizes the costs of economic sanctions. It is therefore optimal for the government to choose efficient projects and technologies. Government intervention to contain economic sanctions will, however, remain necessary in the presence of repudiation externalities.

9. Borrowing taxes have been proposed, for example, in Edwards (1984b) and Aizenman (1989a), and have been analysed in detail in Aizenman (1989b).

Chapter 9

1. Instances of debt renegotiation go back to the 19th century. Debt re-

negotiations have considerably increased in number since the outbreak of the crisis in the early 1980s (see for example Özler, 1989).

2. This does not exclude the possibility that lenders take this opportunity for some 'arm twisting' in order to obtain better terms for new loans.

3. For example, see Luce and Raiffa (1965).

4. For example, see Rubinstein (1982).

5. With incomplete information there will be real time bargaining.

6. In Fernandez and Rosenthal (1990), in applying the non-cooperative bargaining approach to sovereign debt rescheduling, it is presumed that the debtor country continues to service debt during debt renegotiations to the maximum of what lenders can expect. Furthermore, the debtor country has no credible outside option available. It is shown that in a bargaining equilibrium creditors reap the entire cake under negotiation. It is intuitively clear that the bargaining equilibrium must have this property, as, for as long as negotiations continue, lenders are in the best conceivable state of the world.

7. In Krugman (1989) it is reported that in the debt crisis of the 1980s Mexico fully honoured her bonds issued abroad while at the same time letting bank loans fall into arrears. The model we entertain provides a theoretical explanation of why it was optimal for Mexico to do so.

8. For this view see, for example, Eichengreen and Portes (1986).

9. For this view see also the bargaining model of Bulow and Rogoff (1989b).

10. We restrict the analysis to the case where a real store of wealth exists. The analysis without a real store of wealth is isomorphic to the case discussed.

11. If after the failure of negotiations over the gross repayment obligations parties would enter negotiations over the avoidance of economic sanctions the steady state would be at C. Again the direct effect of negotiating gross repayment would be nil.

12. From (9.23) it also follows for $e_{\text{II}}^{*} = 0$ that bargaining over gross repay-

ment, if possible, would neither increase nor decrease the value of the outside option to the debtor country.

13. From the analysis in Section III it follows for $m_{II} = 1$ that bargaining alleviates the adverse selection problem in the steady state compared to the 'take-it-or-leave-it' situation.

14. From the analysis in Chapter 6, in particular from condition (6.15) solvency is the bottleneck constraint and not the incentive to terminate the debt relationship. If banks reap some non-negligible gains from the imposition of economic sanctions then for solvency to remain the bottleneck constraint r^s must exceed n at least by an amount which increases with the gains banks make from imposing economic sanctions.

15. If after the breakdown of negotiations the parties bargained over the avoidance of economic sanctions the bargaining steady state would be at E in Figure 9.2(b).

16. In contrast, compare Footnote 6.

17. In Özler (1989) it is shown that after 1981 bank stocks declined when new information about renegotiations broke in stock markets.

Chapter 10

1. The rationale behind debt-equity swaps will be analysed in greater detail in Section V. See also for example Franke (1989).

2. For an analysis of the differences between foreign debt and the equity financing in the presence of potential capital flight see Eaton and Gersovitz (1989). For an empirical analysis of debt versus equity financing see for example Corsepius *et al.* (1989).

3. Under financial intermediation the discount is at least as large as under bond financing as $r^s \leqslant r^d = r$.

4. For an early analysis of direct investment and the threat of expropriation see Long (1975); for a more recent analysis see Thomas and Worrall (1990).

5. In taking restriction (3.11) we presume that after expropriation bargaining over the avoidance of economic sanctions does not take place.

From Chapter 9 such bargaining could easily be accommodated by replacing $\delta \cdot f^*(k^*)$ in (3.11) by $m \cdot \delta \cdot f^*(k^*)$, where m is given by (9.17).

6. It is easily verified that the same is true if debt is bank-financed. Furthermore, it also holds if, under debt-financing, commitment is feasible.

7. The generalization of Footnote 6 also holds here.

8. The increased incentive to choose inefficient projects and technologies, however, has to be pitted against a possibly decreased ability to choose inefficient projects under direct investment. Whether, on balance, adverse selection is worsened under direct investment is to be answered empirically.

9. In general the requirement that debtors fully repay the principal need not be optimal (Worrall, 1988).

10. Indexation need not necessarily occur with respect to components of the costs of honouring debt. Alternatively, lenders may be able to index the costs of violating contracts to the behaviour of debtors (Aizenman, 1989a).

11. Here we follow Krugman (1988).

12. The model hence provides an explanation why debtor countries so often fail in gaining some debt forgiveness in rescheduling negotiations.

13. We abstract therefore a moment from the option value of holding unserviced claims.

14. That the incentive effect can motivate lenders to forgive debt has been pointed out in Krugman (1988) and Sachs (1988).

15. See, however, the qualifier made at the end of Section III.

16. For an investigation into market based rescheduling instruments see Froot (1988) and Krugman (1989).

17. An example is the Mexico-Morgan-Guarantee deal reported in Krugman (1989).

18. This will certainly be the case if the ability to pay is the bottleneck restriction. It will, however, also be the case if willingness is the binding constraint and the costs of economic sanctions increase with the country's remaining resources.

19. According to Krugman (1989) the observation reported in Footnote 8 in Chapter 9 has let Mexico convincingly argue in the Mexico-Morgan Guarantee deal that Mexican bonds are senior to bank credits.

20. See the discussion on the relative importance of debtor sovereignty under debt and equity financing in Section II for an evaluation of the seniority requirement.

Chapter 11

1. The model we employ in this book is in real terms. Write-down requirements must therefore be interpreted as a forced reduction of dividend payments. Under steady-state conditions dividends withheld forever are valued by the market as if the goods they represent would be destroyed. An important difference between write-down requirements and taxes on financial intermediation then is that under the former, goods not transferred from banks to owners are ultimately withheld from the economy.

2. However, the solvency restriction shifts downward by less because a pure subsidy also increases the value of banks.

3. For the rationale behind rushes on exhaustible assets see the extensive literature on common property, for example Kemp and Long (1980), Sinn (1984), and Mohr (1988c).

4. See, for example, Diamond and Dybvig (1983).

5. Governments, central banks or supranational institutions like the IMF could be the lender of last resort.

6. Compare also Footnote 2 in Chapter 6.

7. For a discussion see, for example, Kindleberger (1978).

8. It is only to accommodate the case $p < 1$ that we need the risk-neutrality Assumption 9.2.

9. In the formal bargaining model, the debtor and creditor countries have their outside options available with the same probability. Although this creates difficulties of interpretation in the present context it is obvious that this assumption is irrelevant for the bargaining solution if $e_{II}^* = 0$.

10. See Footnote 19 in Chapter 2 for a list of such incidents.

References

Abel, A. (1987) 'Operative Gifts and Bequest Motives', *American Economic Review*, **77**, 1037–1047

Abel, A., Mankiw, N., Summers, L. and Zeckhauser, R. (1989) 'Assessing Dynamic Efficiency: Theory and Evidence', *Review of Economic Studies*, **56**, 1–20.

Abreu, D. (1983) 'Repeated Games With Discounting: A General Theory and an Application to Oligopoly', Princeton University, Discussion paper.

Adler, M. (1987) 'On Being Honest and Behaving Honestly', University of California, Davis, Working Paper Series No. 297.

Aizenman, J. (1989a) 'Country Risk and Contingencies', *International Economic Journal*, **3**, 81–102.

Aizenman, J. (1989b) 'Country Risk, Incomplete Information and Taxes on International Borrowing', *Economic Journal*, **99**, 147–161.

Axelrod, R. (1981) 'The Emergence of Cooperation Among Egoists', *American Political Science Review*, **75**, 306–318.

Barro, R. J. (1974) 'Are Government Bonds Net Wealth?', *Journal of Political Economy*, **82**, 1095–1117.

Berg, A. and Sachs, J. (1988) 'The Debt Crisis: Structural Explanations of Country Performance', *Journal of Development Economics*, **29**, 271–306.

Bernheim, B. D. (1989) 'Intergenerational Altruism and Social Welfare: A Critique of the Dynastic Model', *Review of Economic Studies*, **56**, 119–128.

Bernheim, B. D. and Bagwell, K. (1988) 'Is Everything Neutral?', *Journal of Political Economy*, **96**, 308–38.

Binmore, K. (1986) 'Modeling Rational Players', Suntory Toyota International Centre for Economics and related Disciplines, London, No. 133.

Blanchard, O. (1979) 'Speculative Bubbles, Crashes and Rational Expectations', *Economics Letters*, **3**, 387–89.

Buiter, W. (1981) 'Time Preferences and International Lending and Borrowing in an Overlapping-Generations-Model', *Journal of Political Economy*, **89**, 760–797.

Bulow, J. and Rogoff, K. (1989a) 'Sovereign Debt: Is to Forgive to Forget?', *American Economic Review*, **79**, 43–50.

Bulow, J. and Rogoff, K. (1989b) 'A Constant Recontracting Model of Sovereign Debt', *Journal of Political Economy*, **97**, 155–178.

Bulow, J. and Shoven, J. (1978) 'The Bankruptcy Decision', *Bell Journal of Economics*, **9**, 437–456.

Burbidge, J. (1983) 'Government Debt in an Overlapping-Generations Model with Bequest and Gifts', *American Economic Review*, **73**, 222–227.

Carmichael, J. (1982) 'On Barro's Theorem of Debt Neutrality: The Irrelevance of Net Wealth', *American Economic Review*, **72**, 202–13.

Cave, J. (1983) 'Perfection and Entry: An Example', Rand Paper Series, No. 6900.

Coase, R. H. (1960) 'The Problem of Social Cost', *Journal of Law and Economics*, **3**, 1–44.

Cohen, D. and Sachs, J. (1986) 'Growth and External Debt under Risk of Debt Repudiation', *European Economic Review*, **30**, 529–60.

Corsepius, U., Nunnenkamp, P. and Schweickert, R. (1989) *Debt versus Equity Finance in Developing Countries*, Kieler Studien No. 229, J. C. B. Mohr (Tübingen).

Crawford, V. P. (1987) 'International Lending, Long-Term Credit Relationships, and Dynamic Contract Theory', Princeton Studies in International Finance, 59.

Cremer, J. (1986) 'Cooperation in Ongoing Organizations', *Quarterly Journal of Economics*, **101**, 33–49.

Cuddington, J. T. (1987) 'Capital Flight', *European Economic Review*, **31**, 382–388.

Dasgupta, P. (1982) *The Control of Resources*, Harvard University Press (Cambridge).

Devlin, R. (1985) 'External Debt and Crisis: The Decline of the Orthodox Procedures', *CEPAL Review*, **27**, 35–52.
Diamond, D. W. (1989) 'Reputation Acquisition in Debt Markets', *Journal of Political Economy*, **97**, 828–62.
Diamond, D. W. and Dybvig, P. H. (1983) 'Bank Runs, Deposit Insurance, and Liquidity', *Journal of Political Economy*, **91**, 401–419.
Diamond, P. (1965) 'National Debt in a Neoclassical Growth Model', *American Economic Review*, **55**, 1126–1150.
Diaz-Alejandro, C. F. (1984) 'Latin America Debt: I Don't Think We Are in Kansas Anymore', *Brooking's Papers on Economic Activity*, **2**, 335–403.
Dornbusch, R. (1985) 'Intergenerational and International Trade', *Journal of International Economics*, **18**, 123–139.
Eaton, J. (1986) 'Lending with Costly Enforcement of Repayment and Potential Fraud', *Journal of Banking and Finance*, **10**, 281–293.
Eaton, J. and Gersovitz, M. (1981) 'Debt with Potential Repudiation: Theoretical and Empirical Analysis', *Review of Economic Studies*, **48**, 289–309.
Eaton, J. and Gersovitz, M. (1989) 'Country Risk and the Organization of International Capital Transfers', in G. A. Calvo and C. F. Diaz-Alejandro (eds) *Debt, stabilization and development*, Blackwell (Oxford).
Edwards, S. (1984a) 'LDC Foreign Borrowing and Default Risk: An Empirical Investigation 1976–80', *American Economic Review*, **74**, 726–34.
Edwards, S. (1984b) 'The Role of International Reserves and Foreign Debt in the Process of External Adjustments', in International Monetary Fund, *Adjustment Conditionality and International Financing*, IMF (Washington).
Eichengreen, B. (1988) 'Resolving Debt Crises: A Historical Perspective', NBER Working Paper No. 2555.
Eichengreen, B. and Portes R. (1986) 'Debt and Default in the 1930s: Causes and Consequences', *European Economic Review*, **30**, 599–640.
Fama, E. (1980) 'Banking in the Theory of Finance', *Journal of Monetary Economics*, **10**, 10–19.
Fama, E. (1985) 'What's Different About Banks?', *Journal of Monetary Economics*, **15**, 29–39.
Feldstein, M. (1976) 'Perceived Wealth in Bonds and Social Security: A Comment', *Journal of Political Economy*, **84**, 331–36.
Fernandez, R. and Rosenthal R. W. (1990) 'Strategic Models of Sovereign-Debt Renegotiations', *Review of Economic Studies*, **57**, 331–349.
Fischer, S. and Frenkel J. A. (1974) 'Interest Rate Equilization and

Patterns of Production, Trade and Consumption in a Two-Country Model', *Economic Review*, **50**, 555–80.

Franke, G. (1989) 'Economic Analysis of Debt-Equity-Swaps', in H.-J. Vosgerau (ed.) *New Institutional Arrangements for the World Economy*, Springer-Verlag (Berlin).

Frenkel, J. A. and Mussa M. L. (1984) 'Asset Markets, Exchange Rates, and the Balance of Payments', in R. W. Jones and P. B. Kenen (eds) *Handbook of International Economics*, North Holland (Amsterdam).

Friedman, J. W. (1971) 'A Non-cooperative Equilibrium for Supergames', *Review of Economic Studies*, **38**, 1–12.

Froot, K. A. (1988) 'Buybacks, Exit Bonds, and the Optimality of Debt and Liquidity Relief', NBER Working Paper No. 2675.

Froot, K. A., Scharfstein, D. and Stein J. (1989) 'LDC Debt: Forgiveness, Indexation, and Investment Incentives', *Journal of Finance*, **44**, 1335–50.

Grossman, H. I. and Van Huyck, J. B. (1988) 'Sovereign Debt as a Contingent Claim: Excusable Default, Repudiation, and Reputation', *American Economic Review*, **78**, 1088–97.

Hamada, K. (1966) 'Economic Growth and Long-Run Capital Movements', *Yale Economic Essays*, **6**, 49–96.

Harsanyi, J. C. (1977) *Rational Behavior and Bargaining Equilibrium in Games and Social Situations*, Cambridge University Press (Cambridge).

Hellwig, M. (1977) 'A Model of Borrowing and Lending with Bankruptcy', *Econometrica*, **47**, 1879–1906.

Hellwig, M. (1986) 'The Pure Theory of Country Risk: Comment', *European Economic Review*, **30**, 521–527.

Hentschel, J. (1988) 'Managing International Debt', *Intereconomics*, **23**, 126–31.

Hollis, M. (1985) 'The Emperor's Newest Clothes', *Economics and Philosophy*, **1**, 128–33.

Jaffee, D. and Russell, T. (1976) 'Imperfect Information, Uncertainty, and Credit Rationing', *Quarterly Journal of Economics*, **90**, 651–66.

Johansen, L. (1982) 'On the Status of the Nash Type of Noncooperative Equilibrium in Economic Theory', *Scandinavian Journal of Economics*, **84**, 421–41.

Jorgensen, J. and Sachs, J. (1988) 'Default and Renegotiation of Latin American Foreign Bonds in the Interwar Period', NBER Working Paper No. 2636.

Kaempfer, W. H. and Lowenberg, A. D. (1988) 'The Theory of International Economic Sanctions: A Public Choice Approach', *American Economic Review*, **78**, 786–93.

Kemp, M. C. and Long, N. V. (1980) 'Resource Extraction under Conditions of Common Access', in M. C. Kemp and N. V. Long (eds) *Exhaustible Resources, Optimality, and Trade*, North Holland (Amsterdam).

Kierzkowski, H. (1987) 'Recent Advances in International Trade Theory: A Selective Survey', *Oxford Review of Economic Policy*, **3**, 1–19.

Kindleberger, C. (1978) *Manias, Panics, and Crashes*, Basic Books (New York).

Kletzer, K. M. (1984) 'Asymmetries of Information and LDC Borrowing with Sovereign Risk', *Economic Journal*, **94**, 287–307.

Kreps, D., Milgrom, P., Roberts J. and Wilson R. (1982) 'Rational Cooperation in the Finitely Repeated Prisoners' Dilemma', *Journal of Economic Theory*, **27**, 245–52.

Krueger, A. O. (1987) 'Debt, Capital Flows, and LDC Growth', *American Economic Review*, Papers and Proceedings, **77**, 159–64.

Krugman, P. (1988) 'Financing vs. Forgiving a Debt Overhang', *Journal of Development Economics* **29**, 253–268.

Krugman, P. (1989) 'Market Based Debt-Reduction Schemes', in J. A. Frenkel, M. P. Dooley and P. Wickham (eds) *Analytical Issues in Debt*, IMF (Washington).

Kyle, S. and Sachs J. (1984) 'Developing Country Debt and the Market Value of Large Commercial Banks', NBER Working Paper No. 1470.

Lockwood, B. (1986) 'The Folk Theorem for Dynamic Games Without Discounting', University of London, revised version of Birkbeck College Discussion Paper No. 165.

Long, N. V. (1975) 'The Pattern of Resource Extraction under Uncertainty About Possible Nationalization', *Journal of Economic Theory*, **10**, 42–53.

Luce, D. R. and Raiffa, H. (1965) *Games and Decisions*, 5th edition, Wiley (New York).

Moggridge, D. E. (1981) 'Financial Crises and Lenders of Last Resort: Policy in the Crises of 1920 and 1929', *Journal of European Economic History*, **10**, 47–69.

Mohr, E. (1988a) 'On the Incredibility of Perfect Threats in Repeated Games: Note', *International Economic Review*, **29**, 551–55.

Mohr, E. (1988b) 'International Borrowing and Exhaustible Resources: Note on a Liquidity – Creditworthiness Conflict', *European Economic Review*, **32**, 1385–92.

Mohr, E. (1988c) 'Appropriation of Common Access Natural Resources Through Exploration: The Relevance of the Open-Loop Concept', *International Economic Review*, **29**, 307–19.

Navarrete, J. E. (1985) 'Foreign Policy and International Financial Negotiations: The External Debt and the Cartagena Consensus', *CEPAL Review*, **27**, 7–25.

Neher, P. A. (1970) 'International Capital Movements along Balanced Growth Paths', *Economic Record*, **46**, 393–401.

Niehans, J. (1985) 'International Debt with Unenforceable Claims', *Economic Review, Federal Reserve Bank of San Francisco*, **1**, 64–79.

Nunnenkamp, P. (1989) 'Bank Lending to Developing Countries in the 1980s: An Empirical Test of Major Hypotheses on Voluntary and Involuntary Lending', Kiel Institute of World Economics, Working Paper No. 354.

O'Connell, S. A. and Zeldes, S. P. (1988) 'Rational Ponzi Games', *International Economic Review*, **29**, 431–50.

Özler, S. (1989) 'On the Relation Between Reschedulings and Bank Value', *American Economic Review*, **79**, 1117–31.

Persson, T. (1985) 'Deficits and International Welfare in Open Economies', *Journal of International Economics*, **19**, 67–84.

Phelps, E. S. (1961) 'The Golden Rule of Accumulation: A Fable for Growthmen', *American Economic Review*, **51**, 638–43.

Rubinstein, A. (1979) 'Equilibrium in Supergames with the Overtaking Criterion', *Journal of Economic Theory*, **21**, 1–9.

Rubinstein, A. (1982) 'Perfect Equilibrium in a Bargaining Model', *Econometrica*, **50**, 97–109.

Ruffin, R. J. (1979) 'Growth and the Long-Run Theory of International Capital Movements', *American Economic Review*, **69**, 832–42.

Sachs, J. (1982a) 'LDC Debt in the 1980's: Risk and Reform' in P. Wachtel (ed.) *Crises in the Economic and Financial Structure*, D. C. Heath (Lexington).

Sachs, J. (1982b) 'Theoretical Issues in International Borrowing', NBER Working Paper No. 1189.

Sachs, J. (1986) 'Managing the LDC Debt Crisis', *Brookings Papers on Economic Activity*, **2**, 397–431.

Sachs, J. (1988) 'Conditionality, Debt Relief, and the Developing Country Debt Crisis', in J. Sachs (ed.) *Developing Country Debt and Economic Performance*, University of Chicago Press.

Sachs, J. and Cohen, D. (1982) 'LDC Borrowing with Default Risk', NBER Working Paper No. 925.

Samuelson, P. (1958) 'An Exact Consumption-Loan Model of Interest with or without the Social Contrivance of Money', *Journal of Political Economy*, **66**, 467–82.

Schmid, M. (1987) 'External Debt and the Wealth of Nations with Overlapping Generations: The Dynamics of Consumption and Productivity

Shocks', Diskussionsbeiträge aus dem Institut für Volkswirtschaftslehre, Universität der Bundeswehr, Hamburg.

Scott, K. E. (1989) 'Domestic Bank Regulation in a World of International Banking', in H.-J. Vosgerau (ed.) *New Institutional Arrangements for the World Economy*, Springer (Berlin).

Selten, R. (1975) 'Re-examination of the Perfectness Concept for Equilibrium Points in Extensive Games', *International Journal of Game Theory*, **4**, 25–55.

Sheshinski, E. and Weiss, Y. (1981) 'Uncertainty and Optimal Social Security Systems' *Quarterly Journal of Economics*, **96**, 189–206.

Sinn, H.-W. (1984) 'Common Property Resources, Storage Facilities and Ownership Structures: A Cournot Model of the Oil Market', *Economica*, **51**, 235–52.

Sinn, H.-W. (1987) *Capital Income Taxation and Resource Allocation*, North Holland (Amsterdam).

Siebert, H. (1985) *Economics of the Resource-Exporting Country*, J.I.E. Press (Greenwich).

Siebert, H. (1989) 'The Half and the Full Debt Cycle', *Weltwirtschaftliches Archiv*, **125**, 217–29.

Smith, A. (1984) 'Capital Theory and Trade Theory' in R. W. Jones and P. B. Kenen (eds) *Handbook of International Economics*, North Holland (Amsterdam).

Solow, R. (1956) 'A Contribution to the Theory of Economic Growth', *Quarterly Journal of Economics*, **70**, 65–94.

Stiglitz, J. and Weiss, A. (1981) 'Credit Rationing in Markets with Imperfect Information', *American Economic Review*, **71**, 393–411.

Sutton, J. (1986) 'Non-Cooperative Bargaining Theory: An Introduction', *Review of Economic Studies*, **53**, 709–24.

Tirole, J. (1985) 'Asset Bubbles and Overlapping Generations: A Synthesis', *Econometrica*, **53**, 1071–1100.

Thomas, J. and Worrall, T. (1990) 'Foreign Direct Investment and the Risk of Expropriation', Kiel Institute of World Economics Working Paper No. 411.

Williamson, O. (1985) *The Economic Institutions of Capitalism*, The Free Press (New York).

Winkler, M. (1933) *Foreign Bonds: An Autopsy*, Roland Swain (Philadelphia).

World Bank (1986) *World Development Report*, World Bank.

Worrall, T. (1988) 'Debt with Potential Repudiation', University of Konstanz SFB 178 Working Paper No. 69.

List of Symbols

Variables without time index, t, refer to values in period t. Variables with a subscript '$+j$' refer to values in period $t+j$. All asterisked variables or parameters refer to the debtor country. All unasterisked variables or parameters refer to the creditor country. All lower case variables are defined per member of the then living young generation.

b, b^*:	amount borrowed (if $b, b^* > 0$) or lent (if $b, b^* < 0$) (in period t)
c^j, c^{j*}:	consumption of a young household
c^o, c^{o*}:	consumption of an old household
$\tilde{c}^{o*}$:	old-age consumption in the debtor country if debt is honoured
$\tilde{\tilde{c}}^{o*}$:	old-age consumption in the debtor country if debt is repudiated
d^*:	repudiation dummy
e, e^*:	value of the outside option in a negotiation process, defined as a share of the cake to be divided in a negotiated settlement
$f(k), f^*(k^*)$:	production function
$g(\delta)$:	density function
G:	size of the bank-specific production factor in the creditor economy

h:	discount factor applied to the negotiation process
k, k^*:	capital intensity
k^A, k^{A*}:	capital intensities under financial autarky
K, K^*:	size of the production factor 'capital'
L, L^*:	number of households of generation t
m:	share lenders receive from the cake to be divided in debt renegotiations
n:	constant one-period proportional growth rate of population
p:	probability that the outside option is available
r, r^*:	marginal productivity of physical capital
r^A, r^{A*}:	marginal productivity of physical capital under financial autarky
r^d:	deposit rate on bank deposits
r^i, r^{i*}:	interest rate on the foreign component in the portfolio of households
r^s:	interest rate to be paid by the sovereign on bank loans
$\underline{r}^s$:	interest rate on bank loans for which total profits of bank activities is zero
v:	value of the banking system
v^d:	value of bank services
v^i:	value of financial intermediation
w, w^*:	labour income
x, x^*:	quantity of goods available for consumption
x^d, x^{d*}:	quantity of goods available for consumption out of domestic activities
y, y^*:	national output
z:	net transfer in period t from the debtor country to the creditor country
z':	gross transfer in period t from debt obligations from the debtor country to the creditor country
$\underline{z}$:	net transfer from the debtor country to the creditor country for which the value of banks is zero
z^j, z^{j*}:	value of a debt relationship to the young
z^o, z^{o*}:	value of a debt relationship to the old
α, α^*:	production elasticity of capital
β, β^*:	production elasticity of labour
γ:	auxiliary variable
δ:	'gunboat-technology' parameter
$\bar{\delta}$:	upper bound on the gunboat-technology
$\tilde{\delta}$	realization of the state of the world for which the sovereign is indifferent to the alternatives of either honouring or repudiating debt

Δ:	time interval that elapses between two successive offers in a bargaining process
$\varkappa$:	parameter
λ:	production elasticity of bank-specific capital
ζ:	auxiliary variable
ξ:	Lagrange multiplier in various optimization problems
Π:	option value for lenders of maintaining a debt relationship
$\tilde{\Pi}$:	market value of total debt outstanding
$\bar{\Pi}$:	market price of an exit bond
Φ:	probability that debt is honoured
τ:	transfer per member of the young generation in the creditor country to the banking system induced by fiscal policy
σ:	parameter determining the write-down on non-performing loans required by bank regulation
θ:	dividend from financial intermediation
$\tilde{\theta}$:	dividend bank owners receive due to the accounting principles required by bank regulation
Ψ:	variable under control of the sovereign for the containment of economic sanctions
ω	market price of the debtor country's equity
Ω, Ω^*:	time preference factor

Author Index

Subject Index

UNIVERSITY OF BRISTOL
UNIVERSITY OF BRISTOL LIBRARY
WITHDRAWN